THE PERFECTIBLE BODY

THE PERFECTIBLE BODY

THE WESTERN IDEAL

OF PHYSICAL DEVELOPMENT

KENNETH R. DUTTON

CASSELL

Cassell
Villiers House
41/47 Strand
London WC2N 5JE

First published 1995

British Library Cataloguing-in-Publication Data
A catalogue record for this book is available from the British Library.

ISBN 0-304-33230-5

Typeset by Rhys Palmer, The University of Newcastle, Australia
Printed and bound in Great Britain

CONTENTS

FOREWORD

Around the middle of 1985, some friends persuaded me to accompany them to a bodybuilding contest, a form of spectacle to which I had not previously felt any notable attraction and of whose constituent elements I was, at most, only dimly aware.

What I saw that evening made a profound impression upon me. It was not that I found the exhibition especially enjoyable — quite the contrary, if anything — but rather that I found myself puzzled, even mildly disconcerted, by this extraordinary form of human engagement.

One by one, the competitors made their appearance — men for the most part, though with a sprinkling of women as well — and as the rock music blared from the amplifiers, proceeded to put their preternaturally oiled and pumped bodies through a series of flamboyant attitudes and gestures culminating in a fixed pose which suggested that their muscles or veins, or both, were about to explode. The audience roared its approval. Once all the contestants had completed their individual displays, a selected number were called back onto the podium to go through it all again, vying with each other for centre stage and the audience's attention. Finally, the winners were announced, struck a few more poses for the cameras, and received their trophies.

Perhaps it was because I was an outsider that I found myself so bemused by it all, that I left the auditorium with such a curious mixture of alienation and fascination. On the one hand, this was not my milieu, I did not belong here: as an academic, I was out of my element in this world of pure physicality. Yet on the other, as a cultural historian I felt in a sense that I *half*-understood, even if only half, what had been taking place in this curious semantic exchange between performer and audience.

It was, I could discern, a form of theatre — perhaps distantly related to mime or ballet — in which there were actors and spectators. Its components and structure — the heats, finals, judges, winners and trophies — were those of the sporting contest. Yet was this really a sport, or rather a mutant macho version of the female beauty pageant? There were certainly male wolf-whistles for the women competitors, but the latter were only a minor part of the spectacle, almost an entr'acte, and it seemed unlikely that the unequivocally, even aggressively, heterosexual males who dominated the audience were engaged in some form of erotic voyeurism directed at the scantily-clad bodies of the male contestants. Then, there were the elements of ritual or even worship — for it was not so much the athletic movements and heroic poses as the heavily-muscled bodies themselves that excited the crowd's enthusiasm, even something approaching adulation. Was this some kind of late twentieth-century equivalent of a Dionysiac cult of the phallus, or at least of the phallic body?

What, I kept asking myself, had been going on in the auditorium that evening, and what, if anything, did it mean? Conditioned, as an academic, to 'go to the literature', I searched through bibliographies and data-bases in the hope of finding a key to this exotic form of human interaction — surely, I thought, a sociologist's or psychologist's paradise. In vain. Though I came across an occasional article about gymnasium behaviour and some popular historical material on early bodybuilders, I could find nothing that answered the questions going round in my mind. Why did people pay good money to look at other human bodies on display, if not for reasons of sexual voyeurism? Had humans always done this kind of thing, or was it a peculiarly modern phenomenon, a sign of decadence or of a culture in decline? Why did bodybuilding strike me as such an essentially Western pastime, and was there something in our cultural preoccupations that could account for this fascination with conspicuous muscular development? And how was it, if the display of male muscularity was of such distinctly minority interest (as my colleagues assured me), that an Arnold Schwarzenegger could use it to become one of the highest paid and most celebrated figures of our age?

It was out of reflection on these, and a host of associated issues, that this book was written. In the course of my research, I became more and more convinced that what I was exploring was not just an arcane by-way of human behaviour, a hermetic little world of gym aficionados and muscle devotees, but a paradigm of something much larger, more significant, which had to do with the powerful symbolic allusiveness of the human body itself.

What follows, then, is the result of these reflections. By a remarkable coincidence, the day on which I am writing these lines — August 1, 1993 — is precisely the centenary of modern bodybuilding. For it was on August 1, 1893, that the audience assembled in Chicago's Trocadero Theater first witnessed the most celebrated strongman of his day, Eugen Sandow, complete his usual barbell and harness lifts before moving into a sequence of classical poses designed for no other purpose than that of displaying his muscular physique. The ecstatic reaction of the audience that evening was echoed by the newspaper reporters, one of whom wrote:

> 'What a wretched, scrawny creature the usual well-built young gentleman is compared with a perfect man. Sandow, posing in various statuesque attitudes, is not only inspiring because of his enormous strength, but absolutely beautiful as a work of art as well.'

A 'perfect man'? It is not so much the extravagance of the claim as the fact that it could have been made at all, which I find so revealing of our attitude to the human body and its power to excite the imagination.

The pervasive ideal of the perfectible body has been for 2500 years of Western civilisation a reminder that the body is something more than itself — the mirror and form of our human aspirations, the outward and visible sign of human perfectibility. By exploring some contemporary examples and tracing their cultural antecedents, I hope to have opened up for more expert analysis some relatively unexplored aspects of our social behaviour.

INTRODUCTION

UNCOVERING THE BODY

Throughout history the human body has been an object of inexhaustible fascination for its possessors. Not only has it provided the material of endless investigation for biologists, anatomists, sociologists, psychologists and other practitioners of the natural and social sciences, but even in the most primitive of cultures the body has been one of the chief objects of attention and speculation since man emerged from among the hominoid apes. It has been attired, decorated, mutilated, revered, pampered, mortified, and imaginatively interpreted by artists as everything from an obscene assemblage of flesh to an image of the divine spirit.

What subject, after all, could be closer — either figuratively or literally — to our human concerns? The body is the focal point of our individual identity, in that we not only *have* but in a sense *are* our bodies: however distinct the body may be conceptually from the 'self' which experiences and knows it, that which experiences and knows is by its nature an *embodied* self, a self whose social identity and whose location in time and space are contained and defined by their individual embodiment.[1]

We both inhabit and experience our bodies: we know them, as it were, at once from the inside and from the outside. Our relationship with the cosmos is determined by this duality. Whilst the body we can see and feel is our means of transaction with the world, the inhabiting consciousness which feeds upon and is constituted by that transaction tends to see itself as transcendent, as existing over and above the experienced body. The history of imaginative thought is our collective attempt to bridge the gap between our embodied selves and what lies outside them, and the pervasive tradition of the dualism of body and spirit is ultimately grounded in the paradox of a self which both is and is not defined by its body.[2]

The body, then, is both the personal and social symbol of our identity, as well as the means whereby that identity is constituted. The search for identity is the strategy we use in order to deny our meaninglessness, to confer upon ourselves a value within society and within the overall scheme of things. To be aware of our identity and thus move beyond the sphere of unreflecting immediacy is to raise the question of the purpose and function we serve in human existence as a whole. Here, in turn, another and supremely important question is raised, a question first formulated by the ancient Greeks for whom that which was thoroughly adapted to its ultimate end or completion (*telos*) was described as 'perfect' (*teleios*, 'having reached its end'). As Aristotle pointed out in the fourth century B.C., since all living beings develop from a less perfect state (the plant seed, the human embryo) to a more perfect (the grown plant, the adult human), the question is inevitably posed: in what does perfection consist? and further, what kind of perfection can a human being — *as* a human being — reach?

The question has haunted thinkers and religious leaders since ancient times: Hindu and Sikh, Taoist and Christian, have all been concerned with the state of perfection as the ultimate end of the human quest, and have understood human existence as in some sense 'perfectible'. Here, however, we enter dangerous waters. The concept of perfectibility, as Professor John Passmore's important study (*The Perfectibility of Man*[3]) has demonstrated, is susceptible of degradation when attached to morally dubious ideals. Indeed, a number of writers have pointed out, the more general the ideal to which 'perfectibility' permits an approach, the more hazardous the consequences if that ideal is ethically deficient. To seek to be a 'perfect secretary' is a limited but not inherently harmful goal; to seek to be a 'perfect man' is a bolder, and potentially more perilous, enterprise, depending upon the moral value of the absolutes one sets out to attain.[4] To this theme we shall return later in our study.

The role played by the body in the quest for human self-identification and meaningful existence has been the subject of extensive enquiry by social scientists for over a century, and some of the most important advances in our contemporary understanding of the human body have been due to the work of those sociologists and social anthropologists who have set out to explore the body's social dimensions. Pioneered by the French sociologist Emile Durkheim (1858-1917) and later developed

developed by his student Marcel Mauss, this area of research has concentrated on extending our understanding of the body beyond its purely physiological aspects and on exploring the close relationship between the physical and social dimensions of experience. In more recent times, the work of scholars such as Erving Goffman, Jonathan Benthall, Ted Polhemus and Mary Douglas has provided valuable insights into the behaviour and expressivity of man's physical form in the context of the social construction of reality, while others such as Bryan Turner, Peter Brown and Thomas Laqueur have shown how far religious, philosophical or even scientific preconceptions have conditioned our understanding of the body itself as a physical entity. Often interdisciplinary in scope, this field (or set of fields) of study has taught us much about the symbolic capacity of the body and its use as a means of social communication.[5]

The concern of 'Human Social Anatomy' (as this field has been called)[6] is to examine, through the methods of its constituent disciplines, what artists, philosophers, religious thinkers and creative writers had for centuries understood more or less intuitively from their own rather different perspectives — namely, the functioning of the human body not simply as a material organism but as a metaphoric vehicle. Whether as a microcosm of the universe itself, a symbol of mathematical perfection, the 'temple of the Holy Ghost' or the embodiment of the beauty and pathos of created existence, the human body has been the subject of imaginative interpretation in the most distinguished products of the human imagination ever since the birth of civilisation. Ethnologists, psychologists, sociologists, and physical and social anthropologists have increasingly come to recognise the intimate link between the physical body and the social body, and to reject a purely physical understanding of the body and its behaviour in favour of what the sociologist Marcel Mauss has called a 'physio-psycho-sociological' approach.[7] The human body, in this view, can be understood only in the context of the social construction of reality; indeed, the body itself is seen as a social construct, a means of social expression or performance by which our identity and value — for ourselves and for others — are created, tested and validated.

The aim of this book is to focus upon just one facet of this view of the body as metaphor. It takes as its subject what I shall call for the sake of brevity the 'developed body' — that is, the body as presented and interpreted in terms of its muscular development. The field of exploration with which I shall be concerned is the metaphorical or symbolic value that has been attached to highly developed muscularity, whether in the artistic portrayal of the human body or in its social interaction. The scope of such a study is, for obvious reasons, restricted almost exclusively to the male body, though in a number of contexts it will be important to include some reference to the perception and representation of female bodies by way of contrast or comparison.

It is fundamental to my thesis that the social underpinnings of the modern quest for physical development (by which I mean the forms it has taken in Western societies over the last hundred years or so) cannot be understood without an appreciation of certain value-systems originally derived from the Greek culture of the fifth century B.C. and transmitted to Western Europe in modified form at the time of the Italian Renaissance. The capacity of the Christian doctrine of the body to be interpreted in a manner sympathetic to certain Hellenic thought-forms has by no means been the dominant strand of theological understanding, but it was pervasive enough at an imaginative level to carry the theme of the muscular hero-figure as the artistic convention in Europe from the Renaissance until the invention of photography in the mid-nineteenth century. A new concern with supposed 'realism' coming in the wake of the camera has combined with the growing social expectations of the twentieth century to 'democratise' the developed body and make it an accessible object of mass culture and consumerism.

In the public sphere at least, the attention paid to the developed male body from the mid-nineteenth century onwards has been chiefly restricted to men themselves. Whether in the cultivation of their own bodies or in the representation of muscularity in art and photography, it has generally been men who have defined and fashioned the forms and symbolism of muscular development. The role played by homosexual attraction in this process has clearly been significant, though as will emerge later it has not been by any means the sole determinant and the quest for power and enhanced virility or heterosexual prowess have also played an important part. More recently, profound shifts in women's consciousness and the legitimation of women as observers of male bodies have radically altered the pattern of social awareness and discussion, so much so that the objectification of the male body has become a leading element of the contemporary feminist debate.

In bringing together the aesthetic and theological background and more recent socio-cultural analysis, I have sought to provide a historical frame of reference for the contemporary cult of the developed body. At the same time I have tried to suggest that some of the more problematic and socially destructive aspects of modern trends towards physical perfectionism equally have their roots in earlier manifestations.

Let us, then, look at the body in more detail.

As Kenneth Clark has observed in relation to the world of art, every time we criticise a human figure — on the grounds, say, that the neck is too long, the hips too wide or the breasts too small — we are admitting the existence of an ideal or perfect physical beauty.[8] Of the many senses in which we use the word 'perfect' (moral perfection, functional perfection, teleological perfection, etc.) aesthetic perfection is one of the most common. Ideals of beauty (or physical perfection) vary from one society to another: whilst in primitive societies they tend to remain relatively constant over time, in modern Westernised societies they change with astonishing rapidity — a function of our enhanced desire and increased capacity for change. These aesthetic ideals are related to such variable concepts as social status and canons of morality. Female obesity, for example, may be highly prized in societies where only the wealthy can afford to be fat, whilst the notion of female virtue may become closely identified with bodily constriction (wasp waists, tight-fitting corsets, brassieres and garters). In a world of infinitely variable social contexts, some form of transformation of the body — through clothing, bodily decoration or body shaping — is a universal practice, from the most 'primitive' to the most 'evolved' of societies.

It is here, in its very mutability, that the body takes on in the most visible form its function as a metaphor. The presentation of the body in a particular and

recognisable shape or pattern (whether of body decoration or of its sub-species, clothing) represents a kind of *code*, which is meant to be read and understood as an answer to the question: Who am I? First explored by social anthropologists, this notion has been given a wider extension in the work of the French semiologist Roland Barthes, who has analysed a number of examples of body presentation (from all-in wrestling to the world of high fashion) in terms of their function as systems of 'signs' or conventions which can be fully understood only if we know how to read the particular code on which they are based.

The question of how we are to understand (or 'read') the muscular or developed body is the major concern of this book. By its very nature, such a study involves examining the presentation of the body in nude or near-nude form. As such, it raises the complex emotional reactions evoked by the sight of nakedness — many of them related to sexual taboos — as well as posing the issue of cultural differences. A New Guinea tribesman clad only in a penis-sheath may appear to us, to all intents and purposes, naked, even though in his own social context he

is seen as fully clothed. Similarly, whereas in the West the presentation of the nude in artistic works has been an accepted convention, largely free of the taboos surrounding such presentation in everyday life, the idea of presenting the nude or near-nude body as an object of aesthetic contemplation in its own right would simply not have occurred in traditional Chinese or Japanese society, where clothing has been a more potent symbol than nakedness. The code or codes by which we read the presentation of the relatively unclothed body in a Western society where concealment by clothing is the norm, and in particular the way in which we distinguish between the various messages (including the erotic) which are entailed in such a display, are a complex study for which the present book can provide only a few guidelines.

The display of the developed or muscular body as a pattern or metaphor of perfection has in general been restricted to post-Renaissance Western society, its earlier manifestation in the ancient classical world having given way for over a millennium (largely under the influence of Christianity) to alternative models. Its more recent spread to a number of traditionally non-Western cultures has been one of the consequences of their 'Westernisation'. On the other hand, the most naturally muscular of peoples —particularly in Africa and the islands of the Pacific — have developed no such identification: their innate muscularity is accepted as a fact of life rather than an image of perfection, physical beauty residing for them rather in the decoration or at times mutilation of the body. It is tempting to speculate that Western society, whose evolution and political dominance have depended on the scientific and technological extensions of human intelligence rather than on direct physical ability, retains (perhaps for that very reason) a diffused nostalgia for a more purely corporeal existence in which physical dominance was a sign of superiority — a sign now dimly reflected in military epaulettes, padded shoulders, high heels, tall headgear and other modes of fashion aimed at increasing the apparent size of the body.

A fundamental theme underlying the present study is that the symbolism of muscularity in Western societies has been developed within the context of two principal metaphors: the muscular body as power-symbol, and as pleasure-symbol. The pleasure element may take the form either of aesthetic or of erotic pleasure, or it may gravitate ambiguously between the two. Similarly, power-symbolism and pleasure-symbolism themselves may well not be discrete and unequivocal elements of a particular representation or embodiment, but may both be present in varying degrees. Nonetheless, the distinctions of principle remain, and this dual suggestive power of the developed body can be observed in many different manifestations across the centuries.

Whatever system of classification is adopted, the decoding of the developed body as an emblem or metaphor of latent significance is meaningful only within a Western perspective, and the evolution of muscular display as a system of signs can be understood only in the context of evolving Western social attitudes and the images in which they have been reflected. The limited scope of the present work entails a certain selectivity in identifying the more significant stages in this evolution. Even at the risk of generalisation, we must turn our attention initially from one European culture to another according to the extent to which, in a particular era, it contributed to the prevailing Western consciousness of the developed body. Over the past century, the source of those dominant images which have both reflected and moulded Western society's view of itself has shifted from Europe to the United States, and this is nowhere more true than in relation to images of muscularity. It is not by chance that professional bodybuilding — a form of activity which today plays the same role in relation to physical development that *haute couture* plays in relation to female fashion — should be centred upon the USA just as the latest 'look' in exclusive women's apparel is dictated in Paris. In both cases, there are significant cultural reasons for the location. In the case of muscular development, the combination of an affluent consumer society and the Protestant work ethic has been reflected in activities which paradoxically combine disciplined asceticism on the one hand and narcissistic hedonism on the other. Examples are to be found in jogging, dieting, 'keeping fit', aerobics, and similar activities, as well as the success of the gym industry whose income in the US alone from the sale of exercise equipment currently runs into billions of dollars.

Even more important than this shift in focus from one culture to another is the move we must make from the world of high art to that of popular culture. It is critical to my thesis that the contemporary popular imagery of the developed body, in both Western and westernised societies, cannot be fully understood without an appreciation of its origins in the canons of representation developed over centuries of traditional high art and notably in the art academies. The divergence of opinion as to the value of popular culture as a subject of serious academic study occupies a major place in current critical debate from university common-rooms to the pages of scholarly journals, in an age when the number of Ph.D. theses devoted to the pop-star Madonna rivals those devoted to Shakespeare. Yet in no case is this shift in perspective more clearly necessary than that of the presentation of the body as an object of public inspection. Between the invention of the camera and the demise of representational high art a revolution occurred in the public availability of the body, such that its history as a symbolic vehicle throughout the twentieth century is increasingly the history of popular rather than 'refined' social taste.

In tracing these developments, I have tried to avoid, on the one hand, an apologia for the cult of the developed body, and on the other, the kind of denunciation into which even some of the most serious studies of the human body to date have fallen. I have attempted to remain a neutral observer as much as possible, not in the sense of having no personal views but rather in the sense of refusing the extremes either of adulation or of condemnation in order to try to place the cult of muscular development in some kind of proportion as primarily an imaginative pastime. What happens when it takes on the overtones of high seriousness will be obvious from the examples quoted; its fascination when viewed at the level of a sport or even a minor art form, will I hope be evident from the text as a whole.

Equally, given the general rather than academic nature of this work, I have deliberately avoided a doctrinaire critical perspective, whether 'ideological/social' on the one hand or 'structural/formal' on the other; at the risk of methodological inconsistency, I have adopted from time to time whatever viewpoint seemed most clearly to illuminate the issue under discussion. I am well aware that the absence of a defined theoretical framework will displease some academic readers, particularly those committed to the view that only (say) a Marxist critique of patriarchal capitalism or a neo-Freudian/Lacanian theory of fetishistic looking can arrive at a coherent analysis, and that an eclectic approach can result only in a series of at times discrete and apparently unconnected insights. The quest for physical perfection, however, raises so many issues in widely diverse fields that a general overview for non-specialist readers may prove all the more revealing for the absence of a single (and necessarily narrow) theoretical 'grid'.

This book is not intended as an academic study, but as a work for the informed general reader. It certainly makes no claim to originality of scholarship, but attempts rather to take up and expand upon a number of insights which a wide variety of authors and theorists have brought to bear on its central theme. I have deliberately made extensive use of quotations from these sources, both to acknowledge my indebtedness to them and to indicate the extent to which the present work may be considered a series of connected 'readings' in the literature of the perfectible body.

PART I

THE EVOLVING BODY

1.1   **CHAPTER 1**   THE BODIES OF GODS AND HEROES
(Polyclitus, *Doryphorus*, c. 450-440 B.C. (Roman copy). Naples, Museo Archeologico Nazionale.)

1

THE EMERGING BODY

THE BODIES OF GODS AND HEROES

It is an often repeated observation, almost a commonplace, of art history that the representation of the muscular male nude originated and reached one of its supreme manifestations in the sculpture of classical Greece. Even in the twentieth century, those concerned with the promotion of muscle-building exercise have commonly invoked a supposed lineage deriving from Greek classical ideals: in the 1920s, the bodybuilding promoter Charles Atlas promised his clients the acquisition of the 'Greek god type of physique', while more recently the leading international professional bodybuilding contest has conferred upon its winners the title of 'Mr (or Ms.) Olympia'. In 1976, the New York Whitney Museum was to sponsor its most successful exhibition ever under the title 'Articulate Muscle: the Body as Art', a display of bodybuilding accompanied by lectures in which various Professors of Fine Arts expanded glibly on the theme of the muscular body as the inheritor of the Greek sculptural tradition.

It is no doubt true that certain Greek sculptors of the High Classical period were the originators of one particular style of representation of the male figure in which a highly-developed muscularity was one of the chief conventions, yet the very popularisation of this physical style as almost a cliché of our cultural language can lead us to facile generalisations which overlook some of the fundamental questions it raises. What, for instance, was the significance of this achievement in terms of the Hellenic understanding of man; and what was the reason why he was depicted in this physical form?

1.2 One of the best known of ancient female fertility symbols: *The Venus of Willendorf* of 30,000-20,000 B.C. (Vienna, Naturgeschichtliches Museum.)

The present book is not an art history, and our interest in such questions relates not to their intrinsic so much as to their *seminal* importance — that is, to their shaping of an understanding of the body's metaphoric capacity which has inhabited Western consciousness over the centuries and retains some vestige of its symbolic power even in our own age. The fact is that reality has always been interpreted through the reports given by visual images, and that artistic creation was for centuries the chief visual means of communicating cultural values — a role which has been taken over in modern times by newspapers, television and advertising. In relation to ancient Greek civilisation, its art is (together with its literature) one of the two main sources of our knowledge of its world-view. Even in later ages, up to the middle of the nineteenth century, the world of 'high art' was a chief mediator of European society's view of itself and its values. Despite (or perhaps because of) its status as a commodity restricted to an elite, at least until the introduction of public art galleries towards the end of the eighteenth century, its importance cannot be overemphasised: the persons with access to works of art were, after all, precisely those who moulded the social values of their age. Given this general context, and the fact that for most of that period the naked or near-naked human body was the central subject of European pictorial and sculptural art, our exploration or the metaphoric value of the developed body must begin with an overview of its conception and subsequent evolution in the world of painting and sculpture.

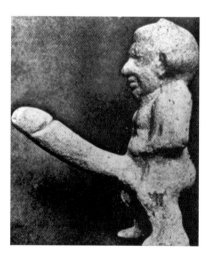

1.3 The hugely exaggerated erect penis is typical of some male fertility symbols, as in this representation of the ithyphallic god Ben. (Ephesus, Museum.)

When as distinguished an art historian as Kenneth Clark boldly claims that the nude is 'an art form invented by the Greeks in the fifth century B.C.'[1], such a statement must command our attention as well as meriting some explanation. To understand Clark's point, it is necessary to grasp his pivotal distinction between the naked and the nude — the former being a reference simply to the unclothed state, the latter referring to the affirmation of the body as a subject in its own right. It is obvious that depictions of the naked human form had existed well before the

1.4 Subservience to mythological ends: the ritualised shapes and postures of some Egyptian funerary art (the falcon-headed god Horus). (Egypt, Temple of Ramses II.)

Classical Greek period. The peculiarly Greek contribution can perhaps best be seen if we compare it, on the one hand, with early fertility symbols (often obese women with large breasts, buttocks and abdomens, or men with exaggerated phalluses), and on the other hand with the stylised representations of Egyptian funerary art. Though many early depictions of the body, some quite sophisticated, lie between these two poles, these at least draw attention to the peculiarly Greek achievement in representing the human body as an *autonomous* entity, distinct — as, for the Greeks, was man himself — from the world of nature on the one hand and that of the gods on the other. Just as, in Greek tragedy, man first confronted his fate and began to formulate

1.5 Before the age of High Classicism, the standing male figure was marked by obedience to mathematical laws of perfection rather than naturalism of portrayal: the only concession to a 'living' portrayal here is in the placement of the feet. [Sculptor unknown], *Kouros, c. 540 B.C.* (Munich, Glyptothek.)

its possible meaning in human terms, so this new consciousness became crystallised in the invention of a new concept: the ideally *human* body.

That most human bodies do not conform to the Greek ideal, far from being a conceptual flaw, was in fact the major point of this form of representation: it depicted man, not as he actually was, but as he could or should be. Here was human self-consciousness, freed from its entanglement with the world of repetitive animality and that of enslavement to mythology. That the gods themselves should be depicted in ideal human form represented in itself an important advance in religious consciousness and a movement towards the insights later to be proclaimed by the great world religions; for it embodied the notion that the gods might be loved for their beauty as well as being feared for their death-dealing powers.[2]

This evolution in artistic consciousness did not develop overnight. The earlier Greek representations of physical perfection — those of the Archaic age (c.600-480 B.C.) — do not, at least to the modern eye, look beautiful. Rather, they incorporate a severely mathematical and somewhat static conception of ideal proportion and a more or less removed nobility of bearing. Not till the beginning of the 'golden age', around 480 B.C., do the sculpted Apollos and Hermes seem to come to life, to take on human attitudes and a sense of arrested movement as the interplay of axes in the living and breathing human body was better understood. It is here — in the works of sculptors such as Phidias and Myron, and later Lysippos and Praxiteles — that the abiding image of ideal beauty was most completely formulated.[3]

In the terms of classical Greek thought, the words 'ideal beauty' might even be seen as tautological, since beauty itself was thought to be an ideal attribute, an indication of that harmony of which the gods supremely partook. Yet the gods were near to men, and could even appear in human form; indeed, they were envious of human beauty as of other forms of human eminence. Since physical beauty was a common bond between gods and men, its depiction could be either an offering pleasing to the divine or else a representation of the divine itself: the same *kouros* (or standing nude youth) might thus be Apollo or an offering to Apollo — a god or a man.[4]

As Greek religion evolved, the gods came to be envisaged less as divine beings in anthropomorphic form than as idealised representations of perfected humanity. In parallel to this movement, as the Archaic age of sculpture gave way to the High Classical age that divine harmony which the figure both represented and embodied came to reside less and less in a preconceived, deductive system of geometrical proportion and more in the harmonious relation of one body-part to another in a naturalistically portrayed human physique. And its most potent exemplar was, for the Greek artistic mind, the muscular male athlete.

What was it about the athlete that so fascinated these artists, inspiring a body of statuary which was to stamp the indelible imprint of the muscular male physique on the visual consciousness of European civilisation many centuries later?

1.6 The weight of the standing figure has shifted onto one leg, bending the trunk and accentuating the sway of the hips in the stance known as *contrapposto*, which will tend to displace the earlier symmetrical stance in representations of the 'ideal' figure. Praxiteles, *Hermes with the Child Dionysus on his Arm*, 330-320 B.C. (Olympia, Museum.)

There are several levels at which one can approach this question. At the simplest, one may look for an explanation in the Greek educational ideal of *arete* (usually translated 'goodness' or 'excellence'), a notion whose relevance went well beyond education in the narrower sense of schooling, and referred to the cultivation of the entire person. For the Greeks, the 'person' was intimately connected with the body, and hence the cultivation of the person and that of the body were closely associated. The three areas into which education was traditionally divided — literature, music and physical education — were of equal importance, so that (as Oswyn Murray has commented) 'it is no accident that two famous *gymnasia*, the Academy and the Lyceum, gave their names to two famous schools of philosophy, those of Plato and Aristotle; for these philosophers had established their activities deliberately in proximity to the exercising grounds'.[5] The gymnasium and the games had both an educational and a social role as the focuses of exemplary activity, the exemplars being the athletes whose exploits functioned symbolically as heroic feats in much the same way as the tournament was later to provide the stage for the display and acting-out of ideals of knightly heroism in medieval Europe. The athlete modelled himself on the *hero* of myth, and in so doing took on much of the symbolism of heroic stature — a symbolism readily grafted onto that family of amatory adventurers and warriors whom the Greeks invented as projections of their cultural obsessions and called 'the gods'. Indeed, although normally conceived as a mortal, the hero attained such godlike status that cult was paid to him and (in the case of Hercules) he might become practically indistinguishable from a god.[6]

But what were the gods? How was their divinity to be conceived, and (more to our purpose) in what form could it be portrayed? To this question every major culture has responded in its own characteristic way, and the religions of the ancient world were to choose widely divergent symbols and myths by which their spiritual aspirations could be translated into recognisable material form. It is not possible to encapsulate in a paragraph or two, at least without gross over-simplification, an issue of enormous complexity to which many volumes have been devoted, but an illuminating glimpse of the peculiarly Greek response can be gained by a comparison of the muscular, heroic divinities of ancient Greece with the very different conventions in which the religions of the Far East traditionally represented their gods or the great recipients of spiritual enlightenment.

The contrast between this typically Western approach to the body and that which has tended to characterise Oriental cultures has been analysed in an important and highly original paper by Gilbert Andrieu, who relates these opposing conceptions to the ancient myths of Hercules and Narcissus. While Hercules is seen as the prototype of the 'bulging chest and muscular abdomen' of the Western hero-figure, Narcissus embodies that of the 'sightless stare and soft belly' of the Eastern divinity.[7]

To grasp the implications of such an antithesis, Andrieu argues, it is necessary to understand the deep rather than popular significance of the two mythical figures, and in particular to appreciate the manner of their deaths and subsequent metamorphoses. Hercules, who sets alight his own funeral pyre and rejoins the gods by overcoming earthly suffering, achieves immortality by rising above human struggle; Narcissus, on the other hand, is re-born after drowning in the spring which is the source of his own image, the image which is in reality that of the god within him. In these opposing images — fire and water, rising above oneself and descending into oneself, external effort and absorption into the infinite — Andrieu sees the delineation of two very different views of man's spiritual journey. If Hercules is the symbol of achievement through exploits (the hero, the athlete), Narcissus is the symbol of knowledge through inwardness (the holy man, the contemplative).

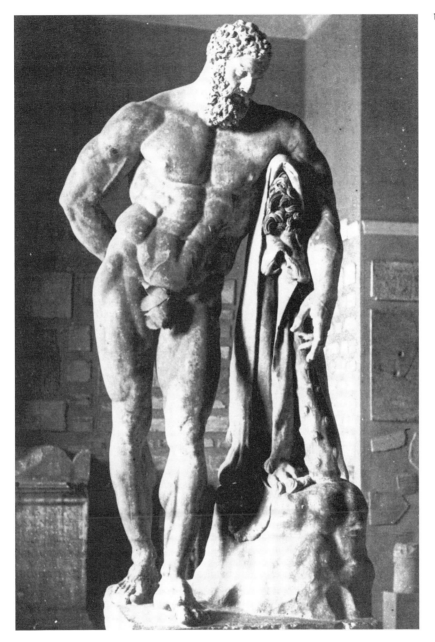

In terms of the bodily depiction which gives symbolic form to these two conceptions of self-transcendence, Andrieu suggests a revealing contrast:

1.8 The earliest Buddhist art tended to be non-figurative. As representations of the Buddha emerged, they tended to adopt a highly ideological stylisation. One of the most common forms is the concave-torsoed Buddha, here shown in the traditional posture known as 'calling the earth to witness'. Thailand, Sukhothai School, early 14th century A.D.

'Alongside ancient Greek statuary we have Indian and Egyptian sculpture, which present to our gaze bodies turned in upon themselves, motionless and concentrating upon an interior life which we can sometimes see captured in the look of the eyes. The chests are not bulging, there is no muscular relief expressive of strength, the stomachs are soft, often rounded, and the posture — seated or standing, sometimes recumbent — indicates how little importance is attributed to the movement of the body. The attitudes reflect a precise tension which frees the individual for an interior journey in search of that other (divine) self which Narcissus meets in his own image.'[8]

1.9 A very different representation of the Buddhist contemplative ideal, though again based on the imagery of circularity, is the so-called 'Fat Buddha', a popular Chinese portrayal of the bodhisattva Maitreya as a pot-bellied figure symbolic of prosperity.

The Greek tradition, on the other hand, is that of a humanity which seeks spiritual elevation through victorious combat against the external, material world, self-mastery rather than self-abandonment to the infinite. Hercules, the 'hero of the bulging chest and contracted abdominal muscles', is in search of a divinity to be attained through deeds and actions rather than by a descent into the self. If we consider for a moment the religious iconography of the ancient East — the lithe and graceful Vishnus, Ramas and Krishnas of Hinduism, or the serenely contemplative Buddhas and bodhisattvas — and compare it with the heavily-muscled, athletic gods and heroes of classical Greece, we can appreciate more clearly the fundamentally activist nature of Greek religion and its fascination with man's achievement of his mortal limits.

1.10 The muscular 'Western' ideal of the body can be discerned in schematic form in early Greek art. The 'Mantiklos' bronze from Thebes (c. 700-675 B.C.), a votive offering dedicated to Apollo, displays the triangular torso and strong thighs which would persist in subtler and more naturalistic form into and beyond the Classical period. (Boston, Museum of Fine Arts.)

Though the earliest representations of the Buddha, particularly those which depict him as a standing figure, betray the vestigial influence of Greek sculpture (notably in the use of drapery and the 'royal' stance), in his more evolved forms he tends to be shown seated in the lotus posture, concave-torsoed and displaying the characteristic signs of the *mahapurusa* or 'Great Man' by which one can recognise every being destined to become a Buddha[9]. In the artistic tradition of Thailand, as exemplified in the Sukhothai school, the seated Buddha depicted in the posture known as 'calling the earth to witness' portrays through his concave body shape the *chakras* or circular bodily symbols which indicate centres of psychic energy. He may be compared with the Chinese representations of the bodhisattva Maitreya, the future Buddha waiting to be reborn on earth: here, the figure is no longer concave but convex or circular, often massively obese as in the popular depiction known as the 'Pot-Bellied Maitreya' or 'Fat Buddha' (mí tuó fó) whose mountainous belly denotes prosperity and good fortune[10]. The circularity of both these portrayals contrasts markedly with the inverted triangle of the Western representation of the torso, seen in its most schematic form in Greek art of the geometric and orientalising periods (up to 600 B.C.). In the 'Mantiklos bronze' of c.700-675 B.C., a votive offering dedicated to Apollo, the strong, cylindrical thighs of the man of action are surmounted by a triangular torso whose outline is reflected in the face. Though later Greek representations would attenuate this starkly geometric symbolism, the outward-pointing angularity of the mesomorphic torso conveys a Western predilection for externality and activism which stands in sharp contrast to the stylised interiority of Eastern religious art.

In a socio-religious system in which athletes were seen as heroes (or, at least, as heroes in the making), it followed logically that heroes should be depicted as athletes. And so the exemplary figure, be it the god himself or the philosophic rationalisation of the divine in human form, bears in classical Greek sculpture the type of

1.11 Hellenism placed a greater emphasis than had Classicism on the effect of violent activity or extreme tension in asserting and even emphasising the muscularity of the 'heroic' body. Hagesandros, Athenedoros and Polydoros, *The Death of Laocoön and his Sons*, *c.* 150 B.C. (Rome, Musei Vaticani.)

physique fostered in healthy young mesomorphs by exercises such as running, javelin and discus throwing, and wrestling. As an emblematic figure, however, he bears this muscular development to an outstanding degree: the aim is not naturalism, and we need not imagine that most young Greeks were endowed with anything like the physical attributes of the sculpted Greek hero-figure. It is precisely in its physical idealism that the sculpture is readable as an aspiration towards, or an invocation of, a perfected state of being.

31

Even outside Greece itself, as in the Graeco-Roman statuary of the neo-Attic school, the influence of the High Classical period remained a potent force in the depiction of the developed body. Indeed, by the later stages of Hellenistic sculpture (2nd and 1st centuries B.C.), the portrayal of advanced muscularity had become even more prominent than in the High Classical age — a function of increased mastery of the sculptor's medium, a closer knowledge of anatomy and a shift in attention from symbolism towards realism. Vigorous action and the depiction of heightened emotions was now a more common preoccupation, and the potent effect of muscular tension in portraying both physical and emotional extremes was exploited to the full. We have moved here from the world of divine serenity and human assurance to that of human striving and human struggle.

In *The Death of Laocoön and his Sons* (Hagesandros, Athenedoros and Polydoros, 2nd-1st century B.C.[?]) and the *Torso Belvedere* (Apollonius [?], 1st century B.C.), the Western world gained two of the most enduring images of the heavily-muscled physique ever created — images whose evocative power has haunted the aesthetic imagination of post-Renaissance Europe as only a handful of other ancient works has done. What these sculpted bodies present is nothing less than a 'muscle-landscape' (to use Kenneth Clark's term[11]), a form in which the attention is directed not so much — as in earlier Greek statuary — to the proportion and balance of the whole, as to the relationships of individual knots of muscle one with the other, to the rise and fall of the body's surface like the hills and hollows of a landscape, a muscularity taken to the very limits of contractile possibility, and the overwhelming impression of physical and emotional energy created by the various structural elements through their suggestion of a surface modelled from within, as it were, by some vital force.

From the early Archaic to the late Hellenistic age, Greek sculpture managed to formulate an entirely original language of the body. The earlier static, geometrical representation of divine perfection in stylised human form was gradually modified and transformed so as to portray at last the potential of the physical body to express a reality beyond and greater than itself. The metaphor chosen, readable through an understanding of this centuries-long evolution, was that of a highly developed muscularity, pointing to the body's self-transcendence.

The perfectible body, and its symbolism, had emerged.

THE ALLURE OF THE ATHLETE

The Greek predilection for physical perfection had the faults of its virtues. Whilst it glorified the well-formed body, it neglected or even deprecated the infirm, the aged, the ugly, the misshapen. As a species of anatomical elitism, this particular form of the pursuit of excellence already contained the seeds of more disturbing developments to which we shall later turn, though fortunately for Greek culture as a whole the cult of the body was held in balance by the parallel flowering of an interest in philosophy and pursuit of the moral and social good which served to protect the social fabric from the dangers of too exclusive a preoccupation with physical perfection.

1.12 The lithe, youthful bodies depicted in Greek vase-painting seem to belong to a different tradition from that of the sculpted gods and heroes. *Attic Youth*, c. 530-430 B.C. (Schwerin, Museum.)

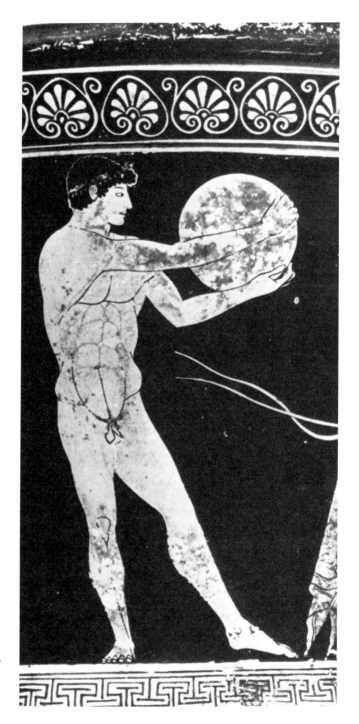

1.13 Athletes were a favourite theme of vase-painting, which often seems as concerned with muscular shape and delineation as it is with sporting prowess. *Athlete with Disc*, Attic style. (Tarquinia, Museum.)

One form of this preoccupation, however, deserves special mention here, in view of its crucial importance not only for an understanding of Greek cultural attitudes but for the attainment of a proper perspective on the developed body as an object of interest in more recent centuries. For it must be recognised that there is a less idealistic, more sensual side to the Greek fascination with the well-developed male body. Indeed, as Edward Lucie-Smith has pointed out, it is impossible to disentangle the artistic portrayal of the nude, at any stage of its history, from the element of erotic attraction.[12] The idealistic, quasi-religious portrayal of the muscular hero to which we referred above is but one of a number of major themes first enunciated and developed by classical Greek art. To it must immediately be added that of the muscular male body as the object of sexual —and in particular homosexual — attention.

The subject of homosexuality in ancient Greece has not always been well understood, and it will perhaps be helpful, even at the risk of over-simplification, to set out a number of general points to which modern scholars have drawn attention.

In the first instance, it needs to be recognised that the so-called cult of homosexuality was not, as is sometimes thought, somehow inherent in ancient Greek civilisation. Without denying the at times overtly homosexual nature of the attraction for the male body to which some Greek art, literature and cultural practices bear witness, we may observe that such public expression is reasonably circumscribed in time and place, having chiefly emerged in certain urban centres (notably Athens) in the fifth century B.C.

The Greek artistic treatment of athletes is instructive in this regard. In the sixth century, the typical athlete as portrayed in art is the strong man, the boxer or wrestler, depicted as a vigorous and heroic male without any suggestion of sexual attraction. He is certainly muscular, and often bearded, the personification of power and endurance. By the fifth century, however, the fully developed adult male tends to be replaced by the athletic youth, not merely strong but also beautiful and graceful — indeed, as remarkable for his physical beauty as for his bodily strength.[13]

Probably the most significant event in organised public life in the intervening period had been the rise of the gymnasium. The domain of the earlier athletes had been the stadium, the place of earnest physical battle; now it became the gymnasium, the place where the youths of the *polis* underwent a period of athletic training. The educational importance of the gymnasium — not so much a building as a recreation or sports ground — made it a popular place for members of the public to observe young men exercising, as was the custom, unclothed (the word *gymnos* means 'naked'). In cultural terms, this nakedness was in itself unremarkable:

'In classical Greece', writes John Boardman, 'athletes exercised naked, warriors could fight near-naked, and in everyday life the bared young male must have been a fairly common sight. Artists did not need to look for naked models of their idealized athlete figures; they had grown up in a society in which male nudity was commonplace and a well developed body was admired. The foreigner found this behaviour disgusting, and the foreign artist depicted nudity mainly for religious, erotic or pathetic appeal. [...] In classical Greece it was not unnatural in life, and in art it required neither excuse nor explanation.'[14]

It was in this climate — in which the horror of actual battle was replaced by a concentration on the technique of movement, on grace and beauty of line and execution —that a fascination with the youthful athletic body was to arise and become a leading theme of artistic representation. So thoroughly was the visible muscularity of the body itself — as distinct from its effective strength in a particular form of battle or contest — the subject of training and thus artistic depiction, that, with the exception of runners, it is sometimes hard to distinguish in a vase painting the event in which the individual athlete was engaged: the artist was often obliged to add a discus or a pair of boxing-thongs or jumping weights to indicate the particular sport involved.[15]

The physical beauty of these youths and young adults, and the sexual overtones of the attraction felt by artists (and other observers) towards these muscular young men, cannot be denied. But it would certainly be an over-simplification to conclude that somehow, in the fifth century, the incidence of homosexuality in the Greek male population underwent a dramatic upsurge, as though the so-called 'gay gene' had suddenly got out of control. From the point of view of the ordinary conduct of civic life, including marriage and the begetting of children, no such conclusion can be drawn. Using the socio-sexual indicators of today, we have every reason to believe that the proportion of Greek males whom we would describe as exclusively homosexual did not vary greatly from one age to another, or from that of modern populations in general. The main distinguishing feature of fifth century Athenians, if one is to be found, lay in the acceptance of that visual pleasure (and, indeed, the pleasure of more intimate encounters) which might be taken in the muscular and graceful bodies of youths by married men otherwise devoted to their wives and families.

If we adopt the view generally held by psychologists that both homosexual and bisexual inclination are the product of a complex interactive 'nature-nurture' equation, our understanding of the Greek predilection must lean heavily towards the 'nurture' rather than the 'nature' end of the spectrum. For what we are talking about

1.14 The abduction of Ganymede by Zeus was a popular theme, illustrating (and perhaps authorising) the pursuit of a beautiful youth by an older man. The youth is deemed to have given his consent by accepting the love-gift of a fighting cock, in this work by the Penthesilea painter, *c.* 460-450 B.C. (Ferrara, Museo Nazionale Archeologico.)

here is more a cultural than a biological phenomenon, the abandonment by a particular society of the social taboo which most cultures have placed on any stirrings of sexual attraction felt by members of the male population towards those of their own sex. Such departures from the cultural norm have been noted in societies other than ancient Greece (the warrior class of the Edo period in seventeenth-century Japan is a case in point[16]), though in most cases the maintenance of 'social stability' and the protection of youth from 'moral corruption' have placed constraints upon such overt expression and severely punished any transgression. Even in ancient Greece itself, the sexual predilection for well-formed youths was by no means universal but was characteristic mainly of the culture of the aristocratic *symposion* or all-male drinking group; this culture had its chief vogue in Athens, where it was regarded as a kind of counter-weight to the family setting and a mode of release for emotions and affections normally repressed in the cause of social cohesion.[17]

This point is of considerable importance for the history of the developed male body, in particular as it helps to explain the abiding interest that the Greek portrayal of male physical beauty has retained even in very different cultures and ages. More particularly, it helps to account for the appreciation of this form of

Greek artistic output amongst those (male) art-lovers who would not consider themselves to be homosexually or, to any significant degree, bisexually inclined. What the Greek system did was remove from the realm of taboo that latent capacity for attraction towards beauty in one's own sex which is by no means uncommon within the population but is in most of its members both successfully repressed and overlaid by a stronger attraction towards the opposite sex.

The cultural difference which in this regard separates modern Western society from that of ancient Greece has been characterised by the French philosopher Michel Foucault in a passage which, although some scholars would see it as over-reflective of his personal preoccupations, is not without insight:

'As matter of fact, the notion of homosexuality is plainly inadequate as a means of referring to an experience, forms of valuation, and a system of categorisation so different from ours. The Greeks did not see love for one's own sex and love for the other sex as opposites, as two exclusive choices, two radically different types of behaviour. The dividing lines did not follow that kind of boundary. What distinguished a moderate, self-possessed man from one given to pleasures was, from the viewpoint of ethics, much more important than what differentiated, among themselves, the categories of pleasures that invited the greatest devotion. To have loose morals was to be incapable of resisting either women or boys, without it being any more serious than that.'[18]

1.15 At a far remove from the diminutive sexual organs of the idealised (Apollonian) male figure, the satyr often bears the giant phallus of the Dionysiac rites, and is not infrequently shown as a bearded or hairy figure. (c. 575-550 B.C.)

Thus, sexual attraction was essentially the same whether it applied to a youth or a woman, though the modes of behaviour arising from such attraction might be very different. 'It was,' writes Thomas Laqueur, 'in no way thought unnatural for mature men to be sexually attracted to boys. The male body, indeed, seemed equally capable of responding erotically to the sight of women as to attractive young men'.[19]

1.16 Ganymede, sometimes depicted as the model of the desirable youth, is characteristically shown without pubic hair. *Ganymede with Cockerel and Hoop*, Attica, c. 530-430 B.C. (Paris, Louvre.)

Richard Davenport-Hines has pointed out that, provided they were the active partners in sodomy, adult men in ancient Greece were not stigmatised or assumed to be sexually indifferent to women; on the other hand, men who were passive sodomites were traduced unless they were youths or transvestites.[20]

To think of Greek homosexuality in the usual sense of the word is thus at best an inadequate, and in some ways a misleading, approach. The sexual attraction which so characterised this particular culture (as distinguished from those of its members who were *exclusively* homosexual) was essentially an attraction towards youthful beauty irrespective of sex — though, of course, most readily observable in the naked young men of the gymnasium. 'When [says Hanfmann] Zeuxis proposed to paint a picture of Helen for the Temple of Hera, he asked the people of Kroton to show him their most beautiful virgins. They immediately took him to the gymnasium and showed him their boys, saying he could imagine the beauty of their sisters.'[21] Indeed in many ancient Greek representations, male and female bodies are distinguishable only by the presence or absence of the breasts and the genital organs.

1.17 Even when the body is so placed that the genitals would not normally be visible, the vase-painters often insisted on showing them, as if they were a necessary part of the convention. Two-handled Attic plate, with youth. (Hanover, Kestner Museum.)

In either case, however, the 'approved' or most desirable youthful figure had a number of standard characteristics, which K.J. Dover has enumerated as 'broad shoulders, a deep chest, big pectoral muscles, big muscles above the hips, a slim waist, jutting buttocks and stout thighs and calves.'[22] From the most minimally sketched vase paintings to the most exquisitely sculpted *kouroi* or statues of gods and heroes, these are the characteristics of the developed body which Greek art was to turn into the permanent and (in modern Western society) universal symbolism of the 'ideal' male physique.

There are two other aspects of the Greek interest in the developed body which have left a distinctive mark on the subsequent conventions of 'ideal' depiction. Curiously, these are non-naturalistic in nature, consisting of the almost universal absence of hair on the body (including, in vase paintings, the virtual absence of pubic hair), and the unnaturally small size of the penis in male figures. By contrast, those figures intended as hideous or loathsome (notably certain satyrs) often have huge penises and are at times extensively covered with body hair.

The cult of the phallus was, to the Greek mind, Dionysiac rather than Apollonian: huge artificial penises were worn by comic actors and large erect phalluses were carried in procession at the festivals of Dionysus in various centres.

But the type of exaggerated phallic representation familiar to us from Pompeii and other centres of Dionysiac (or, in ancient Rome, Bacchic) celebration was foreign to the ideals of the leading Greek sculptors, and even in the more popular vase paintings, as Dover has pointed out, 'the characteristic penis of a young male (human, heroic or divine) is thin (sometimes notably thinner than a finger) and short (as measured from the base to the end of the glans), terminating in a long pointed foreskin, the axis of the penis and foreskin being almost always straight.'[23] The absence of body hair is most noticeable in vase painting, but even in High Classical sculpture it is restricted to a small tuft of pubic hair; even assuming that the absence of chest hair may have been characteristic of some males, the absence of hair under the arms is a sign of the persistence of this rejection of bodily hair from the artistic canon.

It is tempting to conclude from these features of Greek art that the aim was simply to minimise those elements of bodily appearance which most visibly distinguished young males from young females. Such a conclusion, however, does not stand up to close scrutiny, since in vase painting, even when shown in positions where the genitals would normally be concealed from an observer, the young male has them very much in evidence, the penis often projecting horizontally even when not erect.[24] Even in statuary, later examples (particularly of wrestlers or other figures in extreme attitudes) often appear posed so as to present the sexual organs as a chief visual object. The famous *Sleeping Faun* of *c.* 200 B.C., reclining with splayed legs, is a case in point — though the faun or satyr, even when depicted as a well-built rural youth, obviously lent itself to a more openly carnal treatment than the adolescent athlete.[25] Like other (more or less contemporaneous) examples of 'Hellenistic realism', the *Sleeping Faun* marks the entry into the senior art of sculpture of a frank sexuality which two centuries earlier would have been considered undignified or demeaning, fit only for the more popular types of vase painting in which youths were depicted in much the same way (and with much the same intention) as *hetaerae* or courtesans.

A more instructive clue to the significance of these conventions is to be found in what distinguishes rather than what unites the forms of representation in which they appear. For it is in the differences between Greek heroic statuary and popular Greek vase painting that we find the earliest formulation of a distinction which recurs in only slightly different guise in the depiction of the developed male body throughout Western art and can be observed even in contemporary modes of photographic or live representation. In basic form, it can be seen as a differentiation between the 'powerful' male body (the object of admiration) and the 'beautiful' male body (the object of erotic or quasi-erotic interest) —essentially the same distinction of principle that can be observed today between the representation of, say, the male bodybuilder and that of the male pin-up.

1.18 The *Sleeping Faun* (or *Barberini Faun*) of the late 3rd-early 2nd century B.C., whose erotically suggestive posture is still frequently imitated in gay iconography. (Munich, Glyptothek.)

What did this distinction mean to the Greeks of fifth-century Athens? In the first place, we have noted that the convention in question was clearly differentiated from that of the Dionysian cult of the phallus. As opposed to the latter's often crudely misshapen bodies bearing giant penises, both the gods and the athletes are remarkable for the diminutive size of their sexual organs, a contrast accentuated by their visible muscularity; it is also clear that this convention found its significance in the context of an otherwise naturalistic (if at times schematic) depiction of the body. Secondly, we may note that while the sculpted gods and heroes are often endowed with a quite remarkable degree of muscular development, the athletes are depicted with lithe and well-toned bodies but as moderately rather than extremely muscular.

While the gods were admittedly to be held in affection, they were also to be feared, or at least to be respected as embodiments of power. With the hindsight afforded by Freudian psychology, we can read the heavily-muscled body — its capillaries engorged with blood, its surface stretched taut with not an inch of limp or flaccid flesh — as itself a suggestive symbol of phallic power. Indeed, as John Webb has put it, 'muscle operates as more than just the outwardly visible symbol of male power, it is also symbolic of inward rigidity and invulnerability.'[26] Devoid of the soft curvaceousness of the female form, it is erect, hard, supremely virile. Yet it is only symbolically, and, as it were, unconsciously, so: to equip the muscular body with too visibly intrusive a genital endowment would be to replace the universal suggestiveness of symbolism with a restrictively literal and particular meaning, to substitute mere sexual prowess for the universality of divine potency. It is in some such sense as this that Greek artists must unconsciously have understood the need to suppress, or at least attenuate, the overtly sexual message in favour of a more indirect and more widely evocative symbolism.

As distinct from the heavily muscular gods and heroes, the lithe naked youths of the gymnasium were the object of aesthetic and even erotic attention. Their depiction in vase painting, and in particular the treatment of the genitalia, have been carefully and subtly analysed by Dover in his important study.

> 'That a youth or boy', he writes, 'should have a straight, pointed penis symbolised his masculine fitness to become a warrior; that it should be small sharpened the contrast between the immature male and the adult male and assimilated this to the contrast between female and male; a small penis (especially if the existence of the corona glandis is not betrayed by any undulation in the surface of the penis) is an index of modesty and subordination, an abjuration of sexual initiative or sexual rivalry, and the painters' adoption of the ideal youthful penis as the standard for men, heroes and gods is one item in their general tendency to "youthen" everyone.'[27]

It is precisely in this balance between the male subject as virile actor and passive object of erotic attention that the convention can be read in a coherent way. The unambiguously sexual message of the enlarged penis or phallus, along with the hyper-masculine symbolism of body hair, is attenuated or even negated in the Greek artistic convention by a number of key signals of submissiveness and subordination, so as to suggest the role of the male body as 'object of the gaze', of a symbolic and stylised visual encounter in which beauty of form takes precedence over more openly stated messages of masculinity.

1.19 The vase athletes were not young boys, but post-pubertal youths of muscular build, already fit to become warriors. *Athlete with Storage Jar*, Attic style. (London, British Museum.)

The role of art, here as often elsewhere, is to stylise and to some extent idealise desires or relationships which in their actual social setting may well have been purely carnal and even unfeeling. Rosalind Miles has perceptively explored the Greek fascination with youthful beauty from this point of view:

'Love lyrics harp insistently on the boys' pale, smooth, hairless bodies, and there is no pubic hair shown in any of the countless vase paintings of homosexual youths. In marked contrast to later, particularly twentieth-century ideas of what makes a man desirable, the small, delicate penis was much admired. The ideal beloved was not effeminate — the most prized boys were usually champions of the gymnasium, or victors in javelin, discus or running events. But they were very young, since the essence of their appeal was pre-pubertal.'[28]

The social consequence of this predilection, says Miles, was that the youth — like women, slaves and foreigners — was 'no more than an undeveloped and hence inherently inferior being, ordained by the gods to serve the needs of heroes and men.' The feelings and desires of the adult male were the only emotions of any social consequence in such transactions. While this observation undoubtedly carries weight, and the adult male's social right to enforce submission on the desirable youth is to the modern mind one of the more morally reprehensible features of this element of Greek cultural practice, Miles' analysis fails to take account of the role of artistic depiction in sublimating, stylising and even idealising what, in other contexts, often degenerated into practices which most civilised societies would regard as perverted and even barbaric. While some vase paintings admittedly depict the degrading sodomisation of youths by older men, there was also a more noble (and more frequent) vase convention in which the emphasis was entirely upon athletic grace and beauty of form. That the athletes of the vase paintings were already well developed and muscular, moreover, indicates that they were not the 'very young boys' suggested by Miles but post-pubertal youths of at least sixteen years of age[29] who were already fit to become warriors. The artistic convention which (to use Dover's term) 'youthens' them should be seen rather as a stylistic device aimed at mitigating or cancelling the threatening symbolism of hyper-masculinity.

How profoundly these conventions have influenced later displays of the male body (including the contemporary male pin-up and the bodybuilding display) will be discussed in later chapters. For the moment, we may observe that one of the most important legacies of Greek artistic representation, along with that of the 'idealised' male body (the object of admiration), is that of the 'beautiful' male body (the acceptable object of sublimated erotic attention). The success of Greek artistic conventions in simultaneously indicating and repressing the element of sexual attraction has been one of its chief legacies to the later 'mainstream' portrayal of the male body, since it has provided a means whereby the muscular male physique could retain its abiding attraction for artists whilst at the same time disclaiming or consigning to the subconscious level any element of sexual attraction.

SYMBOLIC BODIES

To turn from classical Greece to Imperial Rome is to enter a very different world in respect of the body and its representation. For one thing, the Romans did not share the Greek interest in athletic training; indeed they treated with contempt the practice of training naked, which was regarded as degrading by Roman citizens.[30] Even the athletic movement instituted by the Emperor Augustus was primarily a 'show', the Romans being interested primarily in fighting events such as boxing and wrestling — and, for the general populace, the more bloodthirsty these events the better. Gladiatorial combat, and events in which men were pitted against wild beasts, provided the kind of spectacle in which Roman audiences delighted. Compared with such contests of brute strength, the gymnasium exercises of naked young Greeks seemed not merely tame but effete or even degenerate.

Peace and war were the great themes of Roman art. The triumphs of the Roman Emperor and the deeds of the great Roman leaders, as well as the benefits of the *pax Romana* and the aims of the rulers in imposing law and order on barbaric

1.20 Two portraits of the Emperor Caracalla (Emperor 211-217 A.D.), indicating the ability of Roman portrait sculptors to capture an individual likeness. Despite minor stylistic differences, the subject is clearly recognisable, particularly from the broad ridge of the nose and the V-shaped bulge of the forehead muscles. ((a) New York, Metropolitan Museum of Art; (b) Berlin, Staatliche Museen, Antiken-Sammlung.)

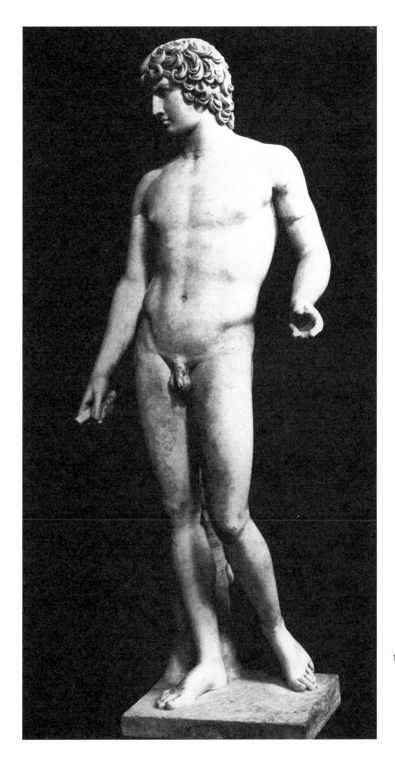

1.21 One of a number of
Roman treatments of
Antinous, whose story
permitted a foray into
the visual language of
youthful beauty. *c.* 130
A.D. (Naples, Museo
Nazionale.)

1.22 The *Augustus of Primaporta*, a propagandist treatment of the Emperor which uses the muscular breastplate –heavily decorated with the symbols of his triumphs – to transform his body into that of the military hero. 19 B.C. (Vatican, Braccio Nuovo.)

tribes, were the subject of triumphal art and the adornment of private life. Military victories and civic order became the favoured themes of Roman statuary, and realism rather than legendary or heroic idealism was a major concern both of the patrician figures who commissioned honorific sculptures and of the wealthy householders who decorated their villas with portraiture and scenes of domestic life and civil or religious celebration.

In its depiction of the developed body, Imperial Rome was (as in so many other areas) less an innovator than an avid and skilled borrower of other, chiefly Hellenic, forms of expression which it turned to its own ends. Greek art provided the models of gods and heroes which were used by the Romans to celebrate the leader of the Roman State and his family and to honour the great rulers and wealthy patrons.

Technical progress in the art of statuary had a significant influence on the form of depiction. Late Hellenistic sculpture had demonstrated such mastery in the rendering of human subjects that few challenges remained. Sculptors had assimilated the art of depicting the most intricate folds of drapery, and with the Roman interest in clothing and adornment the fashion of the clothed statue grew in popularity. As to the nude or semi-clad figure, the new technique of making a plaster cast from an original provided a relatively easy means of using Hellenic models for this purpose. What primarily interested the Romans, however, was the individual: as an Empire ruled by men of powerful character, and noted more for its realism than for the lofty ideals of Greece, Rome was to replace the earlier taste for typification with the close observation of the distinctive individual features of those whom it celebrated in its art.[31]

The nude human figure was studied less and less, and attention passed from the body as a whole to the realistic portrayal of the human head and face. Here we find the beginnings of recognisable portraiture, the culmination of a tendency towards individual observation already discernible in the early Hellenism of the fourth century B.C. The careful observation of facial features and expression makes the Roman Emperors recognisable in statuary in a way that does not apply to the idealised gods and heroes of the Greek Classical age. In a similar way, the *Antinous* (*c.*130 A.D.) in the Museum of Delphi commemorates Hadrian's drowned boyfriend by 'combining a body of mid-fifth-century form with a head which conveys a new emotional intensity' (R.J.A. Wilson)[32].

There is, however, one important legacy of ancient Rome to the depiction of the developed body. This was the *cuirasse esthétique*, the 'decorated breastplate' or upper body armour originally made of leather (French *cuir*) worn by military leaders and those depicted in such a guise. The most celebrated example is the *Augustus of Primaporta* (19 B.C.), the painted marble statue of the Emperor Augustus in which the breastplate is decorated at the top with celestial divinities (the protecting Sky God, the Sun on its chariot ushering in the Augustan age), in the centre with the victories of the Emperor, on the sides with the pacified provinces and at the bottom with a representation of the bountiful earth.[33] Much less realistic a 'portrait' of the Emperor than those of him and his family dating from the late Republic, this unashamedly propagandist representation was one of a number that were created in order to spread to all corners of the Empire the idealised image of the determined and authoritative *princeps*.

1.23 The *cuirasse esthétique* became a convention for depicting the 'man among men' and endowing him with heroic or quasi-divine status. The Emperor Trajan (79-117 A.D.)

1.24 The muscular
breastplate was to
become an artistic
convention for depicting
the heroic body in the
centuries following the
Renaissance. This
engraving from the
Frontispiece of Calvin's
*Institution of the
Christian Religion* (1557
edition) shows the
original 'muscular
Christian', clad in the
armour of spiritual
virtue.

INSTITVTION
DE LA RELIGION
CHRESTIENNE.

COMPOSEE EN LATIN PAR
M. Iean Caluin, & tranflatée en François par luy mefme, &
encores de nouueau reueue & augmentée : en laquelle eſt
comprinſe vne ſomme de toute la Chreſtienté.

AVEC LA PREFACE ADRESSEE AV
Roy, par laquelle ce preſent Linre luy eſt offert pour confeſsion de Foy.

SEMBLABLEMENT Y SONT ADIOV
ſtées deux Tables : l'vne des paſſages de l'Eſcriture, que l'Autheur
expoſe en ce liure : l'autre des matieres principales
contenues en iceluy.

POINT CHARNELLES, MAIS PVIS-

GLAIVE DE L'ESPRIT

HEAVME DE SALVT

HALLECRET DE IVSTICE

BAVDRIER DE VERITE.

BOVCLIER DE FOY

LES ARMEVRES DE NOSTRE GVERRE NE SONT

SANTES PAR DIEV. II. AVX CORINTH. X. CH.

LES PIEDZ CHAVSSES DE LA PRE-
PARATION DE L'EVANGILE
DE PAIX.

DE L'IMPRIMERIE
De François Iaquy, Antoine Dauodeau,
& Iaques Bourgeois.

AVEC PRIVILEGE.
M. D. LVII.

Whether heavily decorated or not, the Roman cuirass took essentially the form of a muscular torso, the full and square pectorals surmounting a prominent thoracic arch and well-defined abdominal muscles. Worn over the toga, the *cuirasse esthétique* had an emblematic value very different from the serviceable oblong of leather armour-plating from which it derived. Making no pretence to realism, it symbolically transformed the most undeveloped of upper bodies into that of a muscular hero. The conventions of late Hellenistic statuary have here been assimilated by the Greek sculptors working in Rome, to the point where the schematised features of the heavily-muscled torso are themselves sufficient to conjure up an image of the 'man amongst men', the embodiment of the physical ideal of the hero or leader.

In its synthesis of Greek art and Roman ideology, the modelled Roman breastplate made a major contribution to the representation of the physically developed male body. Centuries later, in post-Renaissance European art, it was to become the standard convention of the artistic portrayal of heroic figures, thus fixing permanently in the Western imagination the symbolic image of the muscular male torso derived from classical Greece.

By simplifying and stylising the features of the muscular upper body, Roman art turned them into an instantly readable symbol of heroic strength and power. From the neo-classical engravings of the seventeenth and eighteenth centuries to the drawings of 'comic-strip heroes' in modern times, the schematised features of the Roman cuirass have come to represent a kind of artistic shorthand by which the powerful or authoritative male body could be evoked by a few strokes of the pen. The power-symbolism of the developed body had found its definitive Western formulation.

2.1   **CHAPTER 2**   THE BODY RE-BORN
(Michelangelo, *The Risen Christ*, 1521. Rome, Santa Maria sopra Minerva.)

2

THE BODY RE-BORN

THE AMBIGUOUS BODY

The thousand or so years separating the fall of Rome from the birth of the Italian Renaissance saw a prolonged eclipse in the artistic representation of the developed body —and, indeed, of the human body itself. To ascribe this interregnum to the influence of Christianity, though in one sense accurate, is over-simple. For while the dominant strand of Christian thought in the Middle Ages was undoubtedly opposed to the idealising of physical existence, the fact remains that the revival of interest in physical beauty was to take place in the strongly (and at times quite intolerantly) Christian climate of Renaissance and post-Renaissance Europe. That the very concept of 'physical perfection' — which, in most of the great world religions, would be thought a contradiction in terms — should have been a major theme of art in the christianised West is an indication of the distinctive and in some ways paradoxical contribution of Christianity to the history of the human body as an object of artistic and social interest.

The explanation is to be found in the complex and at times ambiguous Christian conception of the status of the physical body. Uniquely among the major world religions, Christianity preached the glorification of the body in the future resurrection life. The Jesus who appeared in bodily form to his disciples after his death was also a transcendent being who had in some sense entered already into the divine glory; in such manifestations he was seen not only as uniquely the Son of God but also as the pattern and 'first fruits' of their own future resurrection. Other world religions either tended to interpret the dualism of body and spirit in absolute terms, stressing total liberation from the body in an ultimately non-corporeal transcendence (the nirvana of Hinduism and Buddhism), or else envisaged physical

2.2 This statue of *The Youthful Christ Teaching*, which depicts Jesus as a long-locked Apollo figure, indicates the extent to which early Christian art in some centres had undergone the influence of the Greek pagan tradition. *c.* 350 A.D. (Rome, Museo Nazionale delle Terme.)

resurrection as basically a return to original sinlessness and the achievement of felicity (the *Paradise* of Islam). Christianity, on the other hand, saw the resurrection of the body as a 'partaking of the divine nature' (2 Pet. 1:4), not merely a continuation but a transfiguration of created, bodily existence which left open a wide scope of interpretation at both theological and imaginative levels.

The Christian doctrine of resurrection is based on a world-view fundamentally different from that of the religions of, say, India and the Far East. Whereas in the latter the cosmic order is basically fixed in a cyclic pattern to which earthly life is believed to conform, Christianity inherited the Hebrew notion of a divine purpose working itself out through a historical process. The death-and-resurrection myths of Oriental religions envisage human life purely as one stage among many in a recurrent cosmic cycle; Christianity, on the other hand, inherited from its predecessors in Europe and the Levant a belief in personal individuality, in an individual destiny to be fulfilled in the purposeful course of history. One of the leading authorities on myth, Joseph Campbell, has pointed to those features of a belief in the afterlife which Christianity and the Greek myths have in common — both of them envisaging the persistence after death of the individual human personality — and which separate them from the Oriental religions (Buddhism, Hinduism, Jainism) in which no such continuity of recognisable personal traits is to be found. In the *Divine Comedy* of Dante, for instance, the voyager through Hell, Purgatory and Heaven can recognise his deceased friends and talk to them of their lives, just as in the classical afterworlds of the *Odyssey* and *Aeneid*, Odysseus and Aeneas readily recognise and can talk with the shades of those recently dead. In the Oriental religions, on the contrary, the mask of the earthly role is dropped at death and that of the afterlife assumed; when the reincarnating nonentity again returns to the earth, it will assume still another mask, with no conscious recollection of any past.

'Whereas [says Campbell] in the European sphere — whether in the classical epics and tragedies, Dante's *Divine Comedy*, or Jung's modern psychology of "individuation" — the focus of concern is the individual, who is born but once, lives but once, and is distinct in his willing, his thinking, and his doing from every other; in the whole great Orient of India, Tibet, China, Korea, and Japan the living entity is understood to be an immaterial transmigrant that puts on bodies and puts them off. You are not your body. You are not your ego. You are to think of these as delusory. And this fundamental distinction between the Oriental and our usual European concepts of the individual touches in its implications every aspect of social and moral as well as psychological, cosmological, and metaphysical thought.'[1]

In inheriting the European and near-Eastern world-view, Christianity was not merely conditioned by neighbouring faiths. It elevated belief in the persistence beyond the grave of the individual human personality, and thus the status of the body in which it is localised, to a degree unparalleled even in those other religions — whether Mesopotamian or Hebrew, Greek or Roman, Celtic or Germanic — which shared both its geographical roots and its belief in the value of the individual.

Christian thought has always distinguished between the physical body of this present life and the resurrected body. St Paul envisaged the resurrection body of the Christian as a spiritual body (*soma pneumatikon*) as distinct from the natural or 'ensouled' body (*soma psychikon*) of earthly existence (1 Cor. 15: 44); and Jesus' own most celebrated reference to the resurrection life (Matthew 22: 30-32) was a rejection not only of the views of the Sadducees, who denied the resurrection, but also of the over-materialistic understanding of the Pharisees. Yet from the empty tomb to Emmaus, what is distinctive about Jesus' own post-resurrection appearances, even as compared to other New Testament theophanies (tongues of fire, voice from heaven, dove, rushing wind) is that it is only in and through his *body* — his individual earthly form — that he is recognisable as the Lord.

The Christian doctrine of the resurrection of the body thus left the way open for a certain latitude of interpretation as to the exact status of the earthly body: subject on the one hand to corruption, it was also capable of being clothed with glory in a future state. From the very earliest days of Christianity, the weight of opinion had swung between an emphasis on the denial and mortification of the earthly body ('the flesh') and a contrary emphasis on the sacred value of embodiment as the privileged point of conjunction between God and man. The Church, after all, was seen as the 'body of Christ', and fed in the most material of forms upon his eucharistic Body. Was the flesh, then, so inherently evil as the result of original sin as to be redeemable only by the eschatological act of God, or were Christians to take literally St Paul's prayer that their bodies might be 'preserved entire without blame at the coming of our Lord Jesus Christ' (1 Thess. 5: 23)?[2]

That the earthly body was imperfect was not doubted even by the great heretics in the early centuries of Christianity; whether or not human nature could be perfected by union with Christ was another matter. If mortal nature was to be perfected in the resurrection life, then the forms in which that nature was expressed on earth could be seen as perfectible — dim reflections for the moment of an ultimate glorification yet to be bestowed. But the concept of perfection was essentially a Greek idea, not part of the Hebrew inheritance of Christianity but rather a product of its early contact with the Greek world. The God of the Old Testament had not been described in terms of perfection but of power, might and holiness. Even among New Testament

2.3 A Greek athlete and a Venus-figure, only their attitudes (hiding their genital organs) indicating that they are meant to represent Adam and Eve. Detail of the Sarcophagus of Junius Bassus, 359 A.D. (Vatican, Crypt of St Peter.)

writers there is at times a discomfort with the notion of perfection: Matthew's account of Jesus' saying: 'You, therefore, are to be perfect, as your heavenly father is perfect' (Matt. 5: 48) is changed by Luke to 'Be merciful, even as your father is merciful' (Luke 6: 36), language much closer in spirit to the thought-forms of the Old Testament (cf. Leviticus 39: 2: 'You shall be holy; for I the Lord your God am holy').[3] Once, however, the Greek concept of perfection (and thus perfectibility) had found its way into Christian thought, it opened up an entirely new way of looking at the relationship between the present life and the 'life of the world to come'.

2.4 Two scenes from a Roman fresco of the 4th century A.D., indicating the 'christianisation' of pagan themes: (a) *Hercules and the Hydra*; (b) *Samson in the Lions' Den*. The figure of the strongman-hero is remarkably similar in both depictions. (Rome, Via Latina catacombs.)

Whilst Christian perfectibilism has more usually tended towards that bodily austerity seen at its most extreme in the teaching and practice of the desert Fathers, there has emerged at certain periods of history an alternative model of Christian perfection based on Christ's teaching of 'wholeness of life' and focusing on the unity of nature and spirit rather than their opposition. Indeed, many of the most important theological disputes throughout the history of Christianity have revolved around the tendency, on the one hand, towards a body-denying asceticism, and on the other towards a body-affirming liberalism. Early Christian theologians such as Clement of Alexandria and Origen opened up Christian theology to the world of Greek thought-forms, as indeed the Christian religion itself needed to be open to a Romano-Hellenic culture if it were to spread throughout the civilised world.[4] While Clement drew upon Stoicism to portray his ideal of the perfected Christian sage who regulates both body and mind with equal diligence, Origen proclaimed the transformation of the physical body, the *vessel of clay*, into 'containers of ever wider capacity, in stages of life that stretched far beyond the grave.'[5] That Origen was anathematised for his teachings on the spiritualisation of the body was a sign that there were limits to the acceptability of such teaching, and in general the role of the early Church Councils was to safeguard the *via media* or 'middle way' of orthodoxy between two opposite heresies. If Manicheism was condemned, so too was Gnosticism.[6] The body would essentially remain open to a limited but real breadth of theological interpretation, its particular status at any given period owing as much to cultural as to religious determinants. Indeed, cultural history — and in particular the history of religious art — affords us an insight into popular Christian belief which goes far deeper than official teaching or theological speculation in revealing the actual status accorded to the physical body at any given period of Christian history.

Such an overview, though necessarily simplified and perfunctory, goes at least some way towards accounting for the fact that Christianity appears to have provided more extensive scope than the other great world religions for the resumption of a 'high' view of the status of the human body where classical Greek culture had left off. The notion of the resurrectible body, indeed, provided an even more organic connection between the present imperfect world and the world of perfected being than the Greek metaphorical imagination had found in the gods or the Platonic ideals.[7]

Early Christian art provides some indication of the ambiguity of attitude towards the body and its portrayal to which we have referred. On the one hand, official Christianity was often concerned to destroy the pagan cult-images, most of which took the form of sculpted representations of the human body. On the other, just as the Christian church had taken over and 'christianised' a number of pagan festivals (Christmas, Easter), so there was at times a tendency to convert pagan artistic motifs into Christian symbols. For a time in late Roman and early Byzantine art, Christ as the perfected Apollo figure or 'Sun of Righteousness' was both a cultural and artistic affirmation, as in the statue of the *Youthful Christ Teaching* (*c.* 350A.D.) where he is shown as long-locked like the Sun God, or the third-century Roman wall mosaic in which he appears as the Rising Sun driving Apollo's chariot. As John Romer has pointed out, 'just as Apollo of Delphi had made a beautiful transformation to become the Roman Sol Invictus, so later he became a Christ of the sun.'[8] Nor did the Christian Emperor Constantine object to being represented in statuary as Helios or Apollo, christianised by the addition of a cross[9]; and in the fourth-century catacombs of the Via Latina in Rome, the strongmen Samson and Hercules are both depicted in frescoes as types or symbols of the power of the spiritual hero.[10]

It was not long, however, before the dominance of asceticism had become established throughout most of the Christian world. Largely under the influence of monastic orders — both the products and the chief proponents of the ascetic tradition —the human body ceased to be a candidate for glorification and became rather a vessel doomed to condemnation unless supernaturally saved by God through the instruments of grace.

The centuries of 'folk-wandering' sometimes known as the Dark Ages were, if anything, concerned with the suppression rather than the maintenance of ancient classical values, though in various learned and mystical traditions some continuity with the ancient world hung perilously on. By the time European society had regained some form of stability, medieval Christianity had so divorced soul and body that open celebration of 'the flesh' was a custom restricted to the diversions of the lower orders, whilst the representatives of the dominant social classes were either enlisted in the service of the Church or involved in the elaborate rituals of chivalry and the concerns of dynastic security. It is in the popular medieval festivals and carnivals that we find the celebration of the body for its own sake.[11] As a warning against such popular excess, the human body — significantly, in naked form — is depicted in the portrayals of the Judgment of the Damned which illuminated missals and decorated cathedral facades, whilst the portrayals of the Blessed entering Paradise show them fully clothed in the raiment of glory.

Apart from the Damned, only three portrayals of the unclad human body exercised the imagination of the medieval mind: Adam and Eve, the crucified Christ, and St. Sebastian. Into the latter, with its vague hints of eroticism, were poured what little the Middle Ages had to offer in terms of the aesthetic contemplation of bodily existence, though the naturalistic portrayal of this Christian martyr is far from the canons of Graeco-Roman paganism. Adam and Eve, who in 359 A.D. could still be depicted in a sarcophagus relief as a naked athlete and a Venus figure — only their gestures and averted gazes representing their sinful nature[12] — were consistently shown throughout the Middle Ages as vessels of despair and decay.

Not till the 'new springtime' proclaimed by the humanists of fifteenth century Italy would the cultural and religious climate enable the body to re-emerge unashamed from the elaborate garments of its medieval winter.

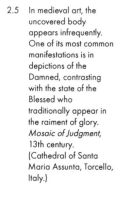

2.5 In medieval art, the uncovered body appears infrequently. One of its most common manifestations is in depictions of the Damned, contrasting with the state of the Blessed who traditionally appear in the raiment of glory. *Mosaic of Judgment,* 13th century. (Cathedral of Santa Maria Assunta, Torcello, Italy.)

Re-discovering the Body

The transformation in attitude to the body which was one of the distinguishing marks of the Renaissance was not merely a return to classical ideals brought about by the revival of study of the ancient world, but a swing in the pendulum of emphasis within Western Christian consciousness from the body-denying to the body-affirming end of the theological range which Christianity had managed to contain. Cultural determinants played an important part in this shift of attention: a revolt against the medieval social control of the body was reflected in Rabelais' celebration of that popular language of the body which had persisted in the Dionysiac tradition of the medieval carnivals; the Hellenistic tradition re-surfaced in the neo-Platonism of humanist scholars such as Ficino and Pico della Mirandola; and the new learning was reflected in the progress of the study of anatomy of which Leonardo was an avid pupil. In these various fields, the focus of attention had shifted from the other-worldly to the this-worldly, for in understanding man, it was believed, we could understand the cosmos itself. The very concept of 'man', of the human species as a whole, was grasped as a guiding principle of study — and man was conceived essentially as 'made in the image of God'. The body is now seen as a microcosm, as God's metaphor for the world.[13] The physical body, which in the medieval period had been drawn purely naturalistically because it was not seen as a figure or type of a higher reality, now took on again the symbolic status which it had abandoned at the break-up of the Roman Empire.[14] The nude could once again take shape as a creative idea.

Belief in analogy — specifically in the knowledge of transcendent reality through the correspondence to it of earthly forms — became so strong a guiding principle that few artistic creations of the Renaissance can be fully understood without an appreciation of their analogical or emblematic value. This is of some importance for the depiction of the body. If the artists of the Renaissance found inspiration in the newly re-discovered works of antiquity, they were nonetheless members (often devout members) of the Christian Church. It was the principle of analogy, inherited from medieval scholasticism and expanded to suit Renaissance ideas, which enabled them to reconcile these two very different thought-forms, for both were seen as analogical references to the world beyond. Works could thus be pagan in treatment and Christian in subject-matter without any conflict being apprehended. Both the Bible for the one part, and for the other the expanding catalogue of ancient works

2.6 The Renaissance
assertion of human
perfectibility: 'the spirit
becomes flesh, purified
and triumphant'.
Michelangelo's Apollo-
like figure of *The Risen
Christ, c.* 1530.
(Windsor, Royal
Library.)

newly come to light again, were avidly searched in the quest for subjects suitable to the display of the body. With Donatello's heroic torso of Christ, we see the first depiction of the body of Jesus in which the beauty of the Christ-figure triumphs over the corruptibility of mortal existence.[15] From now on — in the work of Pollaiuolo, Michelangelo, Signorelli and Bandinelli — the portrayal of the developed body could once again emerge.

What was the specific contribution of the Renaissance to the conception and depiction of the developed body? As to its conception, what was supremely important was that it developed a means of combining in one coherent system both the Greek and the Christian understandings of the metaphoric value of the physical body: what the Greeks had understood largely in terms of anthropomorphism, the Renaissance reconciled with Christian belief through the notion of analogy.[16] It is fair to say that the conception of the body formulated at the time of the Renaissance has been the basis of the entire subsequent history of Western attitudes to the body. We have only to compare the European sculptural tradition with that of, say, India or Thailand, the stylised totems of Africa or the carved Buddhas of China, to appreciate at once the naturalism and the idealism which the European tradition has moulded into one.

In endorsing the Greek bodily canon and modifying it to meet its own ends, the Renaissance was also adopting and 'christianising' the Greek understanding of human self-transcendance of which the heroic body was the symbol.

Such an analysis, though necessarily only outlined here, underlines how much more closely the Greek and Christian notions of self-transcendence resemble each other when seen in contrast with the Eastern understanding. True, there has been in Christianity a mystical tradition which has stressed inwardness and contemplation rather than active involvement in the affairs of the material world; but it is the latter, activist tradition which has predominated in Western Christianity and above all in its art. It is primarily to the Renaissance that we owe the formulation of a language of the body in which the Greek hero-figure becomes the prototype of the Christian hero, the perfectible body becoming the visible emblem of the human spirit victorious in its perpetual combat to overcome the world. Thus, Michael Gill can describe Michelangelo's Apollo-like figure of the naked risen Christ as incarnating 'the idea of human perfectibility', in which the spirit becomes flesh, purified and triumphant.[17] With the exception of classical Greece, no other cultural system has given the muscular hero-figure such pre-eminence as an idealised image as has the post-Renaissance West. Indeed, so thoroughly has the visual symbolism of muscularity become lodged in the modern Western consciousness that it has retained its imaginative potency even in an age when the religious world-view which once underpinned it has largely been abandoned.

2.7 The great models of antiquity provided Renaissance artists and sculptors with the basic visual material for the portrayal of the heroic body. The heavy musculature of the back is often highlighted in the twisting posture of the body. (a) Michelangelo, *Day*, tomb of Giuliano de' Medici, 1519-34 (Medici Chapel, Church of San Lorenzo, Florence.) (b) Apollonius, son of Nestor, *Torso Belvedere*, *c.* 100 B.C. (Rome, Musei Vaticani.) The resemblance is particularly noticeable when the *Torso* is turned through a 90 degree angle.

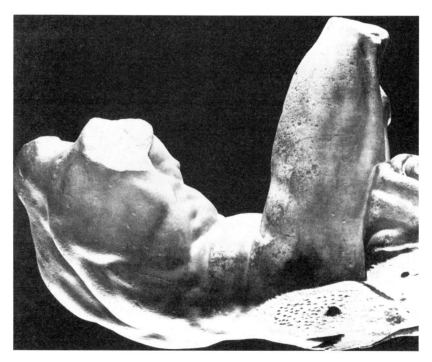

In terms of actual depiction, the peculiarly Renaissance contribution to the portrayal of the developed body (as compared, for instance, to that of late classical art) lies less in its capacity for innovation than in its genius for expressive representation; it is this quality that has led to the persistence of its most celebrated works as cultural icons through the centuries that followed. The sculptures and paintings of the Renaissance and its successor Mannerism have remained enduring figures within the European artistic consciousness even in those ages when both informed and popular opinion have been unsympathetic to the ideals which inspired them.

Whilst the increasing knowledge of anatomy and improvement in technical skills provided the Renaissance and Mannerist painters and sculptors with a far greater expressive range than even the most accomplished of the ancients could command, the great physical models of antiquity — in particular those of the late Hellenistic period —nonetheless continued to provide the basic visual material of muscular portrayal.[18] The body was still, as in ancient Greece, posed erect and resting on one leg in *contrapposto* style (the *Hermes* of Praxiteles: the *Davids* of Donatello and Michelangelo), reclining and supported on one elbow (the *Dionysus* of Phidias: Michelangelo's *Dawn* and his *Adam*), turning a muscular back to the spectator (the *Torso Belvedere*: Michelangelo's *Athlete*, his *Day*), or flexing an arm (the *Death of Laocoön*: Pollaiuolo's *Hercules*, Michelangelo's *Dying Captive*, his *Last Judgment*). By taking up and re-using the classical poses and muscular attitudes of antiquity, the artists of the *quattrocento* and *cinquecento* turned them into standard or archetypal symbols which now transcended the national, cultural and temporal particularity of their original creation. It was they that would define the 'heroic' tradition in European art for the next four hundred years. The achievement of the Renaissance lay not only in its invention of new forms, but in the passing on intact of what it inherited from Greece and Rome: the traditional heroic representation of the male body.

This very expressive range provided the opportunity for discreet forays into the language of eroticism, a possibility more fully developed by the later Mannerist and Baroque schools. By the same token, it raised in renewed form the ancient question of the presentation of the body and the need for contextual signs as to whether erotic messages were or were not intended. That a number of fifteenth and sixteenth-century Italian masters (Donatello, Leonardo, Michelangelo, Signorelli) were either known or suspected to be homosexual posed this issue in explicit terms.

Curiously, it is in the first large-scale free-standing nude statue since antiquity —Donatello's bronze *David* — that the question of erotic ambiguity is raised as sharply as in any other work of the Renaissance. Though not as explicitly sexual in its visual messages as some later Mannerist works, it is much less concerned to conceal them than is Michelangelo's celebrated treatment of the same subject. The

2.8 Donatello's bronze statue of *David* raises the question of erotic ambiguity as sharply as any work of the Renaissance, evoking the sexually enticing boyish fauns or the naked adolescents of the Greek gymnasium. 1430s. (Florence, Museo Nazionale del Bargello.)

majority of art historians are content to refer to Donatello's strictly artistic qualities of proportion, poise and mastery of his medium, while remaining discreetly reticent as to the erotic suggestiveness of the work. Kenneth Clark, for instance, mentions 'the dreamy smile and flexible pose', the suggestion of 'a pagan god returned to earth'; but his reference to the 'tensions and transitions which make the youthful body sensuously appealing'[19] is as near as he permits himself to an acknowledgment of its erotic overtones. Margaret Walters, however, is a good deal more forthright in her appraisal:

'Donatello's nude seems to be a deeply personal work, expressing all the artist's ambivalent feelings toward beautiful adolescence. David almost wilfully eludes all efforts to allegorize and moralize; he is totally unconvincing as a type of virtue. His high boots, the fancy hat shadowing his sensual face, the sword almost too big for him to lift, only emphasize his provocative nakedness. His body is very individual. He is barely adolescent, and the light playing on the bronze focuses our attention on odd details — the swaying stance, the droopy buttocks and the soft stomach muscles. The boy's toes are tangled in the beard of the great severed head at its feet and its helmet plume trails up the inside of his leg to tickle his thigh suggestively.'[20]

The often-remarked fact that Donatello's bronze was not imitated by later sculptors can be attributed to a number of factors, but to those generally advanced one might add the suggestion that its artistic language was rather too ambiguous in its hesitation between admiration and attraction to form the basis of an acceptable new convention of the male nude. It evoked the sexually enticing boyish fauns or the naked adolescents of the Greek gymnasium rather than the reserved heroic adulthood of the sculpted divinity. Not since Greek antiquity had the naked male body strayed so far from the heroic, power-centred convention towards the alternative erotic or pleasure-centred form of representation.

It was not Donatello's but Michelangelo's *David*, combining as it did the head of an Apollo with the body of a young Hercules, that both successfully incarnated the High Renaissance ideal and supremely represented it for the ages that followed. Here as in much of his other work, Michelangelo (though not without inner struggle) was able to sublimate or surmount his erotic impulses by a recourse to the heroic tradition.[21] As opposed to Donatello's slim boyish figure with his undeveloped chest and arms, the torso of Michelangelo's *David* could have been the model for the *cuirasse esthétique* itself. A superbly muscular young adult he may be, but he is primarily a brilliantly original reworking of the Greek heroic convention, a strikingly new embodiment of the Western classical ideal.

Not the least noteworthy feature of Michelangelo's *David* is the naturalistic portrayal of the genitals, surmounted 'courageously', as Frederick Hartt puts it, by pubic locks 'ornamentalized with unprecedented intensity and intricacy.'[22] One has but to compare it with his own idealised Greek figures or his highly conventionalised Sistine Chapel *Adam*, with its almost ludicrously minuscule sexual organs (no doubt symbolic of prelapsarian sexual innocence), to appreciate the boldness of this innovation. It should be contrasted, too, with Donatello's youthful figure whose penis is depicted almost in the exact manner of the Greek vase paintings as if to stress its filiation with the aesthetic-erotic tradition. That anatomical accuracy should triumph in Michelangelo's sculpted figure over the christianised heroic convention so readable in his paintings of male nudes is testimony to the artist's ability to transcend established limits and elaborate a new language of the developed body, suitably Biblical in conception yet thoroughly humanistic and pagan in execution. Neither god nor sex-object, Michelangelo's *David* is a fully human figure with the potential to be both.

In his original analysis of the statue's appearance when viewed from various angles, John Webb concludes that while from the front it appears relaxed and balanced, from the side it seems to be 'defensively recoiling, turning away from threat and revealing significant doubts'. The contradictoriness, the inner tension between confidence and

2.9 '... a deeply personal work, expressing all the artist's ambivalent feelings toward beautiful adolescence ... The light playing on the bronze focuses our attention on odd details – the swaying stance, the droopy buttocks ...' (Walters.)

2.10 The most famous male statue of all time: anatomical accuracy here triumphs over convention to elaborate a new language of the developed body – Biblical in conception yet pagan in execution. 'So modern that he has become the hero of Muscle Beach.' Michelangelo, *David*. 1501-4. (Florence, Accademia.)

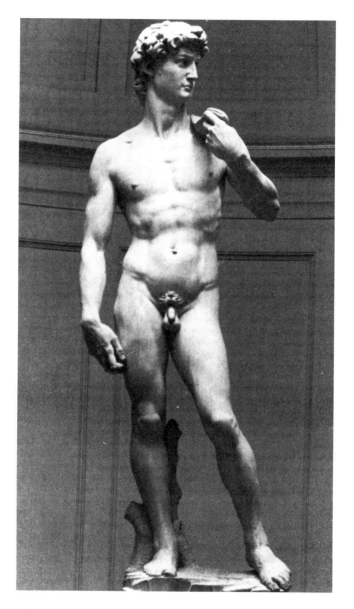

vulnerability, indicate that 'what seems at first to be a statue which endorses an uncomplicated masculinity turns out instead to be one which looks forward to the contradictions of modern masculinity.'[23] Rather more prosaically, Michael Gill has pointed out that the disproportionately thin side aspect of the figure was to some degree conditioned by the shape of the giant marble block from which it was hewn, a fact recognised very early by the committee of Florentine artists who suggested that the statue be positioned in a niche or against a wall. Gill is more inclined to see the modern appeal of the statue in terms of its seminal role in defining the male

2.11 From the side the statue appears 'defensively recoiling, turning away from threat and revealing significant doubts': does it look forward to the contradictions of modern masculinity?

physical ideal: 'so modern is [Michelangelo's *David*] that he has become the hero of Muscle Beach, the most famous masculine statue in the world.'[24] Whatever the explanation, it remains that for the next four hundred years, for reasons only dimly comprehended by later generations, this remarkable synthesis of power and beauty would represent in European art the ideal male physique. Not until modern times would this representation be 'deconstructed' to reveal its essential ambiguity and to explore its implications.

CONVENTIONAL BODIES

If the fifteenth and early sixteenth centuries had endowed the developed male body with a fixed and durable artistic identity, the ages that followed ran the risk of turning it into a mere artistic convention. The philosophico-religious tenets of Renaissance humanism were not even to last out the sixteenth century: religious quarrels, wars and a new pessimism (or at least, as in Montaigne, a resigned scepticism) would erode much of the enthusiasm and perfectionism of the preceding age. In the Europe of the Age of Kings, which was to last until late in the eighteenth century, concepts such as 'the place of man in the cosmos' seemed rather too grandiose to suit the times: 'the place of man in society' seemed a more profitable subject of speculation, and one to be approached much more pragmatically. At one end of a divided social spectrum, religious duty towards God would now become, if not less important, at least an obligation to be held in balance with moral duty towards society; the humane religion associated with some of Molière's characters was seen, if not as a way of making men 'better' — Molière was too sceptical for such a goal — at least as a way of making society more civilised and bearable.

Such a social climate was hardly conducive to idealism, physical or otherwise. The body had become the object of scientific observation, and was understood more and more as a machine. While Cartesian philosophy distinguished between the physical or mechanical body and the rational consciousness, the gradual progress of medicine following Harvey's discovery of the circulation of the blood drew attention to its control by scientific regimens. At the other end of the social spectrum, traditional religious belief seemed to retreat within itself, into mysticism, Jansenism or Puritanism. The body wavered between religious ecstasy and forbidden sensual delight.

In the world of art, such preoccupations were reflected in the turning of established conventions to social or religious ends, in the service (ostensibly, at least) of classical good taste or spiritual edification.

With the excavation of ancient sites in the sixteenth century, the great marble statuary of pagan Greece and Rome had turned the artistic values of antiquity from a vague theoretical concept into specific visible works. Originals were avidly sought by Popes and cardinals, kings and noblemen, and as the making of plaster casts became more skilled and less expensive the appreciation of the most esteemed antique statues gradually spread throughout Europe. The great Papal families of the sixteenth and seventeenth centuries built up extensive collections of originals, of which the finest was that in the grounds of the Belvedere, a villa on the high ground behind the old Vatican palace.

2.12 The marble statuary of ancient Greece was avidly sought by 16th and 17th-century collectors, including the great Papal families. The finest collection was that in the grounds of the Belvedere behind the old Vatican palace. Leochares [?], *Apollo* ('The Apollo of the Belvedere'). Roman copy (of early Hadrianic period) of original *c.* 320 B.C. (Vatican, Musei e Gallerie Pontificie.)

Collected at first as a sign of the inalienable heritage of the people of Rome and to promote the world-wide significance of the city of the Popes, antique statues — or, more frequently, plaster and (later) bronze copies — spread throughout the seventeenth century from Rome to the great European courts of France, Spain and England, as well as to the houses of important families of Florence such as the

2.13 Along with plaster copies, engravings (not always accurate) were the chief means by which familiarity with the most famous antique statues was spread throughout Europe from the 16th to the 18th centuries. Hendrik Goltzius, engraving of the *Farnese Hercules*. 16th century.

Medici. Whilst full-size statuary tended to be restricted, for reasons of size and expense, to the palaces of royal or noble families, smaller copies were acquired by other collectors as the wealth of the high bourgeoisie increased. The capitalist desire for ownership — the wish of the moneyed classes to possess and collect valuable objects — meant that the works of antiquity became the touchstone of 'taste' all over Europe. The very fact of belonging to one of the great collections conferred artistic status upon a work, thus leading to its popularity as a model for casts and copies in private galleries throughout the Western world.[25]

Originally intended as inventories or catalogues of the important works of antiquity, collections of prints and engravings — not always accurate, and at times quite fanciful in interpretation and their conjectured reconstructions — were widely published throughout the seventeenth and eighteenth centuries. For those unable to see the originals, or even good copies, books of prints became the chief means by which familiarity with the most famous and beautiful statues of ancient Greece and Rome was spread throughout Europe.

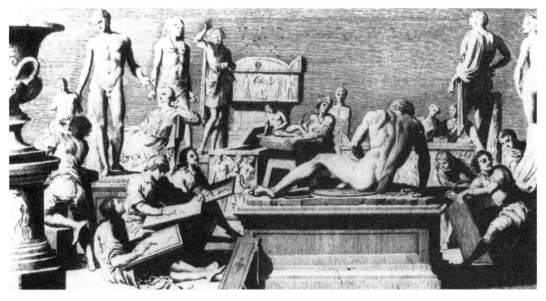

The wide distribution of plaster copies and engravings, and the social prestige attaching to ownership of antique works, meant that for three centuries the production of contemporary artists (notably sculptors, but to some extent painters as well) would be placed alongside and compared with the antique models. Even when the nude male had ceased to become a fashionable subject of sculpted or painted depiction, ancient statuary lived on in the art schools and academies, where it remained until relatively recent times the chief means of teaching students not only human anatomy but the 'classical canon' of posing the body in the attitudes appropriate to high art. From the Academy founded in Bologna by the Carracci at the end of the sixteenth century to the downfall of the academic curriculum with the rise of modernism in the early twentieth century, the 'classical ideal' which flourished in the official academies required that students not begin drawing from life until they had demonstrated their competence in drawing from the antique.[26] Precisely because of their obedience to ancient tradition, the great works of Greece and Rome inspired little that was fresh and original — or memorable — once the years of the High Renaissance and Mannerism had passed. Painters and sculptors were certainly trained in their craft by the imitation of the noble muscular heroes of antiquity, but those of genuine talent were to go beyond such conventional, technically accomplished portrayal to develop their own individual style and vision.

2.14 The academy tradition lasted from the end of the 16th century until the rise of modernism at the beginning of the 20th. One of its main tenets was that students should not begin drawing from life until they had become competent in drawing from the sculpture of ancient Greece and Rome. An 18th-century engraving by Giovanni Domenico Campiglia depicts students drawing and modelling from casts in the Capitoline collection.

The human body in general, as a subject of art, was to reflect the changing tastes and fashions of the seventeenth century. On the one hand, it was depicted more frequently in its socially or religiously garbed form, and the rendering of clothing and drapery became increasingly elaborate and sophisticated not only in painting but also in sculpture. On the other hand, the unclothed body, though retaining an important role in the teaching of art students, turned more and more into a mere artistic convention, largely devoted to allegorical subjects. At its best, as in the work of Poussin, it provided moral lessons and celebrated simple virtue. With the disappearance of deeply-felt heroic ideals, the focus of interest in the unclothed body took more worldly forms, sometimes shifting from idealisation towards eroticism, and the exploration of the symbolic power of the male figure was more and more replaced by a fascination with the sensuous female form. Antique, mythological subjects were still pressed into service, but largely as a vehicle for the seductive portrayal of sexual attraction. Since its development in the late fifteenth and early sixteenth centuries in the paintings of Botticelli, Tintoretto and Titian, and in its subsequent flowering in those of Rubens and Boucher, the female nude was a more powerful inspiration for later Mannerist and Baroque painters than its male counterpart. As to the latter, in opposition to the brazenly provocative boys of Caravaggio we can set only the early Bernini as a major contributor to the European consciousness of the heroically developed male body, and that largely because of the widely-viewed public landmarks he created for the city of Rome.

Bernini's mastery of texture and genius for dramatic construction have ensured him a secure if secondary place in the history of art, though as one of the foremost teachers of his day his recommendation to his pupils that they sketch from the sculptures of Greek and Roman times rather than from nature was to help perpetuate the conventions of what became the 'academy' tradition for the generations that followed. Compared with the leaner, less emphatically heroic athletes painted by Annibale Carracci for the Farnese Gallery ceiling, the monumental figures of Bernini's Roman fountains seem almost intimidating in their muscularity: bodybuilders rather than athletes, the Bernini fountain figures (notably the *Four Rivers* in the Piazza Navona) may at first seem like distant cousins of Michelangelo's four massive *Times of the Day* in the Medici chapel, but their symbolism remains external and decorative and they possess none of the sense of inner tragedy of Michelangelo's recumbent giants. In the Rome of the seventeenth-century Popes as in that of the Imperial Emperors, the developed body had again been transformed from a quasi-religious symbol into a public convention.

2.15 Almost intimidating in their muscularity, Bernini's *Four Rivers* (like the male figures in Michelangelo's *Times of the Day*) seem more like bodybuilders than athletes. Bernini's giant figures seem to lack the sense of inner tragedy which marks those of Michelangelo. Bernini, *The Nile*. Rome, Piazza Navona (*Fountain of the Rivers*), 1648-1651.

2.16 The *Torso Belvedere*, attributed to Apollonius, was one of the works of antique sculpture to which Johann Winckelmann devoted lengthy and enthusiastic discussion in his influential mid-18th-century works. In due course, every significant museum or gallery would possess a plaster cast of the *Torso*, the *Laocoön*, the *Apollo Belvedere* or the *Farnese Hercules*.

2.17 The Tribuna, a room in the Uffizi Gallery, was to become a mecca for visiting tourists anxious to see the best paintings and Greek sculpture. In the late 18th century, the British royal family commissioned the painter Johann Zoffany (*c.*1733-1810) to paint a group portrait of English visitors to the Gallery. (Windsor, Royal Collection.)

2.18 Learned in the art academies, the conventions of representing the body in the Greek mode were to condition the 18th-century depictions of non-European races. The classical influence is evident in this engraving of Captain Cook with natives in Morai, Otaheite (Tahiti). 1770s. (*Cook's Journeys in the Pacific.*)

By the eighteenth century, a fundamentally materialist conception of human nature had become the basis of the European desire for social improvement. Scientific method, education and the forms of social control were the dominant concerns of serious thought, leading to the recognisably modern notion we know as 'progress'. Yet in their rendering of the human body the artists of the age seemed curiously reluctant to explore its expressive possibilities, restricting themselves to sometimes exquisite variations on established styles. Those tendencies in the world of art already visible in the seventeenth century were simply accentuated as the Baroque gave way to the Rococo style. Drapery and clothing predominate over the body in aristocratic and high bourgeois society painting, and in religious work only the cherubs seem to display their nudity. To be sure, a cavalcade of naked nymphs and goddesses can be observed (as one critic has put it) 'cavorting across the ceilings of Europe'[27], but only in a kind of formalised counterpoint to the elaborate fashions of the polite society frequenting the salons below. Engravings on classical themes maintain the *cuirasse esthétique* as one of the conventions of depiction of antique gods and heroes, but such works — turned out in strict compliance with the antique tradition of the art school and the academy — are practically devoid of any originality or freshness of vision.

The one area of art in which classical antiquity inspired any work of genuine creativity in the eighteenth century is that of art history. In two remarkably influential works, *Reflections on the Painting and Sculpture of the Greeks* (1755) and *History of the Art of the Ancients* (1764), the German archaeologist and art historian Johann Winckelmann (1717-1768) was to lay down, not only the foundations of art history as a serious academic discipline, but in particular the intellectual framework and terminology in which all subsequent discussion of classical art has been conducted. His division of ancient art into periods, and his superb lyrical descriptions of certain works — the *Laocoön*, the *Apollo Belvedere*, the *Belvedere Torso*, the *Farnese Hercules* and others — had a profound influence on the thinkers and authors of his day, notably the playwrights Lessing and Goethe, and provoked long-standing discussion of the relations between art, literature and the emotions.

Despite their fundamental significance for the history of aesthetics (and, incidentally, of archaeology) Winckelmann's two great works had no perceptible influence on the artistic movements of his day or those of the generations that followed. What they did, however, quite apart from their ground-breaking importance as works of scholarship, was to popularise a select number of significant ancient statues. From now on, every public art gallery or museum — such as those which began to spring up in the 'museological explosion' of 1790-1850 — would have its due complement of plaster casts of the *Torso*, the *Apollo* or the *Laocoön*, displayed in order to educate the local populace in the lasting value of European or Western civilisation.[28] Even when thought 'shocking', as when exported for display in a still somewhat puritanical America, these heroic male nudes maintained the developed body within the Western consciousness as even more deeply embedded images than those of more recent schools and movements.

So thoroughly had the classical conception of the ideal body permeated the European artistic mind that in the late eighteenth century, when Pacific exploration and Rousseauistic primitivism had introduced and popularised the figure of the 'noble savage', his representation in engravings was characteristically (if not universally) that of a dark-skinned European conventionally drawn in the heroic Graeco-Roman manner of the art class. His torso is the Roman cuirass, his legs and arms full and muscular, his features classically Greek and his general bearing athletically upright. The paradisiac nakedness of the Pacific islander may have been a source of exotic delight to the European mind at a time when the notion of original sin was gradually giving way to that of original goodness, but in his portrayal the Western standardisation of the developed body had now crossed racial boundaries and would, for a time at least, triumph over naturalism.

THE SECULAR BODY

The centuries following the Renaissance had increasingly been affected by the dualism of Western thought. The divisions of principle between Church and State, sacred and secular, mind and body, had gradually freed themselves from the analogical linkages posited by the Renaissance, and concentration would turn more exclusively to a now separate, and purely material, sphere of existence. The development of medical science and a rising concern with public health following the Industrial Revolution led to a new and distinct form of activity concerned with the cultivation of bodily well-being and the overcoming of physical debility. In all of these social changes, a persistent Western impetus towards the improvement of the human condition had been the underlying and unifying factor: moral and religious perfection, which had been a major concern of Western society until the Enlightenment, was gradually to yield to a more purely secular pursuit of perfection, based on the improvement of social and economic order and the advancement of human health through medicine or biological control. Man was primarily a secular, social and physical being, and his further development was believed to lie in these unsanctified fields.

From the nineteenth century onwards, theology was increasingly to give way in the West to the natural and social sciences as the chief explicator of human meanings, the latter now being found essentially in the interrelationship of things (science, technology) or of human beings themselves (history, psychology, sociology). By the end of the century, what Passmore has called 'secular perfectibilism'[29] had taken the form of explicit (though widely varying) social doctrines in the work of thinkers such as Darwin, Nietzsche and Marx, whose detailed philosophical or scientific systems were of less importance as social determinants than the anthropology, or view of man, which they presupposed or promoted. In this process, the ideal heroism provided by religion tended to be replaced by purely cultural hero-systems, the 'hero' being the paradigm or exemplar which defines our significance as human beings and gives our individual self a recognisable value within the world, a way of denying our meaninglessness.

By the early nineteenth century, the classical tradition of the expressive body which Renaissance art had inherited from antiquity and passed on to its successors appeared to have run its course as a wellhead of inspiration for the front rank of creative artists, and had become the lacklustre hallmark of the conservative 'academies' such as the British Royal Academy and the French Académie des Beaux-Arts. In France, the academy tradition flourished briefly at the turn of the century in the neo-classical paintings of a Jacques-Louis David, where a strongly moralistic

2.19 The neo-classicism of the early 19th century saw a revival of ancient themes and heroically idealised bodies. The massive male torso in Ingres' *Jupiter et Thétis* (1811) is on a Michelangelesque scale. (Aix-en-Provence, Musée Granet.)

current justified to the public mind a reversion to antiquity (particularly civic Roman antiquity) which replaced the 'frivolous' wreaths of drapery characteristic of Watteau and the Rococo style. In the work of David's great disciple Ingres, we find one of the last vestiges in painting of the massively Michelangelesque male torso (*Jupiter et Thétis*, 1811). In the carefully posed and unblemished bodies of neo-classicism, at a far remove from the corpulence and sagging flesh that had marked the physical realism of Rembrandt and Rubens, we can observe the final and perhaps the greatest artistic statement of the eighteenth-century *philosophes*' belief in the rational perfectibility of man.

2.20 Neo-classicism produced few sculptors of note, the most celebrated being Antonio Canova (1757-1822) who was considered the equal in sculpture of David in painting. His *Theseus and the Centaur* (1805-1819) shows a typically heroic treatment of the male body. (Vienna, Kunsthistorisches Museum.)

Apart from David and a few gifted disciples such as Ingres and Gérard, the neo-classical style produced few painters of note, and in sculpture only the Italian Antonio Canova stands out above his neo-classical contemporaries as a practitioner of the 'heroic manner'. Students in the *ateliers* continued, as they had for centuries, to draw from the antique, to copy ancient busts and coins and the casts of classical statuary. Nubile maidens, muscular youths and chubby babies were all acceptable, provided that they furnished the subject-matter of moral stories derived from classical, Biblical or mythological sources. Social conservatism could here be reconciled with a competent, if banal, artistic presentation of the human body.

The chief reaction against the neo-classical style came in the form of Romanticism. Variety in composition and the use of colour, light and shade to create a dramatic mood distinguished the work of Delacroix and Géricault from the severely classical style of a David. Paradoxically, the 'flight into Romanticism' served to establish a new interest in realistic portrayal of the body, as flesh-tones, natural lighting and a sense of movement replaced austere classical composition and formal poses. In *The Bark of Dante* (1822) and *The Death of Sardanapalus* (1827), the scale of the figures still betrays a remnant of the heroic tradition but the texture of the pale female and darker male flesh predominates and the overall effect is of a dramatic realism. Though trained in the best 'academy' tradition in the studio of Guérin, Delacroix created a sensation in the Paris *salons* by the startling novelty of such portrayals and their break with convention.

Such a departure into the world of 'novelty' was but a foretaste of the massive upheaval in the world of art which was to take place only a few years later with the invention of photography. The ability of the camera to record the moods and movements of the human body marked not, as Turner had prophesied, the 'end of Art'[30] so much as its fundamental re-appraisal, a more profound exploration of its capacity to suggest the light and colour of a fleeting moment of visual impression: if bodies were depicted, it was not for their inherent physical qualities but for what they might evoke in terms of the relationship of surface, light, contour and association with their setting.

Though sculpture, like painting, was to break away from the academy tradition, it was to do so somewhat later and in different terms. Though the tradition of formalised 'public' statuary continued, well into the twentieth century, to populate

2.21 Breaking away from the classicism of his teacher Guérin, Eugène Delacroix (1798-1863) became the greatest French painter of the Romantic period, replacing the purity of classical line with a concern for dramatic attitude, emotion and the effect of light and shade on the body. *The Death of Sardanapalus* (detail), 1827. (Paris, Louvre.)

parks, gardens and official monuments with uninspired variations on classical motifs — and to take up again the perennial figure of the muscular athlete in pretentious monuments erected in the service of Fascist or Stalinist ideology — it had not completely stifled the ability of isolated geniuses to breathe into the heroic male figure a totally original and altogether memorable expressive capacity.

One of the most striking examples of this creativity was, paradoxically, an artistic creation exhibited in the Paris *salon* — Rodin's 1877 sculpture *The Age of Brass* (*L'Age d'airain*). At its first exhibition in Paris, it created a sensation. Though depicted in the well-established *contrapposto* stance and to some extent influenced by Donatello, the figure transgressed the formal requirement of a clear theme based on some noble human act drawn from history or mythology. Here, as one critic put it, we had not the heroic depiction of a great figure, but 'an astonishingly accurate copy of a low type' — a figure which looked all too much like life itself. The rumour spread that it was a fraud, a *surmoulage*, cast directly in a plaster mould from the body of a model, and a placard to this effect was placed against it by persons unknown. In the scandal that followed, Rodin wrote letters of protest to the newspapers, and demanded (successfully) an official enquiry and vindication by the Ministry of Fine Arts. He even went so far as to have photographs made of plaster moulds of his model, Private Auguste Neyt of the Brussels garrison; the latter, a man of extraordinary physique but little education, understood the sculptor's aims well enough to offer to come to Paris himself to confound the detractors.[31]

The critics who had branded *The Age of Brass* as heresy had failed to see its most important point. It did in fact have a meaning and a symbolism, denoting as its final (though not original) title indicates that prehistoric time when man began to emerge erect from the primitive life of the cave-dweller. This was, in other words, man come of age as a conscious being awakening at last from the long prehistoric sleep to the world of human energy and human potential. That this could be symbolised, not by the apparatus of allegorical accoutrements and props (Rodin

2.22 Rodin's *The Age of Brass* (1876-1877) depicted the male body as an object of art in its own right, freed from historical or mythological interpretations. Its resemblance to 'reality' — a controversial departure from academic convention — was highlighted by being based on the body of an actual and identifiable person. (Paris, Musée du Luxembourg.)

deliberately omitted from the final form of the statue the staff which had originally appeared in the left hand of the figure as if to push himself up from the ground), but by so realistically lifelike a portrayal as to suggest that the human body itself — as it actually was — could contain such imaginative potential, was something totally new to the world of artistic depiction. The outward and visible truth of the human body needed no higher justification than itself.

The significance of Rodin's *Age of Brass* is underlined by the unusual similarities between its exhibition and that, some thirty-two years later, of the finest sculpture by one of his most talented pupils, Antoine Bourdelle. This was the *Héraclès Archer* (Heracles the Archer) of 1909. At its initial exhibition in 1910 at the *salon* of the Société Nationale des Beaux-Arts, a group of other exhibiting artists were so jealous of the work that they ganged up on Bourdelle and moved it into a dark corner. As a counter-measure, Bourdelle gilded the figure and then stood guard over it to avoid any attempted depradations. As in the case of the Rodin, we know the identity of the model (also a soldier): it was Doyen Parigot, an officer in the Cuirassiers and physical fitness fanatic. Far from exaggerating his musculature as has sometimes been supposed, Bourdelle found that Parigot was too well-developed to suit most conventional poses and it was only after a number of experiments that he settled on the extremely demanding 'archer'. The act of posing constituted such a feat of endurance that the model was able to remain in position for only a few moments at a time.[32]

2.23 The plaster model of Rodin's *Age of Brass* draws even more attention to the realism of the body's treatment than does the bronze version of the figure.

2.24 The suggestion of pure physical energy: the body seems to become a muscular spring, coiled to its limit before the moment of release. Antoine Bourdelle, *Héraclès Archer*, 1908. (Paris, Musée Bourdelle.)

The exceptional vigour and dynamism of *Héraclès Archer* raise it well above the 'municipal outlook'[33] of much of Bourdelle's statuary and have ensured it a place amongst the most admired of early twentieth-century sculptures. The body here seems to become a muscular spring, coiled to its limit before the moment of release. Though the work appears to have been inspired to some extent by ancient Greek hunting statues, none of its suggested avatars comes anywhere near it in its suggestion of pure physical energy. Equally importantly, however, in Bourdelle's archer as in Rodin's early man, we are looking in a sense at a 'real' human body, not an idealised figure or conventional symbol but an individual hero who transcends his own individuality by the sheer expressive power of his body.

By the beginning of the twentieth century, the focus of interest in the developed body had shifted definitively from the world of high art and imaginative depiction generally to that of more immediate and popular forms of expression. It seems somehow fitting that, before its final eclipse, the heroic tradition should have been able to draw fresh and original inspiration from the body's metaphoric power while casting a last glance backward in grateful homage to its ancient predecessors.

2.25 As with Rodin's *Age of Brass*, the identity of Bourdelle's model is known: Doyen Parigot, an army officer and physical fitness fanatic. By the beginning of the 20th century, the new interest in bodybuilding and physical exercise was making itself felt, but its incorporation in high art would be of short duration.

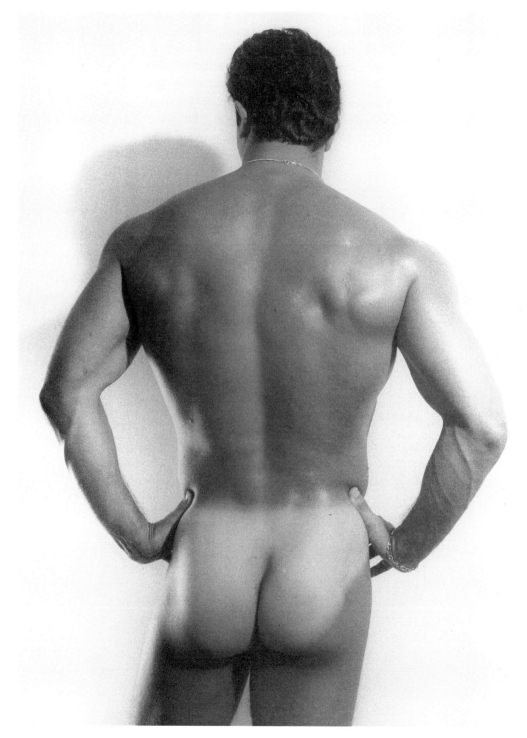

3.1   **CHAPTER 3**   THE VISIBLE BODY
The camera was to bring about a revolution in the 'availability' of the living body for public scrutiny.

3

THE VISIBLE BODY

STUDIO BODIES

The nineteenth century was to mark the most momentous changes in perception of the developed body since the Renaissance, and to lay down the lines of development which have conditioned our understanding even at the end of the twentieth century. Whilst Victorian public morality took up again where the puritanism of an earlier age had left off, a new permissiveness which looked back to the liberalism of the Restoration was increasingly to vie with this social conservatism as the century progressed. The rise of the capitalist bourgeoisie had established monogamous marriages and female chastity as the publicly proclaimed (if often privately flouted) social norms not only in Victorian England but in northern Europe as well, where the stability of family life was promoted as an antidote to the social upheaval that had marked the end of the eighteenth century. The open display of the body was considered a threat to respectability, and concealment by clothing replaced, for women especially, the revealing fashions of earlier periods seen at their most extreme in the French *Directoire*.

While the more zealous of moral guardians completely rejected the depiction of the unclothed body, in general the world of art was considered exempt from the restrictive canons of polite society and 'desexualised' by its reference to the hallowed traditions of iconography. The long and, at times, even distinguished history of erotic art could be conveniently forgotten or overlooked and a painting of a nude could be respectable provided that the ostensible subject of the work could be located in classical mythology (Venus) or Biblical history (Bathsheba). Though the same spurious resort to lofty idealism was used for a time to confer legitimacy on unclad subjects when portrayed by the new technique of photography, even Victorian hypocrisy (and its Continental counterparts) had eventually to come to terms with the frankly voyeuristic opportunities afforded by the new medium.

The early photographic experiments of Niepce and Daguerre (and, in England, of Wedgwood and Talbot) were soon followed by a flurry of interest in the potential of the camera, and from the late 1830s onwards photographic studies attracted increasing public attention. While streetscapes and portraits were produced in abundance, so too were 'artistic' photographs including those of the nude. The early cameras were extremely cumbersome devices of (for their time) great technical complexity, their use largely restricted to the studio. The studio arrangement, with the subject posed motionless (because of the length of exposure) on one side of the room and the photographer behind his machine on the other, made the context almost exactly that of the artist's studio, and it was only natural that photography should soon be seen as a variant, if less lofty, form of artistic activity.[1] The inexhaustible rendering of detail by the camera, and its exact obedience to the laws of linear perspective and chiaroscuro, enabled the photographer to bypass the formal apprenticeship required by the traditional academies. The more progressive and experimental of painters embraced the new medium with enthusiasm, and Delacroix was one of the first members of the Société Française de Photographie. His own photographs of the female nude, as well as photographs of male nudes made for him by Eugène Durieu, were to replace living models as the basis of some of his later paintings.[2] Indeed, the naked human body lent itself so well to photographic reproduction that a trade in pornographic photos did not take long to emerge, and Manet's celebrated *Olympia* of 1863 was influenced by pornographic studies of female nudes.[3]

If painters reached out towards photography, photographers were soon to make overtures towards the world of painting. Skilled photographic portraitists such as Nadar and Carjat in France and Julia Margaret Cameron in England produced camera studies of considerable visual power, and in 1869 appeared the first of many editions and translations of Henry Peach Robinson's influential work, *Pictorial Effect in Photography*. It would be some years before photography would finally establish itself as a visual medium in its own right, and at the same time help painting to extricate itself at last from its long subjection to a literal correspondence to 'real life'.

For a time, however, the advent of photography was to bring about a profound re-appraisal of the human body as an object, precisely because it inherited and continued the European pictorial tradition. Early nineteenth-century photographs were, like paintings, carefully posed compositions. Even photographic portraits of

3.2 A photo (1853-54) by
Eugène Durieu, made
for use by the painter
Delacroix to replace the
use of a live model.
Such photographic
studies, known as
'academies', were put
together into collections
for sale to painters:
their potential for erotic
voyeurism gave them a
much wider audience.
Durieu, *Académie pour
l'Album Delacroix*.

the time became heavy with background props — columns, drapery and painted
scenery aimed at imitating the style of formal painting. The nude body was
photographed, when for purposes other than its anatomical or scientific interest, as
an idealised image, intended to imitate an artist's view of what the naked body should
be like.[4] The fact that the clothing of the time —particularly male clothing — hardly
lent itself to artistic portrayal, either in painting or in photography, further increased
the interest of photographers in capturing the artistic potential of the body itself.

3.3 The close conjunction of photography and painting in the 19th century is visible in a number of works by the leading American painter Thomas Eakins. (a) A photograph (c. 1883) by Eakins of youths swimming; (b) one of Eakins' best-known paintings, *The Swimming Hole*, 1883. (Fort Worth Art Center-Museum, Texas.)

Nowhere is the interaction of nineteenth-century painting and photography more evident than in the work of Thomas Eakins (1844-1916). Today considered by many the finest American painter of his age, he was also one of its most accomplished photographers. Although trained by Gérome in the French academic tradition, Eakins stands out through the vivid realism of his portrayals, particularly those of the human body. While his masterpiece, *The Gross Clinic*, shocked his contemporaries by its depiction of a surgical operation, its frankness was typical of his interest in the human condition, and like much of his work reflects his fascination with the male body.[5] Amongst his best-known works, his depictions of boxers, wrestlers, scullers and naked male bathers (*The Swimming Hole*) did much to establish a new convention in the depiction of the developed body — freed both from the formalised idealism of the art-school and from the exotic imaginings of the Romantics. His suppressed homosexuality, already readable in these paintings,[6] was still more evident in his photographic studies of the male body in motion. In the work of Eakins, heroic muscularity gives way to the lithe muscularity of the athlete, a thematic obsession in his photography as in his painting. The ghost of Donatello rather than Michelangelo hovers over these slim yet muscular bodies.

Eakins' experimental photographic studies of the human body, though less well known than those of his friend and contemporary, the Englishman Edweard Muybridge (1830-1904), did much to establish the photographed nude as an object of serious interest. Eakins' studies have more artistic, even at times erotic, overtones than those of Muybridge, the latter treating the male and female moving body more purely as an anatomical object in the course of movement — often photographed strikingly against a void, as if to stress their clinical nature as kinetic studies. While Muybridge arranged his figures sequentially, Eakins stacked the stages of action on top of each other, distantly foreshadowing the techniques of moving pictures. Influenced like Muybridge by the nineteenth-century scientific fascination with the body's mechanical potential, the French physiologist Etienne-Jules Marey (1830-1904) invented a camera specially designed to capture a series of movements. His influence is evident not only in the development of motion pictures but in the concerns of the early twentieth-century Cubists: Marcel Duchamp's *Nu descendant un escalier*, one of the most influential of Cubist paintings, was directly influenced by Marey's studies.[7]

In the work of Eakins, Muybridge and Marey, the photographed human body began to acquire the nature of a self-sustaining image, at a time when photography generally was beginning to take over from painting a role as the leading visual experience of Western society. As the world of high art had represented a (indeed, the only) socially acceptable means of contemplating the image of the unclothed body, so the purposes of photography could be turned to a socially acceptable means of viewing actual human bodies. Pubic hair — long a taboo subject of art (as it was to remain till the 1880s[8]) and still conventionally hidden by shadows or drapery in much studio photography — was clearly visible in the movement studies of Muybridge which had a wide audience outside the ranks of physiologists and students of kinetics. Medical photography similarly was also at times the subject of widespread public interest.[9] At a less socially acceptable level, the new availability of the body for visual contemplation, whether public or (more particularly) private, gave the photograph a widespread circulation as the currency of erotic voyeurism. The very usefulness of anatomical studies such as those of Muybridge and Marey for scientific and anthropometric purposes made them a convenient subterfuge for those with an interest in the erotic potential they offered. Similarly, the *Akademien* or photographic collections of artists' models in various poses were bought not only by art students but by members of the general public in search of voyeuristic titillation. Other representations of the nude shunned any such sham respectability, and the unashamedly pornographic photograph (or 'dirty postcard') made its appearance as early as the 1840s.

3.4 Edweard Muybridge's collection of photographs *The Human Figure in Motion* (1884-85) consisted of sequential photographs showing the human body – mainly nude –in the various stages of physical actions. Their importance as anthropometric or kinetic studies was equalled by their curiosity value as 'legitimate' photographs of the male and female nude.

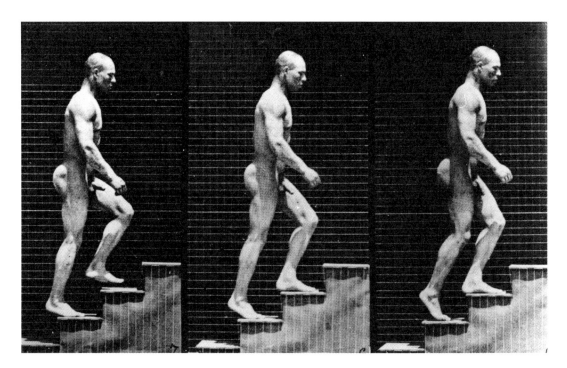

Whilst the female nude predominated within the openly or clandestinely erotic photographic trade, there was in some quarters a not inconsiderable market for the male nude, a trade almost exclusively restricted to homosexual clients.[10] Much of the history of the male nude photograph is outside the scope of this book, since its subjects extend well beyond the depiction of the developed body and include, for instance, the Sicilian youths of Taormina to whose depiction the aristocratic Baron Wilhelm von Gloeden devoted an extensive part of his life, or the boys of Naples in whom von Gloeden's distant relative Wilhelm von Plüschow took such delight. Comprehensive studies of the male nude photograph such as Peter Weiermair's *The Hidden Image* and Emmanuel Cooper's *Fully Exposed* provide informative accounts of the origins, forms and development of this particular genre.[11]

The significance of late nineteenth and early twentieth-century erotic male photography for the development of interest in the muscular physique is nonetheless worthy of some attention. In the first place, it must be remembered that much of the erotic output of those photographers who specialised in the male figure was not openly pornographic: there are no erect penises, for example, and no overtly sexual contact between subjects; at most, eye contact suggests a potentially intimate relationship. As the elaborate pretence of 'art studies' required, the models' poses were often classical in inspiration, the background and props antique, the interest at least superficially anatomical rather than sexual. The distinction between beauty of form and sexual attractiveness is tenuously maintained, and the expression of the subject's face often suggests a lofty remoteness rather than sexual availability or provocativeness. As the attention of some photographers (such as the later Vincenzo Galdi) turned from boyish or adolescent figures towards muscular athletes in heroic poses[12], the contextual signs of the photograph became more and more difficult to read: what was it after all, that distinguished a 'classical' nude statue from a photograph of a nude male of similar heroic build shown in the same pose?

Such devices — often adopted in order to protect against prosecution — at the same time provided a cloak of respectability which enabled this type of photography to be published in well-known photographic journals such as *The Studio*, which were influential in the refinement and development of the art of photography in general. That more overtly pornographic material could be bought privately, or that more suggestive versions of the openly-published work of specialised homoerotic photographers could be ordered by catalogue, did not affect the availability on the general market of these more discreet treatments of the male nude. Given that the nude body (both male and female) was now an acceptable subject of photographic portrayal as it had long been of painting and sculpture, the dividing line between purely artistic depiction and the suggestively erotic remained as elusive as it had been in the other visual arts. And, given that some of the homosexually inclined photographers were among the most accomplished practitioners of their craft — as the homosexual artists of the Italian Renaissance had been of theirs — the studio

3.5 The nude photograph pandered to a variety of tastes. Homosexuals wishing to see nude photographs of adolescent youths (and even pre-pubertal boys) might, at the turn of the century, procure copies of photographs by specialist photographers such as Baron Wilhelm von Gloeden, who posed Sicilian youths in a variety of pseudo-classical settings. Von Gloeden, *Youth*, Taormina, Sicily, *c*. 1900.

photography of the late nineteenth and early twentieth centuries was to become a significant factor in maintaining the developed male body as a subject of acceptable public contemplation.

For most of its history, homoerotic photography was chiefly significant within the restricted confines of the homosexual sub-culture (for which it developed a visual language of eroticism) rather than exercising a direct influence on the cultural mainstream. Only in more recent years has it come to impinge openly upon the portrayal of the male body in the public media. This transformation did not come about overnight, and although the detailed history of the stages by which it took place is not our present concern, reference should at least be made to the work of important figures in the history of serious photography (particularly the 'new realists' and 'pictorialists'), a number of whom made use of the male nude and helped establish it as an acceptable photographic subject. From Frank Sutcliff at the turn of the century to Edward Weston and Imogen Cunningham in the 1920s and, later, George Platt Lynes and Minor White, the male nude gained access, if not to the realm of public acceptability, at least to the canons of depiction recognised by the coterie of serious 'art' photographers, without the suggestion of homosexual voyeurism that had attached to earlier generations appealing to a somewhat different clientele. This does not mean that a degree of emotional involvement was excluded (Platt Lynes' homosexuality, for example, is clearly readable in his work),[13] but rather that the treatment of the subject in the formal terms of photographic art achieved a sophistication which took precedence over (or at least vied with) erotic content. Within this group, Imogen Cunningham (1883-1976) deserves particular mention, her representations of the male body in some ways prefiguring the contemporary feminist interest in the 'objectified male' as well as foreshadowing the work of later photographers (Dianora Niccolini, Grace Lau) who have explored this territory through female eyes.[14]

The invention of photography had brought the 'actual' human body closer than it had ever been to public display, in the Western cultural tradition, since the time of antiquity. For a thousand years or more, many Europeans would hardly ever have seen a completely unclothed body save in the most intimate of domestic circumstances. Painted and sculpted representations of the nude had become more common in the centuries following the Renaissance, and particularly since the creation of public galleries and museums, but none could match the immediacy or sense of actuality provided by the photograph. With the photographer's eye for, and access to, some of the most beautifully formed bodies of his time, the very status of the body as a visual object had been irreversibly transformed.

Thanks largely to the camera, the unclothed human body was on its way to becoming a public object.

3.6 The use of the male nude as a serious photographic subject has helped maintain the developed body as an acceptable object of public contemplation. Though many important photographers of the male nude have been homosexually inclined, the artistic possibilities of the genre have also made it a popular subject of 'mainstream' photography. (John Freund, Pose 39.)

POWERFUL BODIES

Just as in ancient Greece the appreciation of the body and its cultivation went hand in hand, so too in the nineteenth century the awareness of the developed body was accompanied by a renewal of interest in the means of its development. The eighteenth-century concern for scientific method coupled with the study of the body as a machine able to be controlled by scientific regimens, was now joined to a fascination with the modern notions of 'progress' and 'improvement' to awaken a new mode of understanding the human body as an object of exact calculation, capable of being perfected by advances in human knowledge.

In both Europe and America, the public hygiene movement (a form of the impetus towards social reform and mass education) led to the growth of a general concern for sanitary improvement and the betterment of community health. As early as 1811, Friedrich Ludwig Jahn set up the first public instruction in gymnastics on the Hasenheide outside Berlin, thus founding the German School of gymnastics which rapidly spread to France, Switzerland, Czechoslovakia, Austria and other countries of both Western and Eastern Europe. Two years after Jahn, in 1813, Per Henrik Ling, the founder of the Swedish School of gymnastics, was charged by his king with the establishment of a central school in Stockholm for the training of gymnastics teachers.[15] Whilst the Swedish School concentrated more on fluid rhythmic movement, the German School of Jahn and his pupils was concerned with apparatus work of a more formal nature and the fostering of muscular development.

In the 1820s, three of Jahn's pupils took his method to America. One of them, Karl Beck, was to set up with George Bancroft the Round Hill School at Northampton in Massachusetts, the first institution in the USA to have Jahn's equipment. The second, Karl Follen, became a professor at Harvard where he gave instruction in Jahn's exercises, while the third, Franz Lieber (later Lincoln's adviser) set up a swimming school in Boston.[16] The influence of the German gymnastics teachers at Harvard on the American education system was significant, and the general physical weakness and ill-health of the urban populace led Catharine E. Beecher in the 1850s to introduce physical education into American schools. Like Beecher, the newspaper editor and politician Horace Greeley promoted the physical education of the masses as a means of enabling America to emulate the Golden Age of Greece.

Sustained by philosophical idealism or scientific principle, physical culture was to become an increasingly popular activity as the century progressed. In a society where the effects of the Industrial Revolution were becoming evident in the creation of a more sedentary, less physically active workforce, the very biological need of the body for some form of vigorous exercise sought an outlet either in sporting activity or some other systematised form. The international popularity of the German

3.7 By the second half of the 19th century, 'physical culture' had become a popular pastime in increasingly sedentary Western societies. The vigorous swinging of weighted Indian clubs was intended to develop strength in the upper body, as in this 1860s exercise manual.

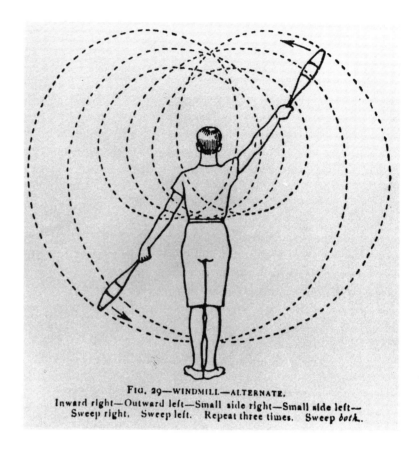

FIG. 29—WINDMILL—ALTERNATE.
Inward right—Outward left—Small side right—Small side left—
Sweep right. Sweep left. Repeat three times. Sweep both.

and Swedish systems of exercise led to the formation in 1881 of the Federation Internationale de Gymnastique, which promoted competition amongst European countries. Weightlifting, which had become increasingly popular as sport during the nineteenth century, had become sufficiently widespread by the 1890s to stage its first world championships (1891) and was one of the sports included at the first modern Olympic Games (1896).

By the middle of the century, the first manuals of physical exercise had already begun to appear. *Mainly Exercise* (1865) provided the gentlemen of the Victorian era with a complete guide to such activities as fencing, running and riding, and to the means of achieving physical fitness through callisthenics, Indian club swinging and the use of light dumbbells. The proper dress for such exercise was as follows:

'A very light covering on the head, such as a straw hat, is best; the shirt collar should be open, the breast being either exposed or thinly covered; the waist-band of the trousers should not be tight, and the boots or shoes should have no iron in them.'[17]

The exerciser was advised to go outdoors in the early morning and seek a grassy plot or sandy beach, though he was admonished first to check for such hazards as 'chasms, stones and stakes'.

It was not long before competing systems of physical development were being placed before the public, and a vast panoply of machines and devices was readily available. William Blaikie's *How to Get Strong and How to Stay So* (1898), as well as providing a complete array of conventional exercise movements, supplied diagrams of machines which users could have constructed and set up in their homes, while the Whitely Exerciser in the early 1890s made effective use of elasticised strands attached by pulleys to a stationary point to develop the arms and torso through the movements of 'throwing', 'hoisting', 'rowing', 'bowling' and 'putting the shot'. Professor D.L. Dowd was the first to make use of 'before and after' photographs to provide proof of the progress in muscular development available to purchasers of his physical culture manual.[18]

3.8 Louis Cyr, a famous Canadian strongman of the turn of the century, had the typical barrel chest and large girth of the stage Samson. Prodigious feats of strength were popular items on the bill of fare of the vaudeville theatre.

Along with the invention of the camera, the awakening of interest in physical exercise in the second half of the nineteenth century was one of the chief focuses of the emerging fascination with the visual appearance of the actual human body, as distinct from the idealised and conventionalised bodies of traditional art. The body had now become an object of interest *in itself*, and the developed body was promoted as being within the reach of the ordinary citizen. No longer the exclusive province of gods and heroes, no longer the outward form of an indwelling divinity or superhuman striving, it was man himself — or, at least, man as the age of scientific progress could enable him to become.

3.9 'Professor Louis Attila' (Ludwig Durlacher) was a former stage strongman who became a teacher and a
promoter of strength competitions. Much decorated by his royal pupils, he was to achieve even greater fame
as the teacher of a young circus acrobat called Friedrich Müller.

At a more popular level, the later nineteenth century was to see a remarkable development in one of the longest-established of contexts for bodily display — the popular theatre. Since the festivals of ancient Greece and Rome, the itinerant bands of players in medieval times and the fairs and entertainments of the seventeenth and eighteenth centuries, popular performances had always stressed the element of physicality, whether through earthy ribaldry of word and gesture, the display of human wonders or deformities, or the acrobatic skills of tumblers, balancers, jugglers and other performers who took physical prowess to its spectacular limits. It was the late nineteenth century, however, which took up these disparate elements, brought them within the walls of the theatre (sometimes theatres expressly built for the purpose) and exploited their capacity to attract huge crowds and turn a healthy profit for their promoters, whether in the form of revue, vaudeville, music hall or burlesque.

In these four main guises — distinct in principle, but in practice often overlapping — the popular audiences of the 1890s were exposed to an astonishing variety of stage acts, from song and dance routines to magicians, trained animals, knife-throwers, ventriloquists, comedians, jugglers, escapologists (notably Houdini) and even — at the Paris Moulin Rouge — the prodigiously flatulent *Pétomane* (Joseph Pujol), who could extinguish a candle by breaking wind from half a metre away. While the element of bawdy at times predominated, the vaudeville and music hall moved gradually towards respectable family entertainment as the century progressed. Burlesque and revue, on the other hand, retained an emphasis on the female form: in France, the popularity of the titillating and exhibitionistic *can-can* in the 1830s dance halls led to its regular appearance after 1844 in music hall and revue. The Folies-Bergère, in its own theatre from 1869 onwards, moved in 1894 to augment the traditional vaudeville fare by the new vogue of the strip-tease, which soon turned into a *spécialité de la maison*; by the early twentieth century, female nudity had come to overshadow all the other attractions of the Folies.

Displays of physical strength had always had a place in the menu of attractions served up by the variety and vaudeville stage: poker-bending, lion-wrestling, and various forms of weight and harness lifting were popular spectacles, and professional strongmen could make a handsome living from such theatrical feats. Self-promotion and showmanship were vital ingredients of success, and the resulting celebrity was turned to good account when the strongman set himself up (as was often the case) as a teacher, or 'professor', of physical culture. As distinct from the organised sport of weightlifting which began about the same time, theatrical weightlifting was a form of entertainment, often beset by trickery and the arts of illusion.

3.10 Attila's star pupil,
Friedrich Müller, was to
change forever the
perception of the
muscular male body.
Under his stage-name of
Eugen Sandow, he
would become one of
the world's most famous
and wealthy men.

One of the most significant figures in this world was the German Ludwig Durlacher, who called himself 'Professor Louis Attila'. A competent stage performer himself, he reached his greatest celebrity as a teacher (boasting among his pupils Czar Alexander III, King George of Greece and even the corpulent Edward VII of England) and as a promoter of strength competitions in circuses and variety halls. The title of 'Strongest Man in the World' had been devised in the 1880s as a means of attracting publicity to such contests, and the claimants included such notable strongmen as the aptly-named Frenchman Charles A. Sampson and his herculean colleague 'Cyclops' (Franz Bienkowski of Poland). On the evening of 29th October 1889, at the Royal Aquarium in London, the challenge thrown out by Sampson was brilliantly met by Professor Attila's star pupil, a relatively unknown 22-year-old German by the name of Friedrich Wilhelm Müller.[19]

Born in Königsberg, East Prussia, Friedrich Müller (1867-1925) was, like many Germans of his generation, influenced in his formative years by the physical culture movement which Jahn had founded in the early years of the nineteenth century. His athletic prowess in the local *Turnhalle* or gymnasium having considerably outstripped his academic performance, he left both school and his family in search of a career as a circus acrobat. Finding himself without a job when the travelling circus to which he was attached went bankrupt in Brussels, he happened upon a demonstration of weight-lifting by Professor Attila and, joining in the activity, handled the weights so easily that Attila immediately took him on as an assistant. Under the tutelage of the 'Professor', he worked not only on his physical strength but on the stage presence required of the theatre strongman, later branching out into wrestling and athletic feats.

Following his victory over 'Cyclops' in 1889, Müller continued his career as a music hall strongman in England and on the Continent, interspersing his feats of strength with displays of muscular tension, and was soon much in demand for exhibitions as an example of the benefits of physical culture. In December 1892, one of his exhibitions for army cadets was even described in *The Lancet* — including his ability to 'make his biceps rise and fall in time to music'; those present were invited to run their hands over his torso, a sensation described as 'like moving your hand over corrugated iron', while 'the action of the muscles of the back caused them to look like snakes coiling and uncoiling themselves under the skin'.

Müller's remarkable physical development was to stand him in good stead. Under his stage-name of Eugen Sandow, he was not only to become one of the world's most wealthy men but was to change forever the public perception of the muscular male body. He was to become the founder of bodybuilding.

BARE BODIES

Thanks to the ability of Renaissance thinkers to endow the nude body with a positive moral significance and accompanying symbolism, the depiction of nudity had become an accepted convention of Western art and was thus considered exempt from the cultural and religious canons applying to everyday life. Photography stretched this convenient social fiction beyond its limit, and the photographed nude would never achieve quite the same privileged status as academic painting and sculpture. Not until the later twentieth century, when the notion of a 'higher purpose' attaching to artistic work had in any case been abandoned, would it be thinkable to display nude photography in public galleries and exhibitions; until then, its appreciation would be restricted mainly to specialist photographic magazines and private collections.

The depiction of nudity was one thing; its public display was quite another. There was no 'glorious tradition' to fall back on, since even the Renaissance had not taken its admiration of Greek antiquity to the point of condoning or encouraging the public nakedness of which the gymnasium had been the prime example. To appear naked, other than in bed or (in certain cultures) at the bath-house, had been considered since early medieval times not only barbaric but sinful.

True, there were occasional exceptions to this rule, even in christianised Europe —a product of that ambiguity in respect of the body which Christian doctrine had never totally resolved.[20] The prelapsarian innocence of the naked Adam and Eve, and the presumed nakedness in which mankind would appear before God in the final Judgment, were potent images for a small number of Christians who professed a paradisiac nudity as a symbol of the state of grace or salvation. The influence of the Adamites, a fourth century millenarian cult which held that man's primitive innocence could be restored by the practice of nakedness, lingered on among a number of Christian sects such as the twelfth-century Waldenses and the Dutch Anabaptists of the sixteenth century. Some art historians have even detected Adamite themes in Hieronymus Bosch's early sixteenth-century painting *The Garden of Delights*.[21] But such departures from the cultural and religious norm were rare, and in general Christian teaching tended to adopt the Jewish proscription of public nakedness.

3.11 At various times, Christian sects have taught that nakedness is a sign of man's primeval innocence. Some art historians have claimed to discern vestiges of this teaching in an allegorical triptych by Hieronymus Bosch. Bosch, *The Garden of Earthly Delights*, detail of centre panel. *c.* 1500. (Madrid, Prado.)

3.12 Early German naturism was heavily ideological, preaching the virtues of the open air, vegetarianism and abstinence from alcohol and tobacco. From the beginning, however, the philosophical tenets of nudism have been inseparable from a curiosity as to the bodies of others. Hugo Erfurth, *Bogenschütze*. 1908.

It was a concern for physical rather than spiritual well-being that prompted the beginnings of nudism as a cultural movement in modern Europe. The growing interest in public hygiene and physical improvement which marked the later nineteenth century led to a number of movements of Utopian idealism based on the promotion of health and the avoidance of disease. To some extent a reaction against the effects of urbanisation arising in the wake of the Industrial Revolution, such movements preached a return to the 'natural' world as a corrective to the problems of modern civilisation, and it is significant that ideologically-minded nudists were for many years to call themselves 'naturists'. Along with physical culture, vegetarianism, dress reform, and the promotion of various 'natural' medicaments, tonics and panaceas, the practice of nudism was conceived as one of the means of improving physical and mental health through the restoration of man's original harmony with the natural world.

Major impetus was given to the nascent movement by the appearance in 1905 of the work *Die Naktheit* ('Nudity') by the German Richard Ungewitter — an apologia for the therapeutic value of fresh air and sunlight combined with vegetarianism and abstinence from alcohol and tobacco. Other German enthusiasts either shared or took up Ungewitter's theories, including the somewhat inappropriately-named Dr. Heinrich Pudor who organised the first modern nudist ('Naktkultur') group and Paul Zimmermann whose nudist spa near Lübeck became the prototype for the 'nudist colonies' that were to follow.[22]

European in origin and always at its strongest on the Continent, the nudist movement was to spread to England, the USA and Canada after World War I, though it was to remain an essentially underground activity in America until the 1930s. Although inspired by German nudism, the American variety was from its inception a more socially than ideologically driven movement, free of the unrelieved intellectual earnestness of its German progenitors and the strict dietary and athletic practices they prescribed. Allegations in the sensationalist tabloid press of 'lewd conduct' in nudist camps, not to mention the occasional police raid, both increased the public's awareness of the nudist cause and led to a growth in club membership; at the same time, the fear of adverse publicity encouraged a particular sensitivity on the part of club officials and often entailed the imposition of an even more puritanical code of conduct within nudist associations than was required in the society around them.

3.13 By the 1920s, German nudism was developing its interest in a natural and healthy life into something more approaching bodily perfectionism. Joseph Bayer, *German Naturist.* c.1920.

The sexual motivation of some nudists, though for a time denied in most of its organisations, was more openly acknowledged from the 1960s onwards[23]. Such motivation may of course take many forms, from mild erotic voyeurism to an openly predatory intent. Though the latter has not been condoned by most organisations, the sexually 'therapeutic' nature of nudism is sometimes claimed by practitioners, who also point to nudist marriages as a sign of the healthy sexuality engendered by the movement. Whilst 'social nudism' has abandoned the sometimes eccentric and Utopian claims of the movement's founders, the beneficial effects of the nudist way of life continue to be proclaimed by journals bearing titles such as *Sunshine and Health* or *Health and Efficiency*.

Though it remains a distinctly minority activity, nudism has a threefold importance for the history of the body in society. Firstly, its origins and early development point to the growing interest in the unclothed body which was already gaining momentum towards the end of the nineteenth century and had clearly become a noticeable trend by the beginning of the twentieth. As such, it was a by-product of a wider social movement concentrated on the liberation of the body from traditional constraints — a movement of which gymnastics, physical culture and dress reform were also a part. Its emphasis on health and the physical cultivation of the body were part of that new interest in fitness which the nineteenth century introduced and which continues today in 'health crazes' and the booming gymnasium and aerobics industries.

Secondly, the message of nudism was spread among — and well beyond — its adherents by books and magazines copiously illustrated with photographs of naked bodies.[23] From Ungewitter's seminal volume onwards, curiosity as to the naked bodies of others could openly be satisfied by the purchase of nudist publications, and their readership amongst devotees was far exceeded by that of seekers after readily-available (if mild) erotica. It is interesting to speculate just how high a percentage of the sales of nudist magazines was accounted for by their popularity amongst adolescent males (at least until the recent widespread availability of more explicit material). Censorship required the careful posing of figures or the air-brushing of photographs to conceal the genital area, but the very fact that the subjects were naked was sufficient to make nudist publications for some decades the only publicly-available means whereby the erotic potential of the unclothed human body could be open to visual inspection and imagination. In an age when 'art photography' of the nude was restricted to a small circle of specialists, and explicitly erotic material was either banned or obtainable only at some risk, nudist publications played a significant role in opening up the representation of the human body — under the ideal subterfuge of a wholesome concern with health, fitness and nature — to the wider public.

Finally, nudism was highly influential in modifying social attitudes towards the public display of the naked body. Although it had been common, until the middle of the nineteenth century, for men to swim in the nude, either on their own or in

3.14 Social nudism retained only a few vestiges of the ideologically-driven naturist movement. Dogged by controversy and accusations of sexual impropriety, it has spawned organisations ranging from those which strictly moderate sexual behaviour to those which openly pander to voyeurs and sexual 'swingers'.

groups such as that depicted in Eakins' *The Swimming Hole*, the practice became unacceptable once seaside bathing had become common amongst women. 'Bathing machines' were introduced to nineteenth-century beaches, and beach inspectors were introduced to ensure the maintenance of decent and acceptable standards of dress. Until the 1960s, mixed nude bathing save on a small number of European beaches and in the 'skinny dipping' which was sometimes fashionable at wild evening parties was an extremely rare occurrence. Over the last generation, however, the sanctioning by local authorities of a limited number of 'topless' and, later, nude beaches has become an accepted practice even in a number of traditionally conservative Anglo-Saxon countries.

The public fascination with nudity reached a peak in the late 1960s with the rock musical *Hair*, written in 1967. Largely dedicated, like the 1969 Woodstock gathering (another festival of dishabille), to the popular counter-cultural causes of the day — the psychedelic drug culture, the hippie movement, environmental and

3.15 Film nudity, once considered daring and 'continental', has become common and almost unremarkable since a number of trail-blazing movies of the 1970s. An Australian example was *Alvin Purple* (1973).

pacifist concerns and pseudo-Eastern mysticism — *Hair* was also intended to shock audiences by the inclusion of a brief (and dimly-lit) nude scene. It was followed, more daringly, by the revue *O Calcutta!* which contained a considerable number of fully-lit nude scenes including a sensuous 'love ballet' and *pas de deux*. The two shows enjoyed long seasons on both sides of the Atlantic, their box-office success revealing a popular fascination with 'nude chic' on which a number of theatrical entrepreneurs capitalised by staging similar productions. In more recent years, incidental nudity on stage and on screen has become, if not common, at least more and more unremarkable, though the voyeuristic appeal of nakedness continues to be exploited in some game-shows on European and US cable television in which contestants strip for the camera. In the latter case, the motivation for wishing to appear naked in the public arena may share with other forms of social nudism a basis in exhibitionism as a form of approval-seeking behaviour, the attainment of self-esteem and recognition through reassurance that one possesses a 'desirable' body.

While nudist organisations continue to exist, and new and expensive nudist resorts are still being opened in various parts of the world, the majority of those who choose to bathe and sunbake on nude beaches would not consider themselves committed nudists or wish to join a nudist association. Whether attracted by the feeling of physical liberation afforded by throwing off all one's clothes, or merely by the aesthetic appeal of an all-over tan, they would see themselves primarily as sharing a lack of inhibition in respect of the human body which has now become widespread in liberal Western societies. In their curious sociological study *The Nude Beach*, Jack D. Douglas *et al.* do provide considerable anecdotal evidence of overt sexual behaviour on a nude beach in California, but they concede that the fundamental 'deviance' involved is that of intentional departure from the Western norm of the clothed body. The 'culture' of the nude beach provides a structured social context in which various forms of status and dominance can be displayed: as in other social groups and clubs, it enables insiders to feel superior to outsiders, and establishes a hierarchy within which the more adept can enjoy and exercise their dominance. Thus, for instance, the all-over tan becomes a status symbol — the 'sign of the brahmin' while 'the tourist-white is a sign of the outcaste'[25]. Competition, status and dominance are as important here as in other forms of social life:

> 'What the naturalists are really doing, largely unrecognized by themselves, is proposing and creating a new form of naturalness in which they are the dominant people ... In a society of unclothed dominance, they obviously have the advantage ... If the whole world were to uncover, then these people would be the sexually dominant group insofar as body-sex displays go, and they surely know it. That is an ultimate reason most people are unlikely to uncover easily.'[26]

Whether for this reason or for others, the fact remains that, even in those cultures where nudism and nude bathing are officially tolerated, the practice has attracted relatively few devotees, and the resurgence of interest in the naked body which marked the later 1960s appears to have lost its impetus. A revival of *Hair* in 1991 was both promoted and publicly received more as an exercise in 1960s nostalgia than for any residue of 'shock value' attaching to the nude scene.

The availability of the 'live' naked body, as distinguished from its artistic or even photographic representation, for public scrutiny remains a problematic affirmation in most Western societies. The lingering mystique of reticence which still attaches to the completely naked body is not simply a matter of its erotic messages, as witness the fact that on many public ('clothed') beaches the sexual overtones of skimpy bikinis for women and brief trunks for men tend to create a much more overtly voyeuristic atmosphere than is observable on most nude beaches. In this context, Stephen Bayley has correctly observed that 'concealment stimulates the imagination to a degree that exposure cannot hope to emulate.'[27] Even in the world of professional stripping (both male and female) a distinction is made between those who go 'all the way' and those who retain a minimal vestige of genital covering, the former being considered somehow less a 'class act' than the latter. As Ben Maddow has remarked:

3.16 Many of those who are prepared to bare all on a nude beach would not consider themselves 'nudists'. Nonetheless, the nude beach has its own culture, creating a new form of social hierarchy in which some people are the dominant figures.

'Nude is what we are; yet we are unfamiliar strangers, even to ourselves. After all, we spend most of our waking time hidden in the woven shell of our clothes. Naked briefly as we dress or undress, or bend ourselves in the bath; from a high angle in a morning shower, or in the mirror of our privacy, we come to see our bodies, if we look at all, with a sense of tender shock.

Nudity uncoils our emotions: good and bad, ugly and beautiful; and we invent illusions to soften the truth of our own feelings.[28]

There remains, then, a certain defencelessness about the totally naked body, such that the young woman in her minimal bikini can feel as protected from the total scrutiny of others as the New Guinea native clad only in his penis-sheath: both are 'dressed' for the social purposes of their surroundings. The point is perhaps borne out by the story related by the female model who was posing nude for an art class when she became aware that she was being observed through binoculars by a Peeping Tom in a building across the street. 'Suddenly', she later remarked, 'I felt naked.'

Though the nudist movement had an undoubted influence in altering Western attitudes towards the body and emancipating them from much of the inhibition of earlier ages, this influence has been tempered by the general unwillingness of our society to follow the nudist path unreservedly. As a social movement, nudism remains something of a by-way, a minor manifestation of that curiosity about the body which marked the close of the nineteenth century and beginning of the twentieth. In part at least, its failure to command wide acceptance can be attributed to a paradox which is inherent in its very nature as a social system.

Both social and (to a lesser extent) Utopian nudism held as a central tenet that the naked body can, indeed should, be looked at without shame or inhibition; yet the extent to which this notion can be put into practice is hardly straightforward. In most non-sexual contexts in which people see each other naked — the locker-room, for instance —eyes are kept carefully averted, particularly in respect of strangers or persons with whom one is not engaged in conversation. When conversing, one is careful to look one's interlocutor straight in the eye, a practice which is of course normal even when both speakers are clothed, but even more sedulously observed in the context of nakedness where to allow one's eyes to wander would be considered intrusive, not to say deviant. Theoretically at least, no such bashfulness should apply within the nudist context; yet most available evidence suggests that the norms of acceptable conduct within nudist clubs (at least those which promote a 'family' atmosphere as distinct from clubs for 'swingers') do not usually extend to the overt scrutiny of the bodies of others. As on the nude beach, any obvious interest in the anatomy of other people is likely to be considered voyeuristic and even potentially prurient behaviour. Though Magnus Clarke, in his balanced study of Australian nudism, agrees that 'most nudists are voyeurs', he also concedes that voyeuristic observation by outsiders — those who seek to observe without themselves being exposed — is generally unwelcome.[29] Although in theory such constraints should not apply, in reality there are very real limits imposed on the ability of nudists to practise what they preach.

At the opening of the twentieth century, an unprecedented question had arisen. If photography had rendered the human body more accessible to the gaze than ever before, what was the next logical step in the same direction? How, in fact, could the actual *living* body be emancipated from centuries of convention and become an object of accepted public display?

3.17 Whether or not they promote a family atmosphere, nude beaches tend to foster a wariness of 'outsiders': those who wish to observe without baring their own bodies to scrutiny are usually considered voyeuristic and prurient.

To this question, nudism offered one answer, though an answer which was to lead to an unconquerable impasse. The naked body would be openly exposed as a public object, in a context which would demonstrate that social intercourse could be conducted with total propriety without the unnecessary constraint and artificiality of clothing. Yet the very requirement that nudism should protect itself against accusations of immorality placed a limit on the extent to which the bodies of others could become the objects of intimate scrutiny or curious attention. Social relationships must be regulated so as to preserve commonly accepted conventions, and in their physical attitude towards one another nudists must behave *as if* they were clothed.

There was, however, an alternative approach to this same fundamental question, an approach in its way just as socially radical as that provided by nudism. The body would be publicly displayed, not totally naked but in as near-nude a state as custom would allow — clad, perhaps, only in a G-string or imitation fig-leaf. In a context conveniently provided by imitation of the great statues of antiquity, a muscular man would offer his body as the subject of a theatrical spectacle. Thus it was that, from 1893 onwards, a respectable matron and her dignified husband might be found seated in an American theatre observing a near-naked man as he flexed his muscles to a musical accompaniment. Even more improbably, this reputable couple would have felt no reticence in stating (if not in such direct terms) that they had come to the theatre for one reason and one reason only: to gaze in wonder and admiration at the body of the man who stood, living and breathing, before them.

The unselfconscious public scrutiny of an actual, living body — a body presenting itself for no other purpose than to be looked at — had at last become possible. The age of bodybuilding had arrived.

4.1   CHAPTER 4 THE BODY BUILT
A peculiarly Western, and relatively modern, concept —the live male body as public object.

4

THE BODY BUILT

THE HERO: SANDOW

Significant social developments, like significant historical events, are never unprepared. They tend to occur when a number of different forces or tendencies, often in quite disparate spheres, happen to converge at a particular moment in time. Their convergence discloses a common movement or direction underlying them all, and they seem uniquely to suit and give expression to the aspirations of their era. It is then, and only then, that some catalyst appears which brings them together and can be seen, usually in retrospect, as the decisive breakthrough. So it was with 'Sandow the Magnificent': if his particular innovation lay in the public display of aesthetic muscularity for its own sake, this achievement itself lay essentially in his combining and giving concrete expression to a number of already discernible trends. Notable among them were the German physical culture movement, the emerging influence of the popular stage as a focus of physical display, and the growing importance of photography as a medium of the aesthetic contemplation of the body which had earlier been restricted to painting and sculpture.

Unlike the robust and stocky strongmen of his day, whose barrel chests and massive girth made them appear rotund and even obese, Müller was a man of remarkably athletic appearance, whose physical resemblance to the muscular statues of the Greek Classical age was a source of frequent and admiring comment. Thanks to Attila, he was able to pick up part-time work as a model for a number of artists and sculptors to supplement his income. Many of these works were forgettable, but among them were sculptures by the Flemish Jef Lambeaux and the better-known French sculptor Gustave Crauck; for the latter, he was the model for the Lapith in the statue *Le Combat du Centaure*. In 1889, in Venice, he met the American painter E. Aubrey Hunt, for whom he posed dressed in a leopard-skin costume in the guise of a gladiator.[1] In London he was photographed, clad only in a fig-leaf, by the fashionable photographer van der Weyde. Through these encounters with artists and

4.2　The young Eugen Sandow, photographed (c. 1890) by van der Weyde. The pose has some Classical antecedents, but is also a forerunner of the later repertoire of stock bodybuilding attitudes.

120

photographers of the time, Sandow (as Müller now called himself, in an anglicised from of his Russian mother's maiden name, Sandov) had become accustomed to the standard repertoire of classical poses.

Sandow had always been conscious of the strength and beauty of his muscular physique. But if it was Professor Attila who had first enabled him to capitalise on the potential of this remarkable combination, it was another promoter who was to comprehend its mass appeal and exploit it to the full.

In 1893, the young Florenz Ziegfeld Jr. was desperately seeking original stage acts for the opening of his father's new Trocadero Theater in Chicago, which was to be one of the main venues of the World's Columbian Exposition. Having scoured Europe without much success, Ziegfeld found himself in the Casino Theater in New York where the musical farce *Adonis* was playing. At the end of each performance, the curtain would be lowered on the principal actor who stood on a pedestal posed as a statue, then raised again to reveal that the actor had now been replaced by ... Eugen Sandow. The New York newspapers, in their reviews of the play, had praised Sandow's appearance as 'having the beauty of a work of art', with 'such knots and bunches and layers of muscle [as the audience] had never before seen other than on the statue of an Achilles, a Discobolus, or the Fighting Gladiator'. Ziegfeld reacted at once, not merely to Sandow's performance, but to the enthusiastic response of the female members of the audience: he knew that he had found his 'act'. Sandow was hired forthwith, and left for Chicago.

Once the legendary Ziegfeld flair for publicity was applied to Sandow, his national and international celebrity became enormous. Following his weightlifting and posing performances at the Trocadero, Ziegfeld signed Sandow up for a four-year contract which returned the promoter a quarter of a million dollars (and Sandow considerably more) from performances in England and the USA. On his definitive return to England, 'The Great Sandow' (as he was now known) set up four gymnasiums and opened a lucrative business selling physique training apparatus, books and magazines. Such was his fame that he was appointed by King George V as 'Professor of Scientific Physical Culture to His Majesty'.

Himself an astute businessman with a gift for self-promotion, Sandow nonetheless owed much of his success to the remarkable insight of Ziegfeld, who saw his opportunity to exploit the new fascination of audiences with the public display of an outstanding physique. It was his inspiration to promote Sandow, not as the world's strongest, but as the world's *best-developed* man. As in so many of his later ventures, the American impresario had correctly sensed the mood of the time. It was not necessary to devise a new performance medium, for it already existed in the variety theatres which had become accustomed to seeing acts billed as the 'world's strongest' (or tallest, or most flexible) man or woman. From there to presenting the World's Most Perfectly Developed Man was but a small step. Inspiration could also be drawn from the somewhat more risqué burlesque theatre, where scantily clad (or even unclad) female bodies were sometimes posed motionless for *tableaux vivants* supposedly representing scenes from Greek or Roman mythology.

Though the context of Sandow's performances was well established, his great innovation lay in the shifting of the audience's attention from the strength of the male physique to the look of the physique. By the use of poses, audience interest could be maintained for the duration of a stage act, and the scene was set for the development of muscular display as a mode of public entertainment in its own right. Sandow's posing introduced a revolutionary concept: that of the live display of a male body in the public arena, as an object to be admired solely by virtue of its advanced muscular development. The social significance of this new element — that of live public display — can hardly be overestimated. The developed body, henceforth, was no longer an object restricted to the context of artistic representation, at one remove from physical reality, or to less openly avowed or even clandestine (but essentially private) encounters. It was transposed into a new domain, to become a socially acceptable focus of aesthetic attention on the part of mass audiences.

4.3 'The Dying Warrior', one of the most celebrated of Sandow's studio poses. There has been speculation as to the symbolic positioning of the sword, though the age of popular Freudian psychology had not yet dawned.

4.4 At the beginning of the
20th century, this was
the best known body in
the world. Hundreds of
thousands had come to
the theatre to see it with
their own eyes, and
millions more had seen it
in publicity photos such
as this.

By the beginning of the twentieth century, Eugen Sandow was one of the best known men in the world. Perhaps just as significantly, he was the possessor of the world's best known body. At the end of 1903, he had already toured all the British provincial cities, much of the United States, Australia, New Zealand, South Africa, India, Burma, China and Japan. His body had been seen and admired by hundreds of thousands of people, and was known to millions more through the publicity photos that accompanied his appearances and were sold wherever he performed. His name itself had entered the English language ('a veritable Sandow'), and his arrival in far-flung colonial outposts and national capitals alike was inevitably greeted by brass bands, civic receptions and huge crowds of curious onlookers. Never before had the body of a living person excited such universal interest.

Though his legendary feats of physical strength accounted for much of the attraction of his performances, Sandow made sure that the appearance of his physique remained an integral part of his celebrity. No performance was complete without a dramatic disrobing and a display of muscular poses performed in minimal attire. The most accomplished photographers of his day were eager to capture him in classical attitudes: Sarony in New York, Steckel in California, Bernard in Melbourne, all published studies of the famous Sandow physique, their commercial distribution earning them (and him) sizeable profits. The word 'perfect' became more and more common in newspaper accounts of his physical development: the Brisbane *Courier* of 31st October 1902 reported that 'as Mr Sandow stood upon the stage, he indeed looked the embodiment of perfect manhood'. Though one art lover in San Francisco perspicaciously remarked that 'he could not have been a model for Donatello', Professor R. Lankester, director of the Natural History branch of the British Museum, made a (not very successful) plaster cast of Sandow's naked body intended to be included in the Museum collection as representing 'a perfect type of a European man'.

Once again, perfection implied perfectibility, and a vogue for physical culture in the early years of the twentieth century held out to its devotees the possibility of 'perfecting' their bodies. The model was not some theoretical ideal, but the living Sandow. A new term, 'body-building', had entered the English language to describe the building of muscularity — as distinct from increasing one's strength or improving one's health — by means of physical culture using weights or exercise machines. Once, however, the physical culture vogue had died out, as it had by the time of the First World War, it would be left to a more restricted band of devotees to maintain the cult of bodily perfectionism.

Sandow amongst others had recognised the lucrative market that existed for books, and particularly periodical magazines, devoted to the development of the body. As early as 1898 he had started a magazine entitled *Physical Culture*, re-named the following year *Sandow's Magazine of Physical Culture*. Earlier in 1898, the eccentric American Bernarr Macfadden (1868-1955) had begun the magazine *Physical Development*, the first in a remarkable string of publications including its successor *Physical Culture* which brought him a considerable fortune. Often considered a charlatan, a confidence trickster and even a madman, Macfadden wrote books and music, opened a chain of vegetarian restaurants, wrestled, lifted weights, and posed for photographs naked or in a lion's skin; by the 1920s he was a millionaire, the owner of various hotels and sanatoriums, the proprietor of several newspapers including the New York *Daily Graphic*, and as well known to the average American as Jack Dempsey.[2] A more serious and even earlier contributor to the literature of physical development was the French Edmond Desbonnet (1868-1957), whose magazines *L'Athlète* (1896), *Education physique* (1902) and *La Culture physique* (1904) were highly influential in the growth of European bodybuilding. With *Sandow's Magazine* and Hadley's *Health and Strength* in England, and the magazine *Kraft-Sport* in Germany, the opening of the twentieth century saw an efflorescence of periodicals often copiously illustrated with physique photographs including in most cases those of the magazine's owner.

4.5   An astute businessman, Sandow saw the commercial possibilities of linking his name to gymnasia, health and fitness magazines, and the sale of bodybuilding apparatus of various kinds.

4.6   Often considered a charlatan, a confidence trickster or a madman, Bernarr Macfadden was a publicist (and self-publicist) of genius. The pseudo-classical nude pose is typical of its time.

4.7 Macfadden's magazines, like his other activities, were aimed at promoting himself and his often eccentric ideas, which included bodybuilding as the key to 'virile manhood'.

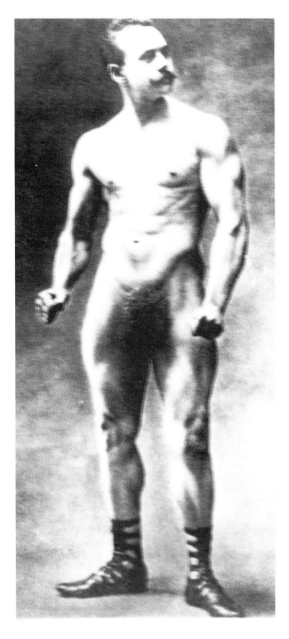

4.8   The Frenchman Edmond
Desbonnet, one of the
first publishers of
bodybuilding
magazines, was a
significant figure in the
spread of interest in
muscle-building in
Continental Europe.

As part of the publicity campaigns aimed at enhancing the sales of such magazines, their founders began to organise physique competitions. The first of these contests, organised by Sandow himself, was held on 14th September 1901 in the Royal Albert Hall in London. Some 15,000 spectators assembled to watch the 60 finalists chosen by Sandow from various regional trials throughout Britain as they were judged on the balance and tone of their muscular development, general health and skin condition. The judges were persons of considerable public standing at the time: the sculptor Sir Charles Lewes and the creator of Sherlock Holmes, Sir Arthur Conan Doyle. After the competitors had assumed a number of prescribed poses, twelve finalists were selected and a winner (William L. Murray of Birmingham) finally chosen. The event was favourably reported in no less eminent an organ than the London *Times*.

Macfadden, never a man to let pass an opportunity for self-promotion, was not long in organising a series of similar contests in America. Hiring Madison Square Garden as the venue, he offered a prize of $1,000 (an immense sum at the time) for the winner of his title as the 'Most Perfectly Developed Man in America'. The victor was a physical education graduate of Harvard University, Albert Treloar (1873-1960), a former assistant to Sandow, who was to capitalise on his newly-won title by the publication of *Treloar's Science of Muscular Development* (1904) and a series of theatrical bookings under the name 'Albert, the Perfect Man'. In 1906, he became Director of Physical Education at the Los Angeles Athletic Club; it was from this location that he was to introduce the practice of bodybuilding to Southern California, where it was later to establish its unofficial world headquarters.[3]

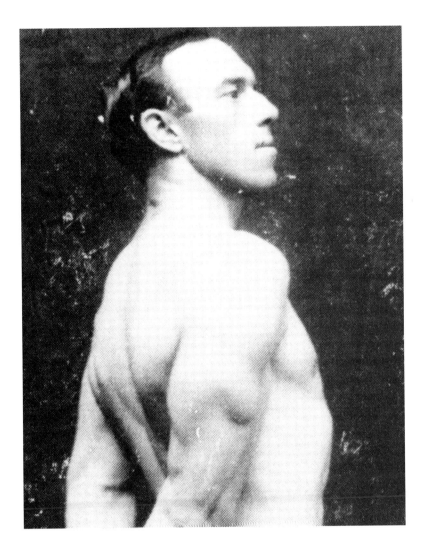

4.9   Albert Treloar was the
first winner of Bernarr
Macfadden's 'Most
Perfectly Developed
Man in America'
competition. After a
career as a stage
bodybuilder ('Albert, the
Perfect Man'), he
introduced bodybuilding
to its later unofficial
world headquarters –
Southern California.

Other such contests were organised sporadically over the early years of the century, by Desbonnet among others, but only Macfadden maintained them on a regular basis, his most celebrated 'Perfectly Developed Man' being the 1921 winner Angelo Siciliano — a somewhat overweight specimen but with an entrepreneurial flair to rival any of his predecessors. Under the name of 'Charles Atlas' he was to maintain for many years his series of back-page magazine advertisements in which the 'seven-stone weakling' was transformed into a muscular bodybuilder by the use of Atlas' 'Dynamic Tension' method of physical development.

THE FAUN: SANSONE

Until the 1930s, most of the practitioners of bodybuilding were also weightlifters, usually making their living from theatrical and circus performances and instruction in physical culture. Their bodybuilding activity, in the form of posing, remained a part of their stage act as it had done for Sandow, or took the form of posing for photographic studies to be used as promotional material. Men like Max Sick of Bavaria (who called himself Maxick), Treloar's pupil Orville Stamm ('the boy Hercules') and Georg Hackenschmidt ('the Russian Lion') were essentially stage weightlifters, though all had themselves photographed posing in skimpy attire. Gradually, however, as the vaudeville theatre declined in popularity, the 'strongman' stage act became a less lucrative way of making a living and its exponents could no longer earn the salary of a Cabinet Minister. At the same time, weight-training techniques were becoming more sophisticated: by 1920 weightlifting had become an Olympic sport, and its practitioners had discovered that the type of training required for building massive strength was different from that required for achieving a muscular look. Posing in the near-nude seemed, in any case, far too frivolous and 'arty' an activity for serious international sportsmen.

The transition from bodybuilding as an adjunct to weightlifting to its emergence as an autonomous activity took some years. Despite the public fascination with Sandow's 'physical perfection', he remained until his death in 1925 the symbol of the strong man as much as that of the developed man. It took a gradual shift in perspective for the representational interest of the body to free itself in the public mind from its instrumental function — a shift which has never been totally accepted in the community at large and which even today leads to the popular criticism that bodybuilders are not actually strong and that their muscularity is 'useless'.

This shift in the nature of bodybuilding from a by-product of the body's instrumental use in weightlifting and health-oriented physical culture to a distinct form of representational display took place in the years following Sandow's death, in the later 1920s and early 1930s. The increasing sophistication of public taste was seized upon by a number of influential trainers and photographers who placed a new emphasis on the formal aesthetic quality of the posed figure. Amongst the bodybuilders and trainers was the man whom many considered Sandow's natural successor, Siegmund Klein (1902-1987). Klein had been brought from Germany as a young child to live in the USA where he observed the vaudeville strongmen and followed for a time in their footsteps. Having married the daughter of 'Professor Attila', he re-opened the Attila gymnasium before beginning his own physical culture studio in 1926. In his instruction and numerous magazine articles, including those in his own publication (*Klein's Bell*), he was to place the primary emphasis on what he called 'training for shape', developing and teaching the types of exercise that would bring out the musculature of the body as distinct from increasing its strength. Frequently photographed in bodybuilder's trunks or brief 'posing strap', he embodied in his own physical development and passed on to his pupils a much more exclusive concern with the aesthetics of muscularity than the 'professors' of physical culture (including Sandow) had traditionally fostered.[4]

Without skilful and sympathetic photographers, however, bodybuilding could not have extended its appeal beyond a small number of devotees. Although a number of earlier professional photographers (Sarony, Eisenmann) had made something of a specialty of 'strongman' photographs, it was not till the 1920s that there emerged a new group who devoted themselves exclusively to what became known as 'physique photography' or the photographic depiction of 'expressive posing'. The first of these was John M. Hernic, a former bodybuilder who in the 1920s opened a mail-order photographic gallery which sold 'The Apollo Art Studies' featuring the leading bodybuilders of his time.[5]

4.10 Siegmund Klein was Sandow's successor as the leading bodybuilder of his day. Through his publications and gymnasium instruction, he helped to transform bodybuilding from the domain of the stage performer into a popular pastime amongst athletically-minded young men.

4.11 Klein's emphasis on the aesthetics of muscularity helped break the nexus between bodybuilding as a representational display and weightlifting as an instrumental activity. The grace and elegance of this pose owe much to the photographer, Edwin Townsend.

The most accomplished of early physique photographers was Edwin F. Townsend of New York, who did away with the pseudo-classical props of the earlier generation and posed his models in relaxed or balletic rather than heroic attitudes. Sophisticated lighting, rich finishing and a meticulous concern for detail made Townsend's work stand out in sharp contrast to the often crude products of his predecessors. The historian David Chapman has commented that

'Townsend often printed his photographs in sepia tone and softened the focus to make his subjects more romantic and dreamy looking. He apparently liked the contrast between the vague, almost feminine image and the hard muscularity of the subject. So while Sarony viewed his subjects as characters in a cosmic drama, Townsend tended to see his as idealised visions of perfection unconnected with the world around them.'[6]

Townsend produced some elegant studies of Sigmund Klein in 1921, but it was some years later that his most memorable work was done — a series of poses by his favourite model Tony Sansone. These not only made his own reputation but did much to re-establish the developed male body as an object of aesthetic contemplation after its abandonment by the world of high art. None of his predecessors in the field, however accomplished, had produced work of such beauty of composition, which at times matches in visual power the contemporaneous nudes of the internationally famous Edward Weston and prefigures those of Bruce Weber and Robert Mapplethorpe in more recent years.

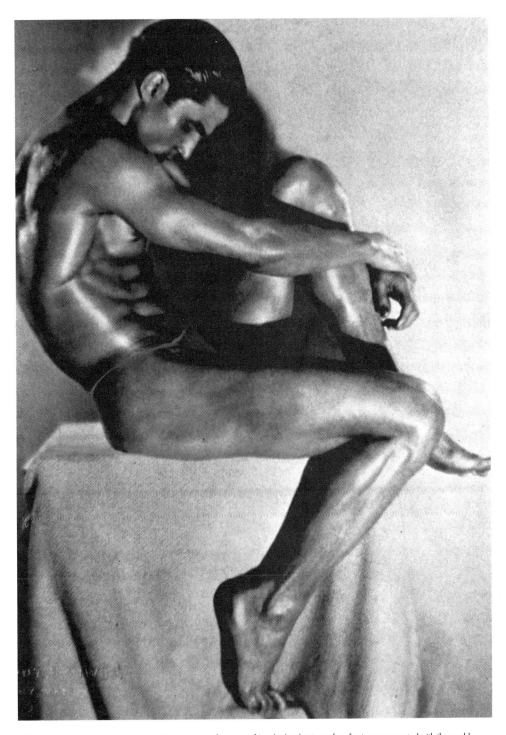

4.12 Townsend's favourite model, Tony Sansone: one of a series of '... idealised visions of perfection unconnected with the world
around them.'

It was not only Townsend's reputation that was made by these studies, but even more so that of his model. Tony Sansone (1905-1987) was a native of New York who had attempted to overcome a number of childhood illnesses by taking up athletics and physical culture. Inspired by photographs of well-developed bodies in Bernarr Macfadden's *Physical Culture* magazine, he began to take an interest in bodybuilding, and a chance encounter with Charles Atlas on the beach in Coney Island in 1921 led him to follow the Charles Atlas course. By the following year, he had won an Atlas contest for progress and development and for the next few years dedicated himself passionately to bodybuilding. Having worked for a short time as an actor and dancer, he later chose to devote his career to the instruction of others in bodybuilding, and in his mature years operated three different gymnasiums in the Manhattan area.[7]

4.13 None of Townsend's predecessors had produced work of such beauty of composition, their cool and elegant detachment suggesting 'a Classical and contemplative Elysium of the soul'.

Sansone's place in the history of the physique rests on two slender volumes of photographs, *Modern Classics* (1932) and *Rhythm* (1935). Mainly by Townsend, though with some by Achille Volpe, they show the athlete posed against a simple background, either almost black (only a dimly lit wall and curtain breaking up the space) or almost white (the shadow of his body reflecting his pose). His body is sometimes relaxed —recumbent, seated or standing casually — sometimes taut, a simple prop suggesting an antique theme. Chapman rightly speaks of the 'cool and elegant detachment' of these poses, the serenity which draws upon 'images of a Classical and contemplative Elysium of the soul'.[8]

What is it that gives these two relatively meagre collections of photographs such an important documentary status in the social history of the body and that makes Sansone such a significant figure despite the totally unremarkable nature of his public career? There are at least three aspects of this question which deserve our attention.

First, these are for the most part nude photographs. From Sandow's time until the end of the 1930s, it was by no means uncommon for bodybuilders to be photographed nude, though only from an angle at which the genitals were hidden. The body was either turned away from the camera, or photographed from the side so that the near leg could be placed forward of the body and conceal the genital area. In a frontal shot, the model (if not wearing tights, trunks or some other form of clothing) was required to sport the somewhat ridiculous 'tin fig-leaf' in order that modesty should be preserved. (Though Sandow's plaster cast for the British Museum shows him totally nude including genitals, this could no doubt have been justified on 'scientific' grounds.) In the case of Sansone, however, the genital area is often completely visible, no attempt being made to conceal it by an artificially adopted pose.

The circulation of the photographs in their original form was highly restricted. In the two volumes in which they were published the genital area was carefully air-brushed, giving it the appearance of a black triangle of hair which is curiously, and disconcertingly, similar to that of the female pubic region. In other versions subsequently reproduced, a fig-leaf has been painted on in the appropriate spot — like air-brushing, a common practice of the time as was the addition of a painted 'posing pouch' or G-string. Air-brushed or not, Sansone was very clearly intended to be seen as a nude figure — and, in many of the photographs, a nude figure in repose. The classicising vocabulary of stage props had disappeared, but so too had the equally classical reference-frame of the defiant heroic stance which was part of the justification for the nudity of the subject. Never before had the image of the bodybuilder been handled with such voluptuousness, or come so close to an overtly erotic treatment.

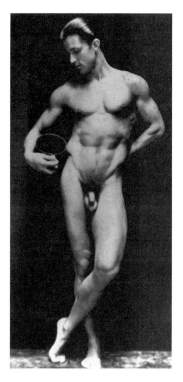  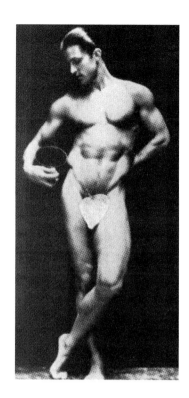

4.14 Three versions of one of Townsend's most famous studies of Sansone, reflecting the social and legal constraints surrounding their publication. (a) The original, highly restricted nude version; (b) with air-brushed genitals, as published in *Modern Classics*; (c) with painted 'fig leaf', as reproduced in magazines.

The second important factor is Sansone's renowned handsomeness. A man of striking visual beauty, he was so remarked for his 'sultry Latin good looks' that in 1926 he was approached by motion picture studios seeking a replacement for Rudolph Valentino, who had recently died. Though he declined the offer, there is no doubt that his extraordinary facial resemblance to the great screen idol played an important part in his appeal: the face of a Latin lover surmounting the body of an Adonis. it is hardly surprising that he has remained an 'icon' of gay culture, his photos — including some of the original (unretouched) nude poses — still appearing today in gay books and magazines. In this respect, Sansone marked an important new development in twentieth-century male iconography. Both before and after him, attractive facial features have been seen as at most incidental to success in the world of men's bodybuilding: it is above all the body that counts. What Sansone incarnated was not the 'heroic' bodybuilding convention but the alternative 'erotic/aesthetic' convention — that in which the subject of representation is chosen for his capacity to elicit desire as much as (or more than) admiration. A male bodybuilder may rise to the top of his profession regardless of the handsomeness or otherwise of his features; for the male stripper or centrefold, on the other hand, they are as integral as his muscularity to the role he plays.

4.15 Townsend had made his name as a photographer of the dance, and Sansone had also worked as a dancer. It is obvious that the gestures and attitudes of Nijinsky influenced some of Townsend's studies. (a) Nijinsky in *L'Après-midi d'un faune* (photo: Bert); (b) Tony Sansone (photo: Townsend).

Finally, Sansone's importance can be linked with his popularising of a more lithe and athletic male physique than that displayed by Sandow and his other bodybuilder-strongman predecessors. Indeed, he owes as much to the dancer as to the weightlifter. It is significant that Townsend had been a theatrical photographer before turning to physique photography, having photographed the legendary Anna Pavlova and the modern dance pioneer Ruth St Denis. Photographs of Isadora Duncan had also been influential in studio photography and had often conditioned the choice of poses. As Peter Weiermair points out in relation to 1920s photography:

'The ideal of a man had changed to the physically fit, muscular body, so that dancers and athletes became favourite models. The shot was meticulously produced in a studio, so that the evolving sculptural effect could be gained through lighting. According to social norms, dancers and athletes were allowed to appear as nudes..... The combination of a powerful, self-confident body and a reminiscence of the Greek world creates a surreal mode of reality and ideal.'[9]

There can be little doubt that the dancing of Nijinsky, which had already inspired a remarkable study by Rodin, was an influential factor in Townsend's posing of Sansone. Nijinsky's celebrated performance as the Faun in the ballet *L'Après-midi d'un faune* (which the dancer had himself choreographed to the music of Debussy) had not only caused a furore on account of its 'indecency' but, more significantly, had opened up to the European imagination a new perception of the expressivity of form and gesture of which the male body was capable. One need only compare the photographs of Nijinsky as he appeared in this role with a number of those taken of Sansone by Townsend to observe the striking resemblance of attitude. Having worked as a professional dancer, Sansone would undoubtedly have been familiar with such photos even if he had never seen Nijinsky perform in person.

In addition to the figure of the hero, the faun had been one of the leading motifs of ancient statuary, the Greeks identifying him with (or as an attendant on) the god Pan. Whilst some antique representations depict the faun figure as bestial — half man and half goat — others show him instead as a lithe and vigorous rural youth, either dancing or in a state of repose. His depiction provided the opportunity for a more sensuous portrayal of the muscular figure than that afforded by the noble or heroic gods, especially as when not dancing he is often shown in a languid recumbent posture. When shown standing upright, the sway of his hips is overtly, almost provocatively sexual in suggestion (a theme also hinted at in Donatello's adolescent *David*), and when reclining he appears to be asleep, offering his inconscient body for the viewer's inspection. The potent sexual overtones of these bodily attitudes were certainly not lost on Townsend. Nor were the darkly Italian features of his model, American fascination with an exotic, sensual Italy having reached a peak during the photographer's boyhood through the popularity of Nathaniel Hawthorne's novel *The Marble Faun*.

All of the above factors combined to make Sansone the most important figure since Eugen Sandow in the history of the developed male body. If Sandow was a Hercules of chiselled white marble, Sansone was a seductive and swarthy Pan. The first was the progenitor of bodybuilding; the second became the prototype of the male pin-up.

Sportsmen and Stars

After the death of Sandow, and with the demise of the strongman-poser, the pursuit of physical development as a legitimate sporting pastime had by the 1930s almost suffered an eclipse, 'physique displays' and 'perfect man' contests such as those of Macfadden becoming more of a cabaret curiosity than a significant public spectacle. While gymnasiums slowly grew in number, and Charles Atlas was reaping substantial rewards from the sale of his muscle-building courses, the future of physical development nonetheless seemed problematic. Many of the serious weight trainers were disturbed by the overtones of voyeurism surrounding the 'artistic' displays of physique photography, and the renowned eccentricity of the crank Macfadden hardly promoted the image of weight training as a serious athletic pursuit. Apart from the impressive but overweight movie star Johnny Weissmuller, who was in any case hardly a bodybuilder, there were no nationally known role-models, even in the USA, to serve as a spearhead for outstanding muscular development. The more athletically-based bodybuilding competitions included a lifting component and involved boxers, weightlifters, gymnasts and swimmers as well as specialised physique trainers, while Macfadden's contests were becoming more and more of a sideshow based on his own curiously outdated notions of 'human perfection'.

Matters came to a head in 1939, when a 'Best Built Man' competition was staged by the York Barbell Company in direct competition with Macfadden's 'Most Perfectly Developed Man in America' contest. At this stage the Amateur Athletic Union stepped in and created its own 'Mr America' competition, first held in 1940. Here at last, under the patronage of an official nation-wide athletic organisation, bodybuilding had found a context which would allow it to develop and flourish. It would become a sport.[10]

The fact that, even over fifty years later, there are still many who are unwilling to recognise modern bodybuilding as a sporting activity reflects the ambiguity with which it is still perceived in the popular mind, notwithstanding the formal apparatus of contest rules, judging criteria and accreditation of organisations and officials that have marked its growth as an organised activity world-wide. The reasons for such reluctance and even at times hostility are complex, some of them involving deep-seated taboos and repressed emotional reactions to the display of the human body.

For its followers, however, the recognition of bodybuilding by the Amateur Athletic Union provided the opportunity to endow the pursuit of muscular development with a social acceptability not previously attainable. The codification of rules and judging criteria shifted the focus of attention away from individualistic display onto group competition: compulsory poses were introduced, their execution being defined with technical precision in the rules for competitors; standards of costume were laid down, in a move to reinforce the sporting image and to eliminate

4.16 By the 1940s, bodybuilding had been recognised by the Amateur Athletic Union of the USA, and had taken on many of the characteristics of sporting competition, including rules, standards and judging criteria. One of the leading bodybuilders of this period was John C. Grimek.

any suggestions of indecency or eroticism latent in the G-string or 'posing strap' displays of some earlier exponents; and the practice of a panel of judges independently scoring competitors according to fixed criteria of muscularity, symmetry, proportion, definition and posing ability conferred on the selection of place-getters an atmosphere of almost clinical objectivity. The placing of judges between competitors and audience meant that the latter was now at one remove from contestants, and the general ambience of competition became little different from that of a boxing or wrestling match: the presence of a crowd gave legitimacy to the appreciation of competitors' physical development which would have raised embarrassing questions in the case of a single individual looking admiringly at the physique of another.

Along with its sporting status, bodybuilding was to acquire a new wave of entrepreneurial promoters, most of whom were also purveyors of weight equipment, food supplements and specialised magazines. If AAU affiliation brought respectability to the sport, men such as Bob Hoffman and Joe Weider gave it a public. Hoffman's York Barbell Company published the magazine *Strength and Health*, while the remarkable Joe Weider, who had started out in Canada in the 1930s publishing on a shoestring a little mimeogrpahed magazine called *Your Physique*, was to build the circulation of his later journals *Muscle Builder* and subsequently *Muscle and Fitness* to the point where the latter has today reached a monthly circulation of over 6 million copies and, together with his other bodybuilding enterprises, made Weider a multi-millionaire.

Though the main focus of development of organised bodybuilding was by now the USA, its growth in Great Britain and on the Continent was far from negligible. The UK and a number of European countries were organising national competitions, and titles such as 'Mr Great Britain' and 'Mr France' were contested at a standard not far behind their American counterpart. By 1947, thanks to the organisational flair of Joe Weider's brother Ben, Canada and the USA had joined to form the International Federation of Bodybuilders (IFBB); the number of countries whose associations were admitted to IFBB membership grow steadily through the 1950s and 1960s, and by the late seventies there were more than 100 member associations. The international flavour of competition was reflected in the move in the 1960s to change the most prestigious title from 'Mr America' to 'Mr Universe', a title also sponsored by the IFBB's rival British association the NABBA (National Amateur Bodybuilding Association). Separate titles were awarded to amateur and professional competitors. In the late 1960s, the new international title of 'Mr Olympia' had been created to bring together the world's top professional bodybuilders including 'Mr Universe' winners. The 'Olympia' has since remained the world's most important professional bodybuilding competition.

How far the visibility and popularity of bodybuilding were heightened by the emergence of a number of its exponents who subsequently went on to movie careers can only be conjectured, but it seems likely that without the international celebrity of such top competitors its public impact would have been far less considerable. Steve Reeves (a Mr America and Mr Universe winner) was undoubtedly the best known bodybuilder in the world throughout the 1950s and 60s, thanks to the popularity at that time of the 'sword-and-sandal' series of B-grade movies usually emanating from Italy.

4.17 The 1950s saw the emergence of the bodybuilder-as-star. Steve Reeves was the first bodybuilder since Sandow to become an international celebrity, outside the specialised world of bodybuilding aficionados.

Within the narrower circle of serious devotees, however, the 'heroes of the game' were well known to aficionados regardless of their lack of a high public profile. From John Grimek in the 1940s to Bill Pearl in the 50s, Larry Scott in the 60s, and Franco Colombu and Frank Zane in the 70s and 80s, there were numerous international champions who had not become well known in the popular media. The rise of black bodybuilders had begun in the 1960s with Sergio Oliva (still considered by some the greatest bodybuilder of all time), and the British Harold Poole and the Guadeloupe-born Frenchman Serge Nubret followed soon after; Chris Dickerson, Robby Robinson, Bertil Fox and the subsequent eight-times Mr Olympia winner Lee Haney have established black competitors as one of the dominant forces in the sport and served as role-models to a younger black generation in the USA, Britain and parts of Europe.

The most dramatic turnaround in the public awareness of bodybuilding took place in the 1970s. The generally improved quality of contestants, the popularity of the gladiator movies and the first stirrings of a new interest in health and fitness played their part in the new consciousness, but more than anything else it was due to the emergence of one man — a bodybuilder of extraordinary charisma and determination, and the first since Sandow to become a universally-known figure on account of his extreme muscularity. The age of Arnold Schwarzenegger had arrived.

4.18 The 1960s saw the rise of black bodybuilders, in the footsteps of Sergio Oliva. The Guadeloupe-born Serge Nubret won numerous 'Mr France' and 'Mr Universe' titles, though the Olympia always eluded him.

4.19 Arnold
     Schwarzenegger: a rib-
     cage so massive that he
     could balance a glass
     of water on his flexed
     pectorals. In the first of
     many successive
     personae, he was to
     revolutionise the image
     of the bodybuilder.

As in the case of Sandow, the timing was perfect, and Schwarzenegger (born 1947) had the same capacity as his predecessor for both sensing the mood of the times and fashioning it into concrete expressive form. As Sandow had learned much about the techniques of self-promotion from the entrepreneur Ziegfeld, so Arnold would be taken under the wing of the most successful bodybuilding propagandist of his day, Joe Weider; the lessons learned by both muscle-men from their showman mentors fell on fertile ground, and both were to exhibit a remarkable aptitude for the enhancement of their own myth even after they had broken away from the influence of their early manager-publicists.

Five times Mr. Universe and an unprecedented seven times Mr. Olympia, Schwarzenegger was 188 cm. (6'2") of solid muscle, a huge 145 cm. (57") chest contrasting with a tiny 79cm. (31") waist when in competition trim. His rib-cage was so massive that he could balance a glass of water on his flexed pectoral muscles. The prominent high cheek-bones and wide, square jaw, the high forehead surmounting the piercing, hooded eyes, combined to suggest a self-assured authority of which his demeanour both on and off stage was persuasive confirmation.

Most importantly, the overt sexuality he exuded was unambiguous — it was masculine, dominant, potently virile. Woman could desire him, but men could also watch him with admiration or envy, free from any overtones of sexual deviance. His own exclusively, almost aggressively, heterosexual orientation was as carefully promoted an aspect of his persona as was his physique itself. The movie *Pumping Iron* (1974) showed him on the beach, surrounded by bikini-clad maidens or carrying a bare-breasted young woman on his shoulders. The book that followed (by Charles Gaines and George Butler) had been rejected by one publisher on the ground that 'No-one in America will buy a book of pictures of these half-unclothed men of dubious sexual pursuits', and when it did appear with Simon & Schuster it set out quite deliberately to change the picture of 'bodybuilders as narcissistic, coordinatively helpless muscleheads with suspect sexual preferences'.[11] Bodybuilders were shown with their wives and girlfriends, whilst their relationship with one another was shown in terms of an at times merciless *macho* competitiveness and rivalry.

The Schwarzenegger phenomenon was instrumental in enabling bodybuilding to shake off much of the suspicion of abnormal sexuality which had dogged it for a generation or more. Arnold spoke of women being 'turned on' by his body, and even his celebrated dictum that 'a good pump is better than coming'[12] suggested that he spoke from wide experience. The publicity hype that followed the book and film of *Pumping Iron* centred upon the magnetic figure of Schwarzenegger himself. He was interviewed on the mass audience Barbara Walters TV show, and with consummate charm managed to convince his host (and no doubt many of her audience) that bodybuilders were neither gay, narcissistic nor dumb. By 1976, he was the star of a packed 'live exhibition' at the Whitney Museum of Modern Art from which hundreds of would-be spectators had to be turned away. With Arnold's photo on their front covers, the sales of muscle-building magazines increased dramatically. The unpronounceable name was slipping effortlessly from the lips in breakfast-table conversation across the USA, and young men could fearlessly display his photo on their bedroom wall. Though he was to re-invent himself several times over the decades that followed, Arnold Schwarzenegger had already re-invented the bodybuilder.

4.20 The overt sexuality Arnold exuded was unambiguous —it was masculine, dominant, potently virile. His heterosexuality was as carefully promoted as was his physique.

By the late 1970s, women's bodybuilding had acquired a sufficient following to merit the organisation of national contests for women. Influenced to some extent by the Women's Liberation Movement as well as the new interest in aerobics which had led women to explore the hitherto little-known territory of the predominantly male gymnasium, the building and display of female muscularity raised a number of problematic issues relating to gender-roles and the type of physique favoured by the traditional judging criteria. Under the auspices of the IFBB, women's bodybuilding gained official status in 1978, and by the early 1980s the 'Ms. Olympia' title had been created. Dogged by controversy in its early years, women's bodybuilding has even today not found a definitive niche. The most successful Ms. Olympia contestant of the 1980s, Cory Everson, managed to project an air of femininity which contrasted with the heavily-muscled or anorexically 'stringy' physiques of some contestants, while remaining within the canons of competition rather than veering towards acrobatic or erotic display. Despite Everson's success, women's bodybuilding remains very much a minority activity even amongst athletically-minded women, and amongst male bodybuilders it is often seen as a kind of erotically-tinged curiosity rather than with the seriousness that the male trainers attach to their own sport.

Bodybuilding has today become big business, even local or regional competitions attracting large audiences and generally running at a profit for their promoters or sponsoring organisations. The IFBB now boasts 134 affiliated national bodybuilding associations, and is a member of the General Association of International Sports Federations (GAISF). International competition pays handsomely (the winner of the 'Mr Olympia' is paid $50,000 and some other top contests pay considerably more), though it has not reached the astronomical sums available to top professional golfers or tennis-players. An estimated 34.9 million Americans currently practise some form of bodybuilding with weight equipment.[13] The sale of associated products — weights and training machines, workout clothing and diet supplements — is an annual billion-dollar earner in the US alone, and to this can be added the multi-million dollar monthly sales of specialised magazines and (more recently) videos.

For all this, bodybuilding remains in some ways a curiously obscure sport. Keenly followed by its adherents, it is largely ignored or even denigrated by 'outsiders' to a degree that attaches to few other sporting activities. Its very status as a sport is often questioned, and many significant newspapers, if they report bodybuilding competitions at all, do so in occasional 'feature' articles rather than in the sports columns. The *Encyclopædia Britannica*, though it annually lists the year's achievements in sports such as curling, greyhound-racing and rodeo, omits any reference to bodybuilding; and, despite repeated attempts, it has not had the success enjoyed by synchronised swimming or handball in being included by the IOC as an Olympic sport, though the IFBB is a member of the World Games and has recognition and demonstration status in a number of national and regional Games.

4.21 By the early 1980s, women's bodybuilding had its own international competitions, though the image of the female bodybuilder continued to gravitate uncertainly between that of a 'Playboy bunny' and that of 'a man in a bikini top'. Two of the leading women bodybuilders of the 80s: (a) Rachel McLish; (b) Bev Francis.

Notwithstanding the increasing popularity of weight-training techniques among track and field athletes, footballers and other sportspersons requiring explosive muscular power, such activities tend to be described at most as 'building the body' rather than 'bodybuilding'. Many others who take out membership of a gymnasium or fitness centre and engage in weight training describe their activity as 'keeping fit', 'doing weights', 'having a workout' or even simply 'training', as if euphemisms were required to replace the taboo-word 'bodybuilding'. The three strands of physical culture discernible even in Sandow's day — training for strength, training for health and fitness, and training for muscular development — appear to have maintained their separate identities, and a particular coyness seems to surround the pursuit of the developed body for its own sake. Some of the paradoxes surrounding this phenomenon will be explored in the following chapters.

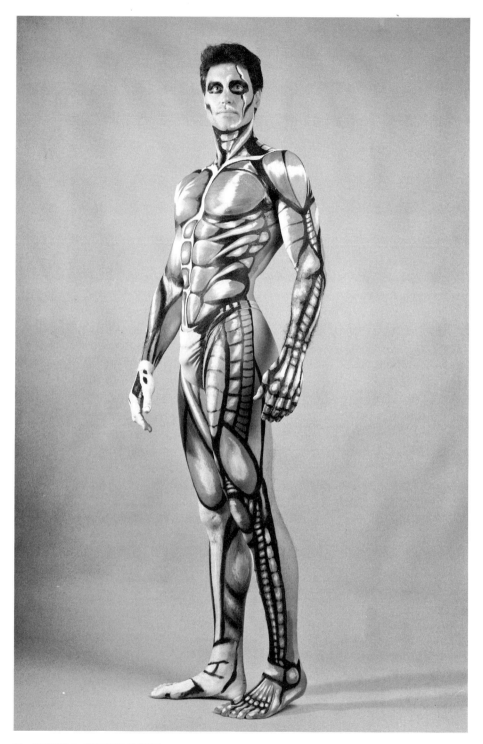

5.1   **CHAPTER 5**   THE POPULAR BODY
With the demise of representational 'high art', the heroically muscular body passed into popular media such as adventure
movies and comic books, where it offered new scope for a nostalgic hankering after primitive physicality or for futuristic
imaginings of superhuman power.

5

THE POPULAR BODY

SAVAGE AND SUPERMAN

Painting had already revolted against the academic tradition at the time of the Impressionist movement. With the advent of Cubism in the early twentieth century, it turned its back on figurative representation in general, and in so doing definitively liberated the body's pictorial portrayal from the long burden of the Greek inheritance. In sculpture, the demise of the figurative tradition was a more drawn-out process, Rodin still remaining active even after the first experiments in geometrical abstractionism. In general, however, the heroic muscular tradition would linger on only in 'official' sculpture of an at times absurdly propagandist nature, while the work of Brancusi, Giacometti and Henry Moore would explore the suggestive power of the body in decidedly non-representational form.

One of the most important outcomes of the Cubist revolution was the breakdown of the traditional barriers between 'high' and 'popular' art. The Cubists had not shrunk from using the collage to stress the visual power of everyday images, and fragments of newspaper pages even made their appearance in the work of a Juan Gris among others. The most celebrated and adept interpreter of Cubist art, the poet Guillaume Apollinaire, had himself described his poetic inspiration as lying in newspapers, billboards and posters; his *calligrammes* — poems written in the shape of various objects — were fascinating illustrations of a new questioning of the limits of a separate world of 'art'. Popular media and commercial images were henceforth to assume the role previously restricted to the beaux-arts in providing the chief visual symbols of their age. Idealised depiction of the body would shift from the world of painting and sculpture into that of the photograph, the commercial drawing and the movie image. None of these media would be more popular, or more influential, in this regard then the cinema, and its role in the evolution of the developed body would be crucial.

5.2   The first Tarzan movie,
Tarzan of the Apes
starring Elmo Lincoln,
was made as early as
1918 — only four years
after the appearance of
Edgar Rice Burroughs'
novel of the same name.

As early as 1894, Sandow had posed for Thomas Alva Edison's primitive Kinetoscope; two years later, this peep-show performance was superseded by four Biograph films in which Sandow's posing was projected onto the movie screen.

Although a number of early films used historical and mythological plots which provided opportunities for actors to display their muscular torsos, the most significant development in this regard was the making, in 1918, of the first Tarzan feature film, *Tarzan of the Apes* starring Elmo Lincoln, one of the first silent films to gross more than $1 million. Other Tarzan films and serials followed throughout the 1920s, and by the 1930s hardly a year went by without a new addition to the genre. Most of the 1930s Tarzans (Johnny Weissmuller, Larry 'Buster' Crabbe, Herman Brix) were former Olympic swimmers, though one (Glenn Morris) was an Olympic decathlon champion. The vehicle provided by Edgar Rice Burroughs' jungle stories for the display of the male physique was eminently suited to bringing the best developed of American athletes before the general public, where their physical prowess and chaste romances with a succession of screen heroines were to make them the role-models of successive generations of adolescent males.

5.3 The first comic strip Tarzan was drawn by Harold Foster as a slim and lightly-muscled figure somewhat reminiscent of Foster's later Prince Valiant.

UNABLE TO DECIPHER THE VIKING SCRIPT, THE APE-MAN HURRIED TO THORIK, WHO GRASPED THE MESSAGE AND READ

In January 1929, the first *Tarzan* comic strip appeared — an adaptation of Burroughs' first adventure novel *Tarzan of the Apes* (1914). The illustrator was Harold R. Foster, a former boxer and commercial artist whose exquisite drawing style emphasised realism and carefully-posed composition. As distinct from cartoonists and comic illustrators, the adventure-series penmen such as Foster were in a sense the true heirs of the 'academy' tradition: the human bodies they invented owed more than a little of their style and emphasis to the anatomy classes of the traditional art school and the drawings (rather than the paintings or sculptures) of the great masters. The body-style chosen by Foster for his ape-man was severely classical, the lithe athlete of traditional art-school drawing. The comic-strip medium required the selection and magnification of conspicuous features, and Foster's Tarzan — who unlike Sandow could well have been a model for Donatello — was shown in the lines of a well-proportioned though not outstandingly muscular figure.

After resigning from *Tarzan* in 1936, Foster was to develop the strip with which his name is still identified, *Prince Valiant*, in which the England of King Arthur was beautifully and painstakingly recreated. Taken over now by a new illustrator, Burne Hogarth, the ape-man was to undergo a transformation, developing his muscle size and definition to a remarkable degree. His shoulders became broader, his waist narrower; his biceps bulged massively, and giant slabs of pectoral muscle contrasted strikingly with the indentations of his serratus and intercostals. He had become a bodybuilder.[1]

Less herculean than his fellow-hero Superman, Tarzan is more exclusively physical. Superman's advanced muscularity is always evident beneath his skin-tight costume, but his wish-fulfilment appeal is based on his reserves of superhuman capacity rather than on his directly muscular prowess, and to that extent he derives from the nineteenth-century interest in quasi-scientific speculation as much as from the quest for physical development. His double identity as the sky-riding avenger and his wimpish *alter ego* Clark Kent appealed to a more fantastic imagination than was attracted to the Rousseauistic Tarzan, and opened up to Americans of the 1940s more universal vistas of triumph over the enemies of freedom and democracy.[2] Like his later emulators — Batman, Captain America, Spider-Man, the Mighty Thor and others — he was to be one of the mythical incarnations of a growing consciousness of the violent clash of world-wide political forces in the years preceding, and following, World War II. The violence of the 'forces of evil' required to be met by the even more effective violence of the 'forces of good'. While Phillip Adams may go a little too far in his claim that 'Superman's belief in might as right and his clear conviction that ordinary people are powerless and useless without a mighty leader at least hinted at Fascism'[3], there were certainly elements in his *persona* of the same saviour-myth that had led to the emergence of Hitler and Mussolini out of the Depression of the 1930s. The darker side of the cult of the muscular hero had again, and not for the last time, come sharply into evidence.

5.4 Once taken over by the illustrator Burne Hogarth, Tarzan increased his mesomorphy and his musculature to a remarkable degree.

155

5.5 Rival Tarzans of the
1930s: (a) Johnny
Weissmuller; (b) Buster
Crabbe. Both were
former champion
swimmers, chosen for
their good looks and
athletic ability. Later
Tarzans would
increasingly be chosen
for their conspicuous
muscularity.

The Tarzan myth, however, was of a different nature — at least in its cinematographic form. Until the 1966 aberration *Tarzan and the Valley of Gold*, where the hero became a kind of super-agent who carried a gun and returned to the jungle only when necessary, most of the Tarzan movies were true to their original concept, and decidedly similar to one another in their story lines, even to the point of repeating earlier footage. Apart from the romantic interest and the performing animals, much of the fascination of Tarzan lay in the juxtaposition of the loincloth-garbed jungle athlete with the conventionally-dressed safari parties, ivory traders and corrupt animal hunters whom he encountered.[4] From time to time, as in more recent if

forgettable films, he would be placed in the even starker contrast of the urban
environment of America or England (*Tarzan's New York Adventure* (1942), *Greystoke*
(1984), *Tarzan in Manhattan* (1989)). By 1991, he was appearing in a new TV
series as a loincloth-garbed environmentalist, 'somewhere [in the producer's words]
between Richard Gere and Arnold Schwarzenegger', protecting the jungle ecosystem
from pollution and poachers. Such situations highlighted his primitive physicality,
and (at a semi-conscious level, perhaps) appealed to the urban nostalgia for a 'return
to nature' — that recurring myth which had taken such diverse imaginative forms as
Rousseau's noble savage and the nudist dream of unclad innocence.

The fascination of Superman lay in his modernity, his very name recalling such progressivist notions of human evolution as had been exemplified in Nietzsche's *Übermensch* and George Bernard Shaw's play *Man and Superman*. Not only at home with, but master of, the technological artefacts of the twentieth-century metropolis, he could leap tall buildings, halt locomotives and outpace aeroplanes. Tarzan, on the other hand, harked back to a nostalgic past, to a jungle Paradise of which natural man could make himself the benevolent king. A more escapist hero than Superman, he rejected the dream of progress for the myth of nature: the purely physical strength and mastery of the human body, rather than its technological extensions, were the imaginative means by which the threat of a potentially hostile world could be overcome. Such mythic status of course required a symbolically muscular physique, rather than the transforming power of a cape and body-suit.

At a more direct level, the figure of a jungle man provided film makers with an unparalleled opportunity for the male star to reveal his athletic body, thus avoiding the need to have scriptwriters invent situations specifically (and often artificially) designed to enable the hero to take off his shirt. Tarzan is unimaginable as a clothed figure, though conceivably he might have been portrayed as fully clad in animal skins. Part at least of his fascination is derived from the sensuous appeal of the unclothed body freed from the restrictions of Western civilisation and its social conventions. The later Tarzans were chosen for the look of their physiques rather than their sporting prowess (they had never been chosen for their acting ability), and Weissmuller's successors from Lex Barker and Gordon Scott in the 1950s to Mike Henry in the 60s and Ron Ely in the 70s were all in a physical mould far superior to that of their predecessors. Curiously, the size of the hero's loincloth grew larger over the years, in tune with changing standards of decency and the demands of the Hays office; from the 50s to the 70s, no screen Tarzan dared emulate Weissmuller's skimpy jungle attire. Not till the 1980s did public taste again turn around, reflecting an age in which male sex-appeal had become more explicit and the display of the unclad body in movies was both more acceptable and more common. By the time of *Tarzan the Apeman* (1981), the loincloth left Miles O'Keefe's buttocks all but bare, and his muscular body became the object of erotic attention on the part of a sexually liberated Jane (Bo Derek). Western society might have moved some distance since the time when ladies in bustles and steel corsets had been invited to feel for themselves the size and hardness of Sandow's biceps, but the sensuous attraction of the developed body had not diminished in the process.

Now spanning more than three-quarters of a century, the *Tarzan* movies are amongst the most enduring film series ever made. Their role in popularising and romanticising the image of the muscular hero throughout the world can hardly be overestimated. It has even been suggested that the classic Tarzan-Jane relationship was the archetype of a number of romantic screen situations:

'The ultimate version of the newborn pinup', writes Michael Malone, 'is Tarzan. A perfect physical specimen, strong and brave and virile. And as innocent as the day he was born. Jane has to teach him everything. How to eat at the table, dress, read, write. She creates him, transforms him into a modern adult male, much as the schoolmarm teaches the cowboy.'[5]

In this mild suggestion of male-female role-reversal, the physically dominant 'hunk' becoming the innocent boy-child whom the woman has to teach about life and about love, Malone and others have recognised the importance of the Tarzan series in developing the concept of the male sex star as 'love-object', thus extending the influence of the ape-man well beyond his jungle setting into the world of the contemporary 'objectified' male.

5.6 A feature of the Tarzan movies was the juxtaposition of the loincloth-garbed jungle hero and the fully-clad representatives of civilisation. Weissmuller's successor Lex Barker (with Charles Drake and Alfred Dekker) in his first Tarzan film, *Tarzan's Magic Fountain* (RKO, 1949).

MUSCLE WARS

If Tarzan had an overseas counterpart, it was in Italy that he was to be found. In 1914 the Italian film director Giovanni Pastrone, seeking a muscular actor to play the part of a slave in the epic *Cabiria*, lighted upon a Genoese dock-worker by the name of Bartolomeo Pagano and signed him up for the role. Set during the Punic wars between Rome and Carthage, *Cabiria* was (along with Enrico Guazzoni's original *Quo Vadis?*) one of the most successful early Italian film spectaculars, and the role of the Roman slave —Maciste — so powerfully appealed to Roman audiences that Pagano dropped his own name and kept that of the fictional slave character created for the film by the Futurist poet Gabriele D'Annunzio. Clad only in a loincloth, Pagano/Maciste bent iron bars, broke chains, and battered Carthaginians with consummate ease, displaying his massive musculature in every scene in which he appeared.[6]

5.7   Bartolomeo Pagano in his first appearance as the Roman slave Maciste, in Giovanni Pastrone's early film epic, *Cabiria* (1914) – the distant ancestor of the later 'sword-and-sandal' or 'gladiator' movies usually emanating from Italy.

So successful was Maciste at the Italian box-office that he was to appear in twenty-nine films between 1914 and 1928. Not all of these were costume epics, like *Cabiria*, *Maciste in the Lion's Den* or *Maciste in Hell*, but even in his more bizarrely fanciful roles —as a detective or a sleepwalker — he retained the character of an amiable giant, the successor of the vaudeville strongman whose brute physical strength was a source of envy and wonderment to lesser mortals.

The original Maciste (Pagano) died in 1947, but so popular a figure had he become that his persona lived on. A little over ten years after his death, an American bodybuilder of Italian background, Lou Degni, was transported back to the land of his fathers to re-create the role. Its days were numbered, however, and although five Maciste films were produced in 1961 it had largely been overtaken in the public imagination by the even more evocative role of Hercules. Under his screen name of Mark Forrest, Lou Degni made a number of Italian spectaculars with titles such as *The Revenge of Hercules*, *Hercules vs. the Barbarians*, *Hercules Against the Mongols* and the extraordinarily-named *Molemen Against the Son of Hercules*. Any last vestige of historical authenticity had of course been long since sacrificed in favour of the apparently insatiable appetite of the Italian (and international) market for musclemen displays, and the years 1961-65 saw the production of over 150 similar adventures set in a heavily fictionalised ancient world. Until their successors, the 'spaghetti Westerns', took over the Roman studios, these poorly acted and badly dubbed costume (or un-costume) dramas were the bread-and-butter of the Italian film industry.

Undoubtedly the most successful of the American bodybuilders transplanted into this fantastic screen world was Steve Reeves. A former Mr. Universe, Reeves had appeared in a few B-grade Hollywood movies and the musical *Athena* before making the transition to the Italian sword-and-sandal genre. His 1957 version of *Hercules* and its sequel *Hercules Unchained* established him as a dominant figure on the European gladiator movie scene for ten years, and he was to become one of the top box-office stars of the 1960s. His emulators included Kirk Morris (*Samson and Ulysses*, *Triumph of the Son of Hercules* and even *Hercules vs. Maciste in the Vale of Woe*), a native Italian and winner of several physique contests whom his countrymen were to label 'the Italian Steve Reeves'. Other bodybuilders such as the three-times Mr. Universe Reg Park (*Hercules and the Captive Women*, *Hercules Prisoner of Evil*, etc.) and Mr. Hungary Miclos (Mickey) Hargitay (*Loves of Hercules*) made similar low-grade films, as did one of the Tarzans of the time, Gordon Scott (*Gladiators of Rome*, *Hercules vs. the Sea Monster*).

5.8 By the late 1950s, Steve
Reeves had abandoned
the world of competitive
bodybuilding for that of
film stardom. The 1960s
were to see an
efflorescence of B-grade
spectaculars set in a
heavily fictionalised and
increasingly improbable
ancient world peopled
by muscular heroes and
bosomy heroines.

The vogue for sword-and-sandal epics, which had begun in the late 1950s,
hardly outlasted the 1960s. By 1970, a movie entitled *Hercules in New York*,
recounting the adventures of Zeus' son in the modern world, was felt by the
distributors to have little prospect of public success; not having been widely released,

5.9 Muscle movies suffered an eclipse in the 1970s, but by the early 80s — spearheaded by Schwarzenegger's *Conan* series — they were making a comeback, as social and political values underwent dramatic change.

it was soon shelved. Its fate must have been a source of disappointment to its potential star, a little-known but already successful bodybuilder who appeared under the name of Arnold Strong. However, 'Arnold Strong' himself might well have vowed prophetically: 'I'll be back'. His real name after all was Arnold Schwarzenegger.

By the time he did return to the genre in 1982, with the huge box-office successes *Conan the Barbarian* and its sequel *Conan the Destroyer*, two significant developments had taken place. In the first instance, technical effects had increased enormously in refinement, and the fantastic landscapes of the *Conan* movies and their look-alikes (such as *The Beastmaster* of 1982 starring Marc Singer) held more interest for audiences brought up in the age of television than did the papier maché antiquity of the 1950s and 60s epic productions. To this was added a greater sophistication in direction, a certain 'distancing' of narrative point of view (what the Brechtians called *Verfremdungseffekt*) which at times almost amounted to self-parody. At the very least, they took themselves a good deal less seriously than their predecessors, and even Schwarzenegger's supposed lack of acting ability lent itself well to the implied joke. Even the TV series *The Incredible Hulk* with bodybuilder Lou Ferrigno appears almost to have been designed more as a comedy or 'send-up' than as serious drama.

Public taste had undergone a major transformation during the 1970s. Writing in 1981, Robin Cross could speak of

> 'a vanishing late-50s world of beefcake, locker room bravado and 'working out' with the boys. A world crammed with slabs of cartilage like corrugated cardboard and Charles Atlas pulling trains along with his teeth. In this sweaty universe, a special niche was reserved for the well-oiled upper torsos of movie musclemen Steve Reeves, Gordon Scott, Reg Park, Kirk Morris and Mark Forrest. Their glistening pectorals and bulging biceps rippled through a series of adventures in which Muscle Beach met Alma Tadema in a delirious cocktail lounge version of the classical world. This phalanx of strongmen provided the exact male equivalent of that great fetish of the day, the startling C-cup charms of perennial B starlet Mamie Van Doren.'[7]

All this is no doubt true, but to see the sword-and-sandal movies only through the eyes of campy 1950s and 60s nostalgia is only part of the picture. Somehow, the technicolor image of a gleaming muscle-man single-handedly slaying hordes of barbarians amidst the flaming ruins of a cardboard Carthage had, as one critic put it, 'lodged itself in the national psyche'.[8] In looking back with gentle mockery on these popular pastimes of an earlier generation, the adults of the seventies and eighties were not only signalling their own liberation from the values of their youth but also that of their society from the values of a more simplistic age.

As early as the 1970s, the *Rocky Horror Show* (1973) had created its own 'send-up' of the muscular American ideal of the previous generation. The bodybuilder Rocky ('a gorgeous hunk of a man, golden-haired and gold-spangled in golden briefs') was a nostalgic throw-back to the heyday of Steve Reeves, an era whose images haunt (as they did for many Americans) his creator Dr Frank'n'Furter: 'If you want something visual that's not too abysmal', Frank suggests, 'we could take in an old Steve Reeves movie.' Frank later goes on to sing the 'Charles Atlas Song':

> '... A deltoid and a bicep
> A hot groin and a tricep
> Makes me shake
> Makes me wanna take
> Charles Atlas by the hand.
> In just seven days I can make you a man.'[9]

The *Rocky Horror Show* was for years to be the focus of sophisticated postmodernist faddism in a number of Western countries — audiences even dressing as drag-queens, bodybuilders or 'middle-Americans' Brad and Janet. Genuine nostalgia, like other forms of sincerity or conviction, seemed by now too naive a response to be openly admitted — it needed to be concealed beneath a modish smugness and a self-conscious superiority over the 1950s values and movie images caricatured and parodied in *Rocky* — yet the knowing winks and mocking self-awareness were in themselves a form of inverted recognition of these images as part of the Western cultural baggage, including that of 'ideal' muscular development as an embodiment of the American Dream.

From the time of its invention, the cinema (and later television) had taken over from high art the role of transmitting the visual images which both reflected and helped create the cultural values of successive generations. The adolescent youth of the 1990s who is moved to take up weight training as a result of seeing an Arnold Schwarzenegger movie is following exactly in the footsteps of Schwarzenegger himself, who was inspired as a youth by the film appearances of his avowed idol Reg Park.[10] Though neither may be aware of the distinguished cultural antecedents of the muscular hero, both are inheritors of a tradition which by now has become deeply embedded in the popular subconscious.

5.10 The *Rocky Horror Show* relied for its world-wide 'cult' status on the fact that its mix of nostalgia and parody appealed to images firmly lodged within the Western psyche, including Steve Reeves movies and Charles Atlas advertisements. (Cast of Theatre Royal Production, Hanley, Stoke-on-Trent.)

PART II

THE LEGIBLE BODY

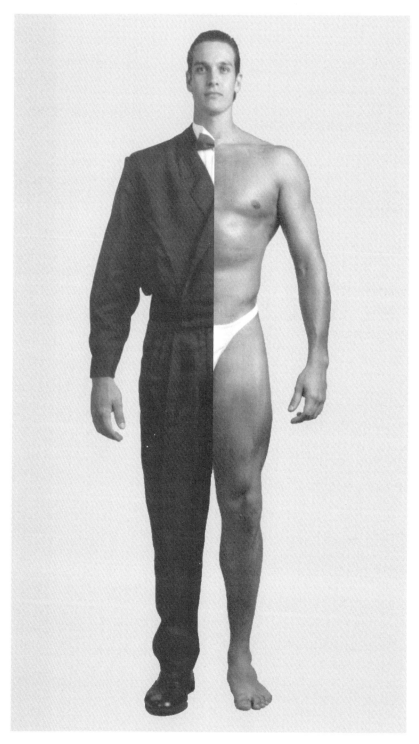

6.1 **CHAPTER 6** THE SOCIAL BODY
As much as the clothes we wear, the kind of body we possess is a determining element of our social existence.

6

THE SOCIAL BODY

READING THE BODY

In our attempt to derive identity and meaning from our social environment, the body is a fundamental resource. It provides us with the most direct clue to our place in society and to the roles we are expected to perform. At an elementary level, as Ernest Becker pointed out in the 1970s, these roles and their performance are based principally on age and sex differences. 'Societies arrange their members in categories of infant, boy, girl, adult male, adult female, old male, old female'.[1] The designation 'old male', which in one culture may enable its possessor to enjoy privileged status as a fount of wisdom, may in another amount to rejection from all significant social interaction. In its more complex manifestations, identification with a particular group may take a benign or a destructive form, as what belongs to our own group is magnified and what belongs to another is diminished. At the harmless end of the spectrum we find play and sport, in which bodies are able to discover their own qualities and aptitudes by matching themselves against other bodies. At the other end, identification with one's group — be it a race, class, nation, or authority in power — can be a more socially destructive outlet for culturally-based chauvinism when rational values become distorted and the urge to excel is concentrated exclusively upon our own particular group.[2] In the closing years of the twentieth century, when the gains made in international co-operation seem increasingly threatened in a number of countries by the re-emergence of a violent nationalism in which the sense of ethnic, religious or regional identity is fuelled by the desire to mark one's own group off from others — to separate 'us' from 'them' — the dangers to which Becker pointed more than twenty years ago are as real as ever they were.

The socially determinant nature of the body has been analysed by Stephen Kern in his cultural study *Anatomy and Destiny*. Kern points to the extent to which, in contemporary Western society, our bodies themselves influence our social existence and our relations with other people, dominating our very personalities. This is especially the case in adolescence and early adulthood when 'the gift of good looks or the curse of ungainliness can dominate entirely our image of ourselves'.[3] Irrespective of age, however, a person who is strikingly fat or thin, healthy or sick, beautiful or ugly, will be profoundly affected by this fact of their corporeal nature, and will need to devise a personal and social strategy to deal with the fact. In an age obsessed with youth, health and physical beauty, Kern argues, the body is a source of great anxiety: whereas earlier ages had coped with bodily frailty and disintegration by belittling the significance and the pleasures of earthly existence, this is no longer the case in a society devoted to the celebration of bodily excellence.

The conformity of the body to the prevailing cultural value-system is a universal human phenomenon, and no society from the most 'primitive' to the most sophisticated is exempt from a code of social presentation of the body. In tribal cultures, an individual's membership of a particular tribe will frequently be indicated by a distinctive form of dress, tribal markings or other visible signs. Ethnologists and social anthropologists have repeatedly pointed to the persistence of this behaviour in professional or social groups in contemporary Western society, from motor-bike gang members to hippies or upwardly-mobile business executives. In societies where clothing leaves much of the body exposed, various forms of bodily marking or decoration have the function of denoting membership of a particular group or status within that group. From tattooing and body painting to scarification and mutilation, symbolic messages of a geographical, hierarchical or sexual nature can often be clearly read in the signs presented by the appearance of the body itself. In Western society, the traditional means of such presentation have chiefly been restricted to clothing (by way of uniform or fashion) and the decoration of the head (by way of hair-style or the application of cosmetics to the face). Whatever the individual form taken by these practices, the manipulation or decoration of the body is less a matter of individual taste than of self-perception, and perception by others, as a person with a recognisable place in the cultural system.

Within this general area of investigation, the social implications of the display of the naked or near-naked body obviously assume some significance. At one end of the spectrum of study, H. Th. Fischer in his influential article *The Clothes of the Naked Nuer* (1964) pointed out that certain tribal societies which to Western eyes may appear naked in fact possess a system of body decoration and adornment which has a discernible social function equating to that of clothing. As Polhemus points out in his comment on Fischer's article:

'A nude body clothed only in a G-string and adorned with paint and feathers — whether that of a Brazilian Indian or that of a stripper in Soho — is not naked. Very rarely is the anthropologist or sociologist justified in studying the human body as if it were stark naked: there are no 'naked savages'.'[4]

6.2   In some cultures, membership of a particular tribe or totemic group may be indicated by distinctive body markings, as in the case of these Aboriginal men from the Liverpool River district, Arnhem Land, Australia.

6.3 'Rarely is the
anthropologist justified
in studying the body as
if it were stark naked.'
Two Tiwi men from
Melville Island showing
cicatrices, representing
the barbs on a spear,
running down their
chests and arms.

The important distinction, made by Kenneth Clark among others, between the naked and the nude underlines this point: a body is naked if it is totally divested of clothing, whereas it is nude if its presentation in naked form is invested with social significance. At the other end of the spectrum from those tribes in which near-nakedness is the normal form of presentation of the body in everyday life, are cultures in which the body is habitually presented in public social life with a significant degree of covering. In the latter type of culture, the appearance of the body in naked or near-naked form may then become a departure from social convention and as such take on a particular kind of meaning. An obvious example is the Western artistic tradition: in a social setting in which clothing has generally concealed the body to a marked degree, the most commonly depicted form of the body in post-Renaissance art has been the nude or semi-nude. In Western art as in classical Greek art, as Clark points out, the nude is 'an idea'.[5]

The particular significance attached to the naked as opposed to the clothed body is by no means universal even in those cultures where a high degree of concealment by clothing has been the public convention. In traditional Japanese society, for example, clothing was highly elaborate and often bore a complex symbolism; yet the naked body did not, as in the West, take on a particular significance arising from its contrast with the clothed state. It was simply naked. In Japan, as Rudofsky points out,

'the nude was seen in daily life but inadmissible in traditional art. Artists showed no interest in rippling muscles and swelling bosoms; they invariably portrayed people dressed to the nines. Even lovers, bedded down on acres of quilts — a favourite subject in art — are always fully clothed, not because the artists were prudes but because the Japanese seem to like making love entangled in each other's garments.'[6]

In Japan, life in the wider society supposed and even demanded a highly formalised style of clothing, but domestic life and the culture of the bath-house made semi-public nakedness common and quite unremarkable. It was certainly not considered attractive, and if anything served as a vaguely uncomfortable reminder of the animal element in the human body. The naked body could be invested with significance and personality only by the art of *irezumi*, in which (at least in its more elaborate forms) almost the entire body was covered by tattoos.[7] This art-form has been continued among the lower social classes in modern Japan, a country which despite Westernisation has retained much of its traditional lack of interest in the naked body for its own sake. Even today, says Bornoff, 'nudity is entirely natural to the Japanese; it is traditionally considered neither aesthetic nor titillating'[8], and even in the *nudo gekijo* or 'nude theatre' it is common for performers to keep the upper half of their bodies clad.

In Western society, there has been a constant duality of attitude towards the depiction or presentation of the unclothed body. At one end of the range of attitudes has been an extreme concern with 'modesty' which reached its apogee — or nadir, depending on one's view — in the puritanism of the Victorian era. In its most absurd (if perhaps apocryphal) form, it required the covering of table legs lest they offend the eye through their resemblance to unclothed human limbs. At the other end of the spectrum, the naked body has been considered a reflection of divine harmony or has been romanticised as a symbol of 'ideal' existence. Whereas in most non-Western civilisations, the naked or near-naked body has tended either to be considered a natural mode of social presentation or at the most regarded with indifference, only in the West (and, to some extent, in Islamic cultures) has the sight of nakedness been regarded as offensive. Similarly, only in the West has the nude body been regarded as *in itself* (as distinct from its adorned or decorated form) worthy of aesthetic or erotic attention.

6.4 Western cultures have
never viewed the naked
body with indifference:
always invested with
significance, it has
gravitated between an
aesthetic ideal and an
object of shame or
disgust.

This peculiarly Western form of interest in the unclothed body has been the outcome of a constant tension between two diametrically opposed views. On the one had, there is the conception of nakedness as shameful or 'taboo', a notion derived largely from the popular identification of the Fall of the naked Adam and Eve with sexual transgression: the naked state became associated with forbidden erotic desire and the 'lusts of the flesh'. On the other hand, at least in art, post-Renaissance Europe had embraced a metaphorical form (the nude) which had been invented by classical Greece to invest the body with positive aesthetic and symbolic value. In neither case was the naked body a matter of indifference, and indeed the tension between the two opposing views served largely to heighten the problematic status of the body and increase its fascination for the Western imagination.

With the exception of the nudist movement, which had concentrated on the fact of the body's nakedness irrespective of its aesthetic appeal, the Western mind has tended to follow the Greek notion that certain types of unclothed body were more worthy of favourable interest than others. In some Greek vases (such as the Attic Kylix of c.520 B.C. in the British Museum) we can see well developed athletes practising the discus and javelin while a flabby, pot-bellied youth and his skinny, undeveloped companion —obviously figures of fun or even disgust — stand arguing.[9] It was clearly not just any display of nakedness that aroused Greek admiration, but only those naked bodies that conformed to the canons of desirability. In both the heroic and erotic traditions, the West has adopted the Greek preference for some body-shapes over others. Whereas in the case of the nude female form taste has varied considerably, from the fleshy maternal nudes of Rubens to the slim, long-legged 'beach bunnies' of today, the ideal male figure has been less subject to swings in fashion. (The corpulent late Victorian or Edwardian gentlemen with his prominently displayed vest and watch-chain may have suggested a desirable affluence, but he was never depicted unclothed as an aesthetic ideal.)

6.5 Modern Western societies have tended to follow the tastes of ancient Greece in their preference for certain body shapes over others· extreme leanness or corpulence have never had the status accorded to athletic muscularity as an aesthetic ideal. Attic red-figure kylix of c. 520 B.C. (British Museum.)

6.6 Western man no longer possesses the natural muscularity still found in many of the native peoples of Africa
and the Pacific, and his fascination with physical development may represent a hankering after a more active,
pre-technological lifestyle

More than any preceding age, the twentieth century has been obsessed with the visible world. The information we receive about what is happening around us has increasingly been conveyed in visual form — in the first half of the century through newspaper and magazine photographs (and, to some extent, the movie screen), and in the second half overwhelmingly by television. No event, however significant, nowadays seems 'real' unless accompanied by graphic visual images. The contemporary Western personality itself is preponderantly a visible self, its identity embodied in external performance: like the events taking place around us, we ourselves seem hardly real or meaningful unless our existence has a value of performance and is validated by an audience (which may include ourselves). A number of social theorists, following Christopher Lasch in the 1970s, have borrowed Freud's psychoanalytic term 'narcissism', using it in a less technical sense to characterise the modern preoccupation with self-observation and our concern for favourable observation by others. Over the same period, the portmanteau term 'post-modernism' has been taken up in a series of modish works from Charles Jencks' writings on architectural design to Jean Baudrillard's polemics on consumerism and the media to denote the contemporary preoccupation with the surface of things, a concern for decorative effect and a commensurate lack of interest in substance or meaningful content.

With the gradual disappearance or breaking-down of fixed class-systems, the attribution of personal value and status have become less dependent on our inherited and essentially immutable place within the social system, and have become a function of symbols more obviously within our control, such as style and fashion. Such commodities permit the creation of successful 'images' — the visible signs of status and value through which our worth as individuals can be observed and approved by ourselves and those around us. The cosmetics industry is aimed both at the affirmation of visible beauty amongst the young and at the denial of visible degeneration amongst the ageing.[10] Recourse to dieting, cosmetic surgery or 'keep-fit' programmes enables us to project the image of perpetual membership of the visually preferred age-group and to deny the approach of death, to achieve an illusory sense of immortality. The 'body bigotry' condemned by some social critics — the devaluation of any physical appearance not seen as socially acceptable (old age, deformity, ugliness) — is more philosophically interpreted by other social analysts as a natural horror at the prospect of physical degeneration and ageing in a society where the 'this-worldly' is the sole or supremely important dimension of existence.

This modern preoccupation (sometimes known as 'bodyism')[11] takes the form of a concentration on the outward appearance of the body, as distinct from that control of the inner body which was of more exclusive concern in earlier centuries. The pursuit of the developed body has here a particular significance. It can be argued that it is merely one component of the total 'bodyist' fixation of contemporary society, to be understood in the same context as other modes of ideal bodily presentation such as slimming, plastic surgery or the use of cosmetics. Equally, it can be understood as part of the syndrome of 'healthism' where it stands alongside aerobics, jogging and other fitness-oriented activities in which a particular form of asceticism ('no pain, no gain') is applied to the simplistic equation exercise = fitness = health = longevity. An alternative explanation sees its fascination for organised Western societies as lying in the effects of evolution and particularly on the accentuated effect of technological advances since the Industrial Revolution. According to this theory, Western man no longer possesses the natural muscularity still found for instance in the native peoples of Africa and the Pacific, and his unconscious 'race memory' leads him to a kind of nostalgia for a more primitive form of existence of which dim memories still remain.

These theories are by no means mutually exclusive, and each of them may contain important clues to the motivation underlying the quest for physical development in the modern Western world. What is crucial is that, with the rising standard of living brought about by modern technology, has come a rising standard of expectation: contemporary Western society, unlike most of its predecessors, is now confronted by an array of ideals presented as within its grasp. The rise of Western democracies has led to an expectation that their members can be actors, rather than mere objects or observers, in the decision of their fate, while the advent of advertising has meant that desirable images are both created and presented to us as attainable ends.[12]

In this process, physical perfectibilism finds a natural place. While it is possible to interpret the rise of mechanical technology in the late nineteenth and twentieth centuries as to some extent replacing the role of the human body in terms of labour potential, it is equally legitimate to see the technological revolution as having extended the body's range of symbolic possibilities and thus magnified its power. In a post-modernist world where appearance and 'image' are both supreme values and able to be more and more effectively shaped and manipulated, not only does the body transmit messages to the society around us, it has itself become increasingly the content of the messages it seeks to convey.

THE TRANSFORMABLE BODY

Within the total range of bodily modifications that have been practised within human society — body painting, tattooing, clothes fashion, incision, circumcision, clitoridectomy, mutilation and the like — the shaping of the body has been one of the most persistent. In his anthropological study of these practices, *The Decorated Body*, Robert Brain has included reference to what he calls 'the plastic body' — that is, the body which is either trained or artificially pressed into a shape determined by the society as reflecting its cultural ideals.

Among the forms of body-shaping practised in contemporary Western societies, Brain lists such practices as dieting, plastic surgery (aimed at the correction of deformities), cosmetic surgery, breast implants, the removal of fatty tissue, hair transplants and the interventions connected with gender re-assignment.[13] He compares the favourable image associated in Western society with thinness with the desirable image of obesity favoured in Bangwa (Cameroon) and other parts of Africa, where fatness is associated with ideas of royalty and maternal abundance. The contrast between these social ideals and the common reality is revealing: in Bangwa, Brain observes,

> 'a plump woman is a desirable woman, and a well-covered girl demonstrates that her family is sufficiently well-off to provide fattening food for her. This plump ideal can in fact only be achieved by upper-class men who have little to do but eat, drink and grow fat, and by nubile girls who are specially 'fattened' prior to marriage. The rest of the Bangwa, men and women, are fit, slim physical specimens, who live high up in the mountains, working in their farms and gardens. In Bangwa, the ideal is fat, the reality thin; in the West, the ideal is thin and the reality often fat.'[14]

Conformity to the body-ideal can thus be seen either to *reflect* status, as among the Bangwa, or to *confer* status as in a society where one's place in the social hierarchy is not foreordained by birth or other factors extrinsic to the body itself. Equally, whereas in more traditional societies the body-ideal tends to be unchanging, in modern Western society it may change dramatically from one generation to another, and be reflected in fashions or styles which accentuate the preferred bodily configuration. As with the Bangwa, obesity in mid nineteenth-century Europe was a sign of affluence and the ability to enjoy a substantial diet without the need for hard physical labour. In contemporary Western society, slimness reflects a concentration on athletic competitiveness and youthful vigour within a system geared to ideals of individual enterprise and material achievement.

6.7 The contemporary
Western ideal is
slimness, reflecting
athletic competitiveness
and youthful vigour
within a social system
geared to promoting
these as ideals.

In some cases, the exposure of a social system to interference from another may result in a transition from one cultural value-system to a different system, and this may be reflected in a corresponding change in mode of body-presentation. A significant example is modern Japan, whose Westernisation goes back to the nineteenth century with the adoption of European forms of dress but where in recent years there has been a growth in cosmetic surgery amongst some women (and, more recently still, some upwardly-mobile businessmen) who have had the shape of their eyes altered in order to give them a more 'Western' appearance. In each case, however, the transformation adopted corresponds to a socially recognised norm reflecting status, beauty, power or some other attribute recognised as desirable.

Social critics have not always viewed such cultural practices with the dispassionate eye of the anthropologist. In one of the more controversial of recent works on the body-shaping aspirations of Western women, *The Beauty Myth*,[15] Naomi Wolf has attacked what she perceives as an obsession with female physical perfection, and particularly with thinness, in the industrialised world. By promoting the idea that to be thin is to be beautiful, Wolf argues, images of female perfection are used as a political tool against women. Such images, conveyed by the media and particularly by women's magazines, are directly responsible for a dramatic increase in the number of women suffering eating disorders and for the social pressures which lead women to undergo dangerous and sometimes disfiguring cosmetic surgery. Wolf sees the concern with female beauty as being economically driven, not only in the more direct sense that huge sums have been invested by magazine and other media proprietors in the commercial exploitation of such images, but also in the use of these images to 'define' women and keep them politically and economically subjugated. Middle-aged, mature or less attractive women are devalued in a way which does not apply to their male counterparts, and the equation of social value with conformity to an ideal of physical beauty divides those women who possess or are led to pursue such qualities from those who are able to fulfil themselves and contribute to society through their intelligence or work skills. By thus pitting women one against another, the manipulators of the beauty myth are able to deny women the power to which they should be entitled in an equal society.

The Beauty Myth provoked sharply divided reactions, as was no doubt its intention. Its somewhat facile equation of 'women' (in general) with relatively affluent urbanised Western women — the biology-transcends-ethnicity assumption — is no doubt appropriate to its polemic, as well as to its readership, though it does tend to limit the applicability of Wolf's thesis. No doubt the social pressures on the women of the Bangwa are as great and perhaps just as male-dominated as those on middle-class American or European women, but they are different pressures and their social consequences are equally different. Similarly, while Wolf is no doubt correct in attributing to the rise of photography an important role in disseminating models of idealised femininity among a mass public, not all of the forces leading women to eating disorders such as anorexia nervosa can be attributed to the desire to shape the body in accordance with cultural criteria of appropriateness, and the origin of this disease, at least for some young women, in a search for individual freedom from the restrictive authority of the middle-class family has been carefully analysed by Turner amongst others.[16]

It should also be borne in mind that the trends of the last century or so in the presentation of the body have not all been socially repressive of women. The 'women's clothing reform' movement of the late nineteenth and early twentieth centuries, which was to emancipate women from the steel corset of Victorian times, was a physically and socially liberating advance. Influenced to some extent by practical considerations such as the shortage of metal and the demands of women's employment, it also owed much to the writing and lecturing of physical culture advocates such as Sandow (who actually invented a less restrictive corset, the 'Symmetrion'), Isadora Duncan and Bernarr Macfadden.[17] Equally, the ideal of thinness, which arose in the decade following the First World War, was related not only to aesthetic factors but also to a new interest in athletic mobility in the wake of the physical culture movement and to the engagement of women in work leading to their emulation of a number of male body-images as a sign of emancipation and the search for female value in areas other than fertility. The boyish 'bob' or 'shingle' hairstyle, the disappearance of the hour-glass figure and even the introduction of the breast-flattener were at least as much symbols of the rising social status and new freedom of women as of the changing language of aesthetic appeal.[18]

6.8 The 'aspirational' male image — tall, lean, tanned and muscular — has a greater influence in defining men's views of themselves (and of other men) in Western societies than is acknowledged by those who believe that only women have fallen victim to the 'beauty myth'.

A less frequently discussed issue in contemporary social analysis than the pressure on women to conform to an aesthetic ideal is that of the pressures affecting men. The physical stereotyping of women in a male-dominated society cannot be attributed exclusively to motives of cynical manipulation of one sex by the other. It is also due, in part at least, to the fact that men no less than women have fallen victim to the 'beauty myth'. Though no doubt less socially repressive than in the case of the images affecting women, the conformity of men to the prevailing body-ideal of their own sex plays as important a role in urbanised post-industrial cultures as the various forms of male body decoration have done in less developed or more traditional social milieux. No less than in most tribal societies, men as much as women are the subject of social expectations in respect of their physical self-presentation. Aspirational images of tall, lean, tanned, fit and youthful (or youthful-looking) males are the stock-in-trade of magazine and television commercials just as are slim attractive young females. Commercial gyms, home exercise machines, diets, health farms and cosmetic surgery are commonly pressed into service for the improvement of the male physical appearance. The American Society of Plastic and Reconstructive Surgeons has reported that in 1990 over a quarter of nose re-shaping and chin augmentation procedures, and more than half of ear pinning operations, were performed on men; less frequent procedures (with male clients ranging from 7 to 9 per cent) included 'tummy tucks', buttock lifts and total face lifts, and the number of requests for male pectoral implants is on the increase.[19] While silicone pectoral implants and calf implants are most popular among bodybuilders, other men (from business executives to movie stars) are turning to 'aesthetic' or 'rejuvenative' surgery such as chin implants, chemical face peels and — reportedly, in the case of Sylvester Stallone — cheek implants. European surgeons have reported that the number of hair transplants for men has become as frequent as breast implants for women.[20] To these may be added the recent innovations in genital surgery, including penile implants, penis engorgement, testicular tucks and testicular implants.

Recent research in both the USA and Australia has indicated that young men suffer the same anxieties about their appearance as do women, that they are desperate to be 'the right shape' and that they see the classic muscular mesomorph as the ideal masculine body-type.[21] Research findings recently presented to the British Psychological Society have indicated that the increased visibility of 'ideal' muscular physiques in the media and popular entertainment (e.g. male strippers) has caused men to feel increasingly uncomfortable about the look of their own bodies. Reporting on these findings, the London *Evening Standard* commented that this insecurity was a fit retribution which had been too long delayed:

'Women have had to put up with nude girlie pin-ups for decades. It is only right that the British male should now submit to the humiliation of being gleefully compared to the oiled beef of the Chippendales' triangular torsos.'[22]

The contemporary cult of physical perfection and the need for conformity to the visual images propagated by the mass media are potent influences within our cultural system, and condition men's social and sexual behaviour just as effectively as they determine women's perception of the gender roles expected of them.

The 'tyranny of beauty' in Western societies has traditionally affected men as well as women[23], though it is only in recent decades that this issue has become a part of the debate relating to sexual politics. The French writer Pascal Bruckner has distinguished between two characteristic responses to the question of socio-sexual inequality posed by the requirement of physical attractiveness. The first, which he calls the 'American response', has been to denounce the 'aesthetic blackmail' applied to women and to attack the culture propagated by the cosmetics industry and popular women's magazines. The second, which he calls the 'European response', has been to extend the vogue of physical attractiveness to men as well as women[24].

6.9 '... Males must now submit to the humiliation of being gleefully compared to the oiled beef of the Chippendales' triangular torsos.' There is evidence to suggest that the public visibility of 'ideal' male physiques has led men to feel increasingly uncomfortable about the look of their own bodies.

Bruckner sees the characteristic American denunciation of the tyranny of beauty as stemming from the residual puritanism of American society, especially when combined with a particular understanding of democratic values which seeks to eliminate differences between the members of society. The European tradition, notably in Latin countries, has always placed a social value on beauty, elegance and sensuality, as well as on the acceptance of individual disparity even within a framework of social democracy. In the European tradition of the 'dandy', for instance, elegant artifice has had an established social role which contrasts with the 'naturalness' valued in egalitarian American society.

Bruckner's sweeping opposition of 'European' and 'American' responses to the beauty cult fails to take account of the importance of male physical attractiveness in the desirable images portrayed by American as much as European popular media, though it is more convincing as an explanation of why the vehement denunciation of such images is more characteristic of American social critics than of their European counterparts. Equally importantly, it draws attention to that paradoxical combination of hedonism and asceticism which characterises American society and has spread to other Western societies to the extent that they have been influenced by American cultural values.

This combination can be observed at a superficial level in television food advertisements, which are largely devoted to fatty, high-cholesterol, low-nutrition 'junk' food or alternatively to diet regimes, low-calorie foods and supposedly 'natural' (i.e. healthy) foods. At a deeper level, this combination has been analysed by Bryan Turner in his work *The Body and Society*. Turner has demonstrated a significant link between social and individual motivations in the contemporary cult of the body, showing how the rise of capitalism has produced a paradoxical combination of the asceticism of production, embodied in the work ethic, and the hedonism of circulation, residing in the ethic of personal private consumption. The 'new hedonism' identified by Turner may at first appear contradictory, but it is not oppositional: it is perfectly geared into the market requirements of advanced capitalism and promoted throughout the class system as various forms of apparent bodily asceticism (largely centred upon a preoccupation with health, fitness and slimness) are combined with a hedonistic fascination with the body and the notions of competition and success.[24] Turner's analysis allows us to understand the contemporary cult of the body as both inward-looking and outward-looking: it provides a means of achieving personal identity at the private level, and at the same time gives us a public value in accord with the prevailing social ethic.

Whatever the extent of its influence for good or ill, the shaping of the body to reflect culturally-determined values has been one of the most significant forms of self-presentation in twentieth-century Western society. In respect of the male body, the continuation in popular visual media, notably film and photography, of 'ideal' images earlier embedded in the European artistic tradition has endowed athletic physical development with a distinctive status as a commodity of social transaction.

ARCHETYPAL BODIES

The purpose of body-shaping in inter-personal transactions is to reinforce the 'natural', or at least the commonly accepted, body-images conveyed by the body itself. The particular shape pursued will depend largely on culturally-determined values and expectations and on the extent to which rapidly changing societies modify or alter their value-systems. In some cultures, as we have seen, these systems remain relatively unchanged over successive generations; in others, they vary considerably from one age to another and are reflected in fashions or styles which may last only a year or two.

If the reinforcement of mutually understood social messages is the basic purpose of the various forms of body-shaping, a further step in this direction is the exaggeration of these messages by taking the reinforcement to extreme lengths. In some African societies, where a long neck is considered a sign of female beauty, young women have their necks encircled by a series of bands which are gradually added to until by adulthood the neck has reached an inordinate length and can no longer support the head if the bands are removed. The traditional Chinese practice of foot-binding for women was another example of exaggerating, to the extent of bodily mutilation, a sexually attractive message, in this case associated with small feet. Such exaggeration, in Western societies, has usually been in the form of the adoption of extreme shapes in clothing, most (though not all) of which have avoided the deformation of the body itself. In female fashion, the crinoline and the bustle exaggeratedly increased the apparent size of the hips and buttocks, while an appearance of unnatural height has been provided by *chopines* or high platform-shoes and, in the eighteenth century, immensely high hair-styles and wigs. An example in the world of male fashion is the Tudor predilection for wide, padded shoulders tapering down to a tightly fastened waist, accompanied by the wearing of a codpiece of at times remarkable dimensions. The padded, wide-shouldered 'power-dressing' adopted by some female business executives in the 1980s and early 1990s has reflected a similarly heightened message of command and authority (though the codpiece has not yet made an appearance in this quarter).

6.10 The V-shape of the torso is a biological marker of masculinity which can become a 'super-normal stimulus'. The primitive grounding of this stimulus-display has been explored by a number of ethologists and social anatomists.

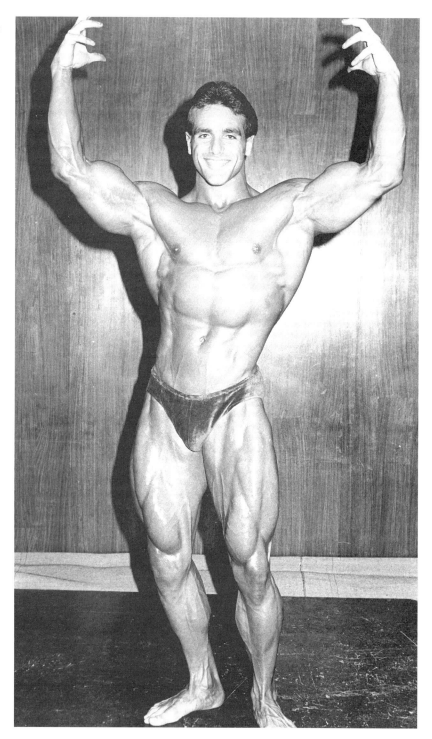

Whilst examples of exaggerated body-shapes can be found in many societies, the means of their creation have differed from one time and place to another. Desmond Morris, in his book *The Human Zoo*, has pointed to the human tendency to create what he calls 'super-normal stimuli' aimed at increasing responsiveness, and this is especially so in an age when the complexity of urban life and the sheer variety of experiences to which society is exposed have removed much of the novelty of existence. Such super-normal stimuli include those provided by the human body, particularly those reflecting gender differences:

> 'At puberty there is a marked difference in the growth rate of the shoulders in males and females, those of boys becoming broader than those of girls. This is a natural, biological sign of adult masculinity. Padding the shoulders adds a super-normal quality to this masculinity and it is not surprising that the most exaggerated trend occurs in that most masculine of spheres, the military, where stiff epaulets are added to further increase the effect.'[26]

While Morris' analysis extends mainly to the exaggerated or super-normal stimuli provided by bodily additions and accretions such as clothing and cosmetics, we can better understand in the light of his argument the shaping of the body itself to exaggerate and reinforce similar messages. The comic strip illustrators whose heroes are endowed with massive pectorals and biceps and impossibly narrow waists (just as their heroines are exaggeratedly curvaceous) are responding to their readers' — and perhaps their own —fantasies of 'super-normal' masculinity and femininity, and it is not surprising that such fantasies should equally be projected onto the shaping of the actual body. Just as the muscular Roman breastplate provided a form of apparel which permitted its wearer to project an image of 'super-normal' masculinity befitting the military leader or (in artistic portrayal) the mythological hero, so the possibility of developing the advanced muscularity of the body itself by the techniques associated with physical exercise may enable healthy males to use their own bodies to emit similar heightened messages as a means of reinforcing a desired self-image.

In both individual and social terms, then, the cultivation and development of the body can be seen as a response to very powerful stimuli. More importantly from our present point of view, the modern Western requirement of visual reinforcement of the messages transmitted and received in our transactions with ourselves and others has meant that the contemporary fixation upon the body cannot be divorced from observation and visual scrutiny — of our own bodies and those of others. A body must be on display and available for inspection, whether in visual representation or personal form, in order for us to comprehend the particular messages it is conveying. To increase their effectiveness, these messages need to be amplified and exaggerated, in such a way that (to use McLuhan's language) the medium actually *becomes* the message.

6.11 Bodybuilding is a form
of social display in
which the configuration
of the body itself emits
heightened messages
aimed at reinforcing
desirable images (or
self-images) as a mode
of social exchange.

It is in this context that we can most fruitfully approach the phenomenon of bodybuilding, an activity often seen as meaningless or futile. If indeed it were so, it would be well-nigh unique among the procedures in which human beings engage, since every mode of human involvement with the world or the self, however trivial in appearance, has a motivation and thus a discernible significance. In the light of the preceding discussion, it seems reasonable to advance the hypothesis that the practice of public (that is, organised and usually competitive) bodybuilding has articulated a 'language' of muscular development which is readable in cultural terms even if its messages are generally apprehended at a subliminal or sub-conscious level by those to whom they are addressed.

In the specific terms of the body's physical development, the bodybuilder represents the extreme degree of reinforcement or exaggeration of the messages emitted by muscularity. The Western cultural tradition having rendered muscular development readable — that is, conferred upon it a particular symbolic significance which can be generally understood against the background of commonly accepted conventions — the bodybuilder from Sandow onwards has presented his body in such a way as to make its physical configuration itself the 'content' of the display, by dint of an extreme muscularity developed to the point where it dominates or even excludes all other visual messages.

If the message being conveyed is the developed body itself, the social transaction with the audience is meaningful only because the developed body is as much a cultural and imaginative construct as it is a physical object: it carries with it the whole cultural baggage of perfectibility, localising and giving shape to half-formed human fantasies and aspirations. At its most elemental level, it represents to a physically-fixated audience the fulfilment of their desire to find meaning in the sheer fact of their physical existence. By establishing a hierarchy of physical values, in which the bodybuilder approximates more or less closely to the highest point on the scale, it gives intelligibility and purpose to the body's otherwise meaningless existence as a mere object in time and space. It was not by chance that early enthusiasts of bodybuilding could slip from reference to a practitioner of the sport as having 'a perfect body' to reference to him as 'a perfect man': in a world where ultimate meanings can be found only at the physical, material level, bodily perfection and human perfection are readily equated.

.

The pursuit of the developed body, however, goes far beyond the relatively limited confines of bodybuilding as an organised competitive activity. Indeed, it goes beyond the activity of those who practise some form of weight training for physical development, many of whom (as we have observed) would reject the term 'bodybuilding' in relation to their pursuit. The developed body has in fact acquired a public status in modern urbanised society which extends into the everyday images purveyed by the media, entertainment and advertising which do much to shape our perception of the contemporary world. The relationship between the specialised universe of bodybuilding and the more common images of physical development can perhaps best be approached by following the semiological analysis proposed by Roland Barthes.

In his seminal 1952 essay on all-in wrestling (*Le Monde où l'on catche*)[27,] Barthes was the first to apply Saussure's system of semiology (the study of signs in social life) to a phenomenon lying on the borderline between sport and popular entertainment. This world of wrestling, Barthes observed, worked as a spectator sport because of formalised codes or conventions which could be read by the spectators (and anyone else who learned them) but would otherwise make the spectacle pointless or unintelligible. The fact that the wrestlers were not actually hurting each other and that the cheating was obvious, far from detracting from the match, was precisely what the audience wanted: it expected the 'good guys' to win regardless of their ability compared to that of the 'bad guys'. The aim, unlike the world of boxing, was not contest so much as ritual — an attempt to make the world intelligible in terms which the audience could grasp by understanding the meaning of the conventions. Like language or literature, Barthes claimed, the world of the all-in wrestling match worked by means of a *code* — an internally self-consistent system of signs. The 'meaning' of the activity was intelligible, not by reference to some reality or object lying behind the signs, but only by the differences between the elements of the code — that is, only the context created by the signs themselves could explain their meaning. Here, as in classical art, Barthes concluded, form triumphed over content.

If Barthes' analysis lends itself well to the bodybuilding contest — an activity which many outsiders find pointless precisely because they do not understand the internally consistent 'code' of bodily presentation within which the ritualised signs become intelligible — his 1967 work *Système de la mode*[28] helps us to understand the relationship between a highly specialised world (in this case, the world of high fashion) and the everyday world (that of the general commercial fashion industry) which derives its intelligibility from reference to the images or ideals established by the former world, a world from which grey hair, fatness, middle age and work all seem equally absent. The dumpy shop-girl who reads high fashion magazines and

6.12 Bodybuilding makes the body itself the 'content' of the visual transaction, by developing muscularity to the point where it dominates or excludes all other visual messages.

spends most of her salary on clothes actually inhabits a more 'real' world than that of the preternatural models of the *haute couture* salons, but that is not the point: it is the language or system of signs presented by high fashion — in itself an essentially arbitrary language — that defines the shop-girl's view of herself and the self-assertion she makes to other people.

6.13 The ritualised language of the bodybuilding display is comprehensible only as a form of 'code', readable within a system which creates its own context and establishes its meaning.

Barthes' theory of the role of codes, or specialised systems of signs, does much to explain the role of bodybuilding in establishing a language of the body which has shaped our contemporary perception of physical perfection. Following his analogy of the 'exemplary' function of the world of *haute couture* in relation to that of everyday fashion, we can see the competition bodybuilder as incorporating to an extreme or archetypal degree the 'messages' of the developed body, whilst recognising that by no means all those who pursue the cult of muscularity will themselves be led to imitate or attempt to replicate these messages in such extreme form in their own bodily development or display.

This is not to suggest that organised bodybuilding, as a human social activity, is confined to the somewhat elemental level of the transmission of heightened bodily messages or 'super-normal stimuli'. These may indeed be the dimly-acknowledged substance of the social transaction, but the form of that transaction is constructed in a way which closely replicates that of more conventional sporting activity — in the pitting of players one against another in competition, the application of rules, game-strategies, the emergence of winners and losers, the hero-system attaching to champions, and so on. All of these are the common denominators of participant or spectator sports, and as such require no justification beyond the element of play and diversion they provide. Most sports, indeed, have their origin in quite primitive and elemental practices, including inter-tribal battle (football, hockey), beating with sticks or clubs (cricket, baseball, tennis) or taking aim at an object from a distance (golf, netball). In their evolved form, however, they have retained only remnants of their earlier function and operate mainly as recreation or as tests of skill, strength, tactics or agility, without any utilitarian goal. Viewed in purely operational terms, competitive bodybuilding functions in much the same way as other forms of recreational or sporting competition.

It remains, however, that it is the body itself which is the primary focus of attention in the bodybuilding display. Even if the aesthetic movement of the body (in the posing routine) is a criterion of official judging — as is also the case with sports such as gymnastics, diving or formation swimming — it is doubtful whether this element is of major interest to most spectators, for whom the muscularity of the physique is the chief object of engagement. The rules of competition do no more than provide a context, perhaps even a pretext, for the display of muscular development: they give the spectacle a form, a progression and a culmination, as well as providing a competitive ranking through the comparison of individual bodies both with each other and (implicitly) with the hypothetical point to which all aspire.

The social significance of bodybuilding, then, does not lie in its relatively small following as a competitive pastime or sport, any more than that of *haute couture* lies in the number of those attending a fashion parade. Any man who looks in a mirror and concludes that he looks too skinny or out of condition, not to mention the man who undertakes an occasional light work-out just to 'firm up', is acknowledging — even if sub-consciously — the possibility of a more highly developed appearance with which his present appearance is compared. That he may not, and probably does not, wish to emulate the extreme muscularity of the advanced bodybuilder, is not the point: the very fact of a qualitative comparison of a 'less developed' with a 'more developed' body implies the criterion of an archetypal bodily configuration to which physical development conforms to a greater or lesser degree.

By its very exaggeration of certain physical features, the bodybuilder's physique adds to the number of visual 'codes' by which we filter the reality we see. Standing as it does at one extreme of the total spectrum of recognisable bodily configurations, it thereby alters our perception of configurations situated at other points along the continuum. Let one example suffice. The appearance of Arnold Schwarzenegger in a number of highly popular movies from the early 1980s onwards introduced to the screen such a visually overwhelming impression of muscularity (even compared to the earlier 'gladiator' genre) that other actors called on to display their physiques in these movies tended to look undeveloped by comparison, even though in other contexts they would have appeared impressively muscular. Since the release of the early Schwarzenegger movies, film-makers requiring well-developed heroes have been obliged to look for actors in a physical mould far superior to those of even a generation ago. Just as successive Tarzans had been of more and more impressive build through the 60s and 70s, so Schwarzenegger set a new benchmark for the muscular hero in the 1980s. Even in children's entertainment, the bodybuilders' physiques of 'Teenage Mutant Ninja Turtles' seem to be a product of the Schwarzenegger generation, so profoundly has the image of advanced muscular development affected the popular landscape of the body.

Most of the six million monthly readers of *Muscle and Fitness* magazine do not resemble the exaggeratedly muscular specimens whose every pectoral striation is faithfully depicted in close-up in its pages, any more than the majority of ancient Greeks resembled the Hermes of Praxiteles. Still less do the bodies of the majority of mass consumers in urbanised societies resemble the less exaggerated but still recognisably muscular physiques associated with the advertising of beach and leisure wear, soft drinks and other products of a consumer-oriented society. What is common to them all is the visual language that is used, a language built up over centuries of cultural tradition even if, for the most part, it is apprehended only at a sub-conscious level.

6.14 The rules of competition are meant to give form, progression and a culmination to what is basically a fixation on muscularity. They create a context, even perhaps a pretext, for muscular display.

7.1   **CHAPTER 7**   THE BODY POLITIC
From prowess in individual combat to membership of a militaristic elite, the developed body has often been used to symbolise an aspiration to political dominance.

7

THE BODY POLITIC

DOMINANT BODIES

In a society as impressed by body imagery as ancient Greece, the perfection of divine being had to be reflected in a form that was free of physical failings. As the gods were tyrants and thus to be feared, they must be depicted as physically powerful; as they were also divine protectors and thus to be loved and worshipped, they must also be portrayed as physically beautiful. In Greek society, physical imperfection was a subject of shame: deformity, weakness or the degeneration of age tended to be looked upon with little sympathy or compassion. Despite its unparalleled contribution to the definition and creation of many of the noblest ideals and achievements of Western civilisation, the example of ancient Greece has all too frequently been invoked in societies obsessed with mastery and dominance by an elite group of 'superior' members over those who, through accident of birth, lack of opportunity or simply a different world-view, were considered less capable of embodying prevailing social ideals and thus of lesser inherent value in human terms. For the Greeks, physical perfection was divine, and those mortals who most nearly approximated it were the heroes. No mere abstract idea or socio-political construct, heroic stature had a recognisable bodily form, and it was seen as the aim of a heroic society to strive towards this physical ideal.

Modern European societies have by no means remained untouched by this particular species of Greek physical elitism, and it has surfaced in a number of variations in social movements over the last two hundred years or so. Curiously, it was in an age when the artistic portrayal of the masculine physical ideal had lost much of its earlier momentum that its social incarnation began to take hold of the imagination. It was in the German Idealism of the late eighteenth and early nineteenth centuries, a more fertile soil than the practicality of British Empiricism or the intellectual world of French Rationalism, that it took its most evident form. The influential art criticism of Johann Winckelmann had eulogised the sculpture of late

7.2 *Der Turnvater*: the 'father' of German gymnastics, Friedrich Ludwig Jahn. His development of systematic physical training in 19th-century Germany would lead to modern gymnastics, weightlifting and bodybuilding —and would be turned to more sinister ends under Nazism.

Greek antiquity — the Laocoön, the Apollo Belvedere, the Belvedere Torso — and prompted his exhortation to his fellow-countrymen that 'the only way for us to become great, or even inimitable if possible, is to imitate the Greeks.'[1] The tenets of Idealism, which proclaimed the uplifting of cultures through the transcending of national and class barriers and the celebration of human dignity and beauty, had a deep effect upon the more romantically-minded of nineteenth-century German moralists and social reformers, and in a century of profound political upheaval and gradually emerging national unification the promotion of a stronger and more heroic society was an attractive (and, in itself, an unexceptionable) goal.

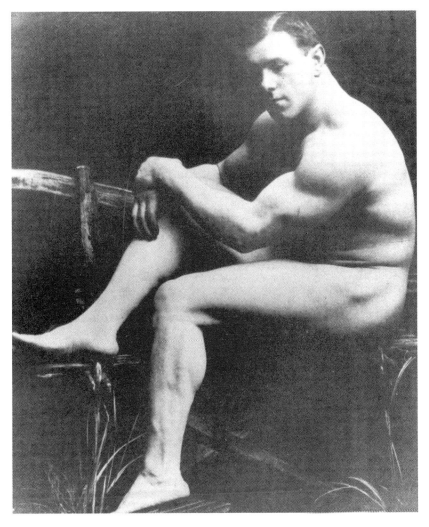

7.3 Though sometimes dubbed 'The Russian Lion', Georg Hackenschmidt was, like many of his contemporary strongmen-bodybuilders, of German-speaking origin. Posing for the camera nude or in skimpy attire was considered unremarkable in his day.

It is in this context that we can understand the aims of the 'father of German gymnastics', Friedrich Ludwig Jahn (1778-1852). The Napoleonic domination of Germany from 1806 to 1813 was reducing his country to such a low ebb politically and psychologically that Jahn felt compelled to call his countrymen to a programme of physical training which, when combined with patriotic idealism and the love of freedom, would enable them to throw off the tyranny of foreign rule. In the spring of 1811, on the Hasenheide near Berlin, he established his first *Turnplatz* or exercise ground for the practice of physical culture which would make young German men capable of bearing arms and prepare them for the imminent war of liberation.[2] The enlistment of physical exercise in the interests of military training was, or course, not new — it went back to antiquity — but Jahn's movement was to give it a peculiarly modern form.

7.4   Like his friend and
countryman Walt
Whitman, Thomas
Eakins was fascinated
by the well developed
male body. A belief in
racial superiority
underlay much of the
19th-century interest in
physical development.
Thomas Eakins, *Salutat*,
1898. (Addison
Gallery of American
Art, Andover, Mass.)

By 1813, Jahn's trainees were ready to answer the call to arms issued by King Friedrich Wilhelm III, and to demonstrate at one and the same time their fitness and their loyalty. Despite numerous setbacks as political alliances shifted, gymnastic societies received official approval in 1842 and numerous societies appeared throughout the country. These *Turnvereine* had as their emblem the monogram of the four-F cross, standing for the words *Frisch, Fromm, Froh, Frei*: literally, 'fresh, devoted, happy, free'.[3] Of particular significance here is the word *fromm*: it is difficult to find an English equivalent which captures all the overtones of idealism and patriotism which were an important part of the German gymnastic movement.

The German influence on the later development of weight training and physical culture was immense. Sandow (Müller), as we have seen, was brought up in the tradition of the *Turnhalle* or gymnasium, and in the great wave of European immigration to the USA from the 1850s onwards the interest in physical development was not the least of the cultural imports brought to the new world by German settlers. Even in English-speaking countries, the identification of physical culture, weightlifting and bodybuilding with a German background was to become so complete in the wake of Attila (Ludwig Durlacher), Sandow/Müller, Klein, Hackenschmidt and others, that the celebrated strongman-poser Louis Hart often billed himself as Ludwig Hardt in order to suggest a German ancestry.[4] The significance of the German emphasis on the building of individual strength and on physical development generally, and its influence in Anglo-Saxon cultures where the stress had traditionally been on recreational team sports, can hardly be overestimated.

In the English-speaking world, meanwhile, a somewhat different (if analogous) current of thought had been stirring throughout the nineteenth century. A new progressivism based on scientific knowledge and technological discovery was working beneath the veneer of the bourgeois social system to awaken a new interest in physical and mental perfectibilism — a movement which would gain momentum towards the closing years of the century. Imaginative speculation, which for two hundred years or more had invented wondrous Utopias where current social orders were reversed, would turn to new fantasies, in which present society itself might be transformed, often in frightening ways, by modern discoveries: from Mary Shelley's *Frankenstein* (1818), through the imaginative work of Poe in the 1840s, Stevenson's *Dr. Jekyll and Mr Hyde* (1886), and later in the translations of Jules Verne and the novels of H.G. Wells, thought was directed to the possibilities of the future, to the control of the body by the mind, and to the ability of scientists to shape and engineer humanity. In the wake of Mesmerism, hypnosis gained increasing acceptance and was a subject of widespread interest by the 1880s. The human body, whose nature as a machine had been first discovered and then explored over the two preceding centuries, could increasingly be controlled and improved; the steady advance of orthodox medical practice and scientific knowledge helped fuel the imagination as to the possibilities that might be achieved in the future.

In the United States, physical perfectibilism was to take incipient form in the work of a number of influential artists and writers. An important aspect of Thomas Eakins' interest in realism, and of his turning away from established European styles, was his consciousness of being American, of belonging to a new nation grappling with the challenges of its environment. It is impossible not to see a strong thread of resemblance in this respect to the writings of his fiercely nationalistic friend Walt Whitman, whose portrait Eakins painted in 1887. Whitman's fascination with the healthy human body, the 'Body Electric', and his own self-promotion in the mythical persona of the model of untainted masculinity, concealed (as in Eakins) an unmistakable undercurrent of homosexual attraction to the 'physical-culture hero' who appears in different guises throughout the various editions of *Leaves of Grass*.[5] Although Whitman's dream of American cultural revolution did not materialise — at least, in the form in which he imagined it — his euphoric humanism had an important effect on other artists of his age.[6] Along with the paintings of Eakins, they were to evoke an image of the muscular male body almost as potent in its symbolic status as the idealised Greek statues had been to the classical age and its imitators.

Whitman enthusiastically embraced the belief in physical development as a means of social improvement and the reversal of 'degeneracy'. In his writings one can discern the darker undercurrents of belief which often enhanced the attractiveness of such theories to some of their more theoretically-minded adherents. The French biologist Lamarck, writing in the early years of the nineteenth century, had held that the organs of animals could be classified according to a hierarchy of complexity, from the lower to the higher stages of life, and that these organs were improved with repeated use and weakened by disuse. The application of Lamarckian theories, particularly as they affect heredity, to the improvement of the human race was a subject of fascination to a number of thinkers who embraced Lamarckism as the foundation of the new science of 'eugenics'. If Lamarckism meant that 'the development and effectiveness of organs are proportionate to the exercise of those organs', then individuals could consciously and substantially modify their bodily organs during their lifetimes. The Lamarckian 'law of exercise' (as it was called) provided a scientific and moral basis for physical education and gymnastic exercise, such as that found in Jacques' *Hints Towards Physical Perfection* which Walt Whitman both read and reviewed.[7]

But popular Lamarckism went further than this. It taught that such temporarily improved organic condition in an individual could promote a corresponding permanent improvement in the individual's offspring. Similarly, the failure to exercise any organ weakened and gradually atrophied that organ in both the creature and its descendants. From here, it is but a small step to the assumption that certain races of men have preserved their organic capacity better than others — in other words, to the theory of racial superiority. Whitman, like a number of other popular Lamarckians of his time, was prepared to accept such quasi-scientific racist propaganda, with the result that his vision of human perfectibility (including physical perfectibility) attributed to the white, Nordic races a considerable hereditary advantage over (for example) 'the nigger' and 'the Injun'.[8]

If such dangerous nonsense was latent in some of the theories surrounding physical education, the latter generally assumed a more benign form of perfectibilism, wherein the healthy development of the human body led merely to a happier and more vigorous society. In any case, the vogue of Lamarckism in scientific circles was of relatively short duration, the work of August Weissmann in 1885 postulating an impermeable barrier ('Weissmann's barrier') between generations which excluded the inheritance of acquired characteristics. Nonetheless, the Lamarckian eugenic theories underlying much of the early physical culture movement should not be underestimated; the belief that individuals could not only improve themselves but, through breeding out less wholesome biological strains, improve humanity itself is one of the more morally ambiguous currents of that evolutionary perfectibilism which so marked the later years of the nineteenth century — whether in Darwinian, Nietzschean or Marxist guise.[9]

7.5 The stage strongman Siegmund Breitbart, nicknamed the 'Iron King' for his ability to break or bite through iron chains, was a victim of nascent anti-Semitism in 1930s Germany.

Two sides of the German physical culture movement were to emerge in the course of the nineteenth century. Many German gymnasts had emigrated to America in the 1850s and a large number of them fought for Lincoln in the Civil War. These 'democratic' gymnasts, who stood for social justice, liberty and progress, also continued in Germany where they were to establish the Workers' Gymnastics League (*Arbeiterturnerbund*). Their attitude towards the Prussian-dominated German imperial state from 1871 onwards set them in opposition to a rival group, the German Gymnasts' Association (*Deutsche Turnerschaft*), which espoused the cult of the Kaiser, the struggle against Social Democracy, the greatness of the Reich and the furthering of its ends through military training. To these were soon added the cult of the Germanic peoples.[10]

7.6 Ideologically 'pure' art of the Nazi period: the official style of public monuments at times came close to comic-strip caricature. Two sculptures by one of Hitler's propagandist artists, Arno Breker: (a) *The Avenger*; (b) *The Sentinel*.

The disputes between the two gymnastic associations continued until well after World War I. While the 'democratic gymnasts' welcomed the collapse of the monarchical authoritarian state, their rival organisation bitterly resented Germany's defeat and instituted a search for scapegoats. In particular, non-Aryan races (especially the Jews) were blamed for the physical and moral degeneration of German society, and anti-Semitism became a feature of a renewed interest in physical perfectibilism. By the 1920s, even Jewish strongmen became the victims of persecution: Siegmund Breitbart, known as *der Eisenkönig* (the Iron King) because of his renowned ability to bite through iron, was a victim of nascent Nazism. Proudly proclaiming his Jewish identity, and sometimes billed as 'the Jewish Samson', Breitbart did not hesitate to perform his feats of strength in front of a large Star of David draped on the stage behind him. Organised disruption of his strongman acts by Nazi sympathisers became

so violent that he was forced to hire bodyguards to ensure his safety.[11] By 1933, under the leadership of Neuendorff, the German Gymnasts Association had instituted anti-Semitic regulations, and its leaders had made a public declaration of allegiance to Hitler and National Socialism.[12]

The rise of Nazism was accompanied by propagandist theories of art which identified the grace and strength of the 'ideal Nordic' (i.e. German) body with superior racial characteristics and contrasted it with the physical degeneration or brutishness of the *Untermenschen* (lower races). Physical education and gymnastic exercise held a place of major importance in the National Socialist state schools, and their militaristic overtones were apparent. The new fighting elite was to possess in physical form the godlike humanity of classical antiquity, and ideologically pure male nudes proliferated in the sculpture of propagandist artists such as Adolf Hildebrand and Arno Breker, given theoretical justification by the writings of compliant art-historians and critics.[13] These derivative and artistically worthless attempts to recreate Hellenic beauty took the conventional form of advanced male muscularity, symbolising German racial perfection through idealised physical 'purity'.

This preoccupation with the body was not restricted to the world of art. From the early 1920s, Major Hans Surén, Chief of the German Army School of Physical Exercise, had promoted the ideal of male physical perfection which (despite his later denials of such intention) became associated with the superiority of the Germanic race. Surén's obsession with nudity — he insisted that his soldiers train naked and often had himself and his pupils photographed in the nude — did not endear his more extreme views to Hitler, who banned naturist clubs in 1933 and was no doubt concerned at the homoerotic overtones of Surén's training methods. Nonetheless, Hitler encouraged the cult of physical perfection and spoke of the beauty of the naked body — a link, in his eyes, between classical antiquity and the healthy Aryan youth of the Third Reich.[14] The Nazi cult of bodily superiority was openly manifested at the 1936 Berlin Olympic Games and particularly in Leni Riefenstahl's propagandist film treatment of German Olympians and their physical prowess. Riefenstahl's film, says Richard Mandell, evoked a kind of Nordic eros. She possessed

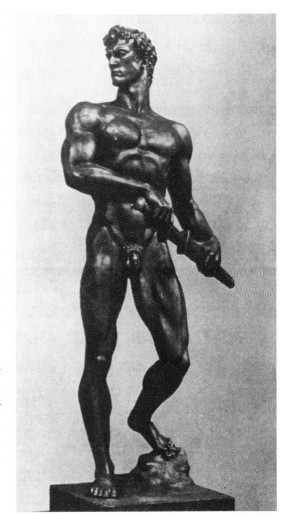

> 'a quality rare among women: a keen appreciation of muscular, male good looks. There are dozens of brief closeups of fine Aryan heads and shoulders,.....[of] sturdy mesomorphs and slender boys in the tent cities'.[15]

To Hitler's chagrin, the Nazi dream of equating German culture with that of classical Greece as the natural leader of a 'golden age' of physical dynamism was dramatically —and very visibly — thwarted by the success of the black American sprinter Jesse Owens who won four gold medals.

Never before had the Western conception of physical development been turned to such blatantly political ends, or the idealised muscularity of classical art been so institutionalised to serve the purposes of the State. In the totalitarian climate of Hitler's Germany, the disparate fields of aesthetics, social morality, bodily development and political ambition were all brought together within a single theoretical framework which rendered all forms of expression subservient to the aims of the Nazi regime.

A similar tendency was evident in Fascist Italy, though without the more extreme overtones of racial purity. A comparable preoccupation with power and the leadership of the autocratic hero as an incarnation of the biological life-force, the elimination of physical weakness and a nostalgia for the glory of earlier civilisations (in this case ancient Rome) all had their necessary reflection in ideological art. The vast, columned buildings and sporting arenas in neo-Roman style erected by Mussolini all used the familiar sculptural image of superbly muscular athletes as symbolic manifestations of the glory and power of a new elite characterised by vitality, virility and energy.

7.7   The training methods of Major Hans Surén, Chief of the German Army School of Physical Exercise in the 1920s, involved training naked – pursuing ideals of physical perfection which were later promoted by Hitler as a sign of Aryan racial superiority. *The Ball Throwers* (photographer unknown). Germany, c. 1925.

The German totalitarian dream, along with its equation of social and physical perfectibilism, was shattered by defeat in World War II. In the new political order that followed, the physically developed body would take on a more subtle, and at times more publicly contested, significance as an embodiment of social values. There must surely be a tragic irony in the fact that, half a century later, members of an extremist Israeli organisation (the Jewish Defence League) should be shown on television doing bodybuilding exercises in preparation for a commando mission against nascent neo-Nazi groups in a newly-reunified Germany.

7.8   Enrico del Debbio's *Athletes* (1938) in the Foro Italico, Rome, reflect the ideals of physical power and nationalistic nostalgia for the glories of Ancient Rome promoted by the Fascist government of Mussolini.

THE AMERICAN DREAM

In the post-War democratic societies of the West, governments were anxious to avoid any suggestion of physical perfectibilism along with the rest of the ideological baggage of totalitarianism. Within the broader scope which they accorded to political pluralism, however, the dominant images of social life — and particularly those of the popular media — continued to endow the developed body with public significance.

In the USA in particular, muscularity continued to bestow quasi-heroic status on its possessors. Comic-strip characters such as Superman and his imitators were visually defined by their powerful physical development, and their adventures were successfully syndicated world-wide. Endowed with various forms of super-normal power, they fought against international villains in defence of democracy and the American way. 'Screen idols' such as Kirk Douglas, William Holden, Robert Ryan, Burt Lancaster and Tony Curtis were cast in roles which required them to reveal their muscular torsos in the process of winning the heroine, while at a less sophisticated level the Tarzan movies provided opportunities for hitherto unknown actors to appear in a loincloth. While the American Steve Reeves displayed his musculature in 'sword-and-sandal' epics (being one of the few non-Italians to do so), Victor Mature brought brooding Italian good looks to the more up-market American treatment of similar themes.[16] The surfing movie (Gidget and its sequels) provided the opportunity for well-built young males in swimshorts to vie for the attention of the heroine, and the tanned, blond, athletic 'all-American boy' (Tab Hunter, Troy Donahue) became a favourite pin-up.

The muscular hero was not uncritically accepted even in the popular images of America itself. The subtle irony of Al Capp's comic strip *Lil Abner*, which for over 50 years conveyed a popular and influential view of backwoods USA, poked fun at many sacred cows of American life and its fads and fashions. Though these were usually introduced in the form of strange characters who came and went over the years, even the pivotal Yokum family were a form of gentle humour directed at the American ideal: the diminutive hillbillies Mammy and Pappy Yokum (symbols of an earlier, pioneering generation) had given birth to a pure-minded and physically well developed son, the embodiment of every red-blooded young American male's dreams. Abner himself changed his shape from the more realistic proportions of the 1930s strips into the huge shoulders, bulging biceps and impossibly narrow waist of the 1950s and subsequent years. His younger brother, Honest Abe, had by the age of $15^1/_2$ the blond hair and super-normal muscularity of the Caucasian bodybuilder of the post-Reeves generation.[17] Though Al Capp directed his more obvious barbs at the humbugs and phonies of the American Right (and, later, the trendy Left), he retained a kindly if mock-naive distance from the muscular icons of his day.

7.9 Al Capp's comic strip *Lil Abner* poked gentle fun at changing American values. Abner's physique evolved to suit the times: the slim country yokel of the 1930s (a) had, by the 1950s, taken on the shape of the 'all-American' muscular mesomorph (b) which was popularised by Steve Reeves.

Perhaps the most striking illustration of the identification of advanced muscularity with socio-political ideals was the rise of the counterculture in the late 1960s and early 1970s. In the context of rising social unrest among middle-class youth and heightened in the USA and some other Western countries by the increasing unpopularity of involvement in the Vietnam War, the alternative culture proposed a physical ideal radically at odds with the prevailing social assumptions. The youth culture of the sixties and seventies spanned a wide variety of social manifestations, from the hard-line protest movement to a more generalised but less politically active population of young people generally disenchanted with the values of their parents' generation. The muscular ideal, with its overtones of patriotic heroism, physical power and even militarism, was starkly at odds with the aspirations of this newly-emerging culture, and the new popular idols tended to be as far as possible removed from images of advanced physical development. Emaciated and androgynous figures, exemplified by Mick Jagger and David Bowie, were directly and deliberately antithetical to the images of manly muscularity conveyed by the movie heroes of the preceding generation.

In this manifestation, most obvious in some of the rock music stars of the 1970s, physicality was at least as crucial to the symbolism as it had been for the tradition against which it was reacting. The upper body was displayed as shirts or jackets were unzipped or torn off on stage, revealing a pale and skeletal torso as vulnerable in its childlike innocence as the tanned and muscular physique of the bodybuilder was armoured and assertive. The hair was long, contrasting with the cropped haircut of the military; the face was emaciated and anorexic, almost feminine; tight-fitting trousers accentuated the slimness of the hips. Only the phallic guitar, its symbolism inherited from Presley, but here used more overtly and aggressively, made the sexual message unambiguously male. This was the culture of the *un*developed body, its appearance as emblematic as a Michelangelo nude and as self-consciously political in its visual message as a German athlete of 1936. Although the organised world of rock music was (and remains) as capitalistic in nature and operation as any other manifestation of Western culture, revolving around concepts of success, hero-worship, the accumulation of extreme wealth and the trappings of luxury, it nonetheless succeeded in projecting a countercultural image in accord with the soft-Left political alignment of a significant proportion of 1970s youth, suggesting a generalised mood of rebellion against established values and authority. In such a context, the political overtones of the undeveloped body were clearly established.

The 1980s brought a swing back to the Right, a new climate of support for the conservative side of American political and social life which saw Ronald Reagan elected as President. The muscular hero was to re-emerge, again laden with political overtones. Rock singer Bruce Springsteen was to cast off his earlier image as a ragged Bob Dylan imitator and to re-emerge in 1985 as a big-biceped post-Vietnam American celebrating working-class values with his hit record 'Born in the USA'. Meanwhile, in a series of unapologetically populist movies, Sylvester Stallone and Arnold Schwarzenegger in particular were to make use of a variety of means, from bare knuckles to technologically advanced weaponry, to exploit the physical stature conferred on the new breed of popular hero by his conspicuous muscularity.

7.10 The counter-culture of the 1970s brought with it the cult of the *un*developed body – just as much on display, and just as emblematic of underlying values, as that of the muscular hero-figure. Pop idol Mick Jagger.

7.11 In the swing back to the political Right which marked 1980s America and saw Ronald Reagan elected President, the muscular hero was to re-emerge. One of its first manifestations was Sylvester Stallone's pugilist-hero Rocky Balboa.

The changing emphases of contemporary bodybuilding are clearly discernible in these physiques, which stress muscular definition, the clear separation of individual muscle-groups and the striation of muscle-bands as much as (or even more than) the overall size and proportion of the physique which were the qualities prized in the earlier generation represented by a Steve Reeves. Stallone, though never a professional or competitive bodybuilder, had been inspired by seeing Reeves' *Hercules* at the age of thirteen and used bodybuilding techniques to build a physique whose surface was a model of lean muscle definition, whereas Schwarzenegger, no longer displaying the steroid-enhanced bulk of his professional bodybuilding days or even of his earlier series of *Conan* movies, was now a 'lean, mean (but overwhelmingly muscular) fighting machine'.

Stallone's series of *Rocky* movies, which had begun in the late 1970s, owed much to the recent example of Muhammad Ali, with his assiduous promotion of the boxer-as-hero and of himself as 'the greatest'. This element Stallone combined with a number of well established film conventions, including the Maciste tradition (the actor closely identified with his film persona, although Stallone had too many other irons in the fire to change his name to Rocky Balboa) and the standard American genre of the boxing movie, which had allowed stars from the age of John Garfield and Errol Flynn to that of Kirk Douglas and Paul Newman to display their torsos and their machismo. A more recent variation is the kick-boxing movie, the training-ground for two European 'hunks' — the Swede Dolph Lundgren and the Belgian Jean-Claude Van Damme — who followed in Arnold's footsteps to become box-office stars in the USA. Brought together in 1992 for *Universal Soldier* (two Schwarzeneggers for the price of one), they have concentrated more and more on displaying their muscularity for its own sake and are frequently featured as role-models in bodybuilding magazines.

The boxing movie had established a tradition in which the pugilist hero undergoes severe punishment: he almost loses the fight, and in some cases actually does lose (though usually, by dint of his indomitable pluck, reaping a 'moral' victory). The parabolic or allegorical significance of the genre is well analysed by Michael Malone:

> 'In American movies, boxers don't win because they're good; they win because they get angry. It's certainly not very professional, but it's much more dramatic, because it's personal, and women as well as men can identify with emotionally evoked violence. Our champions are potentially the biggest and the best, like America, but like America they have to be *forced* to demonstrate this fact.'[18]

7.12 Though dominated by the personae of Schwarzenegger and Stallone, the popular action movie of the 1980s was to see the emergence of a newer generation of muscular stars punching, kicking or shooting their way to stardom. (a) Dolph Lundgren; (b) Jean-Claude van Damme.

7.13 Stallone's *Rocky* series was succeeded by the more disturbing *Rambo* movies: reversing in imagination the American humiliation in Vietnam, they exercised a modish fascination on younger viewers which led to growing public concern at screen violence.

The assumption that the personal motivation of the pugilist-hero can be equated with national aspirations and values lies just below the surface in most boxing movies, but in the case of the *Rocky* series it is beyond doubt: in *Rocky IV*, for example, the hero faces a Soviet boxer who is 'trained to kill'. The context of sporting competition had long been a theatre for the acting-out of politic antagonism and rivalry, and no more so than in the case of the USA and the pre-*glasnost* Eastern Bloc. American resentment against the sheer physical dominance of its traditional adversary, especially in strength sports, translated readily into the terms of the plucky, lithe American David and the massive, brutish Soviet Goliath.

7.14 Schwarzenegger in his later 1980s mode as the 'good guy' avenger symbolically righting his country's wrongs by means of advanced firepower. *Predator*, 1987.

The *Rocky* formula (defined by Graham McCann as 'regeneration through violence'[19]) took a new and disturbing turn in Stallone's *Rambo* series, in which the 'hero' symbolically played out another national resentment: the failure of the American political and military engagement in Vietnam. Once again, the hero needed to be goaded into action, but once engaged — and with sophisticated weaponry now providing a technological extension of his (significantly) bare torso — he would enable millions of Americans to live out the fantasy of what they felt should have happened in Vietnam. The formula of the 'good guy' provoked into violent action was also exploited by Schwarzenegger. In *Commando*, he was a logger battling thugs who had kidnapped his daughter; in *Predator*, the fearless leader of an elite military unit facing a killer alien who skinned his human victims; in *Total Recall*, the quarry of killers (whether real or imagined) who could be overcome only by violent response. Though in part these films can be seen simply as examples of the American vogue of movie violence which characterised the 1980s and early 90s, it is impossible to divorce them from the persona of their hero, from the fantasy of an iron-muscled prodigy who exists somewhere inside the ordinary citizen (or the peace-loving but sorely provoked country) and can, if necessary, be conjured into violent action.

By the early 1990s, on-screen and actual social violence had reached the point where public reaction, both liberal and conservative, demanded a re-appraisal of the psychological effect of screen images, especially on the young. Always attuned to the public mood, Schwarzenegger had already 'softened' his image in *Twins* and *Kindergarten Cop*. In the $100 million sequel to the 1984 *Terminator*, in which he had played a 'bad' cyborg he re-created the role in 1991 as a 'good' cyborg who is taught (by a child) that killing is wrong. In a political climate which had seen the destruction of the Berlin Wall and the dismantling of the USSR, the message could well be seen to reflect its time. The violence, of course, remained — viewed, as in the contemporaneous Gulf War, as a necessary incidental to the greater good. What had changed was the emphasis: instead of the private individual transformed by injustice into a rampaging avenger, we now witnessed the reconciliation of a once violent being to the 'new world order'. Schwarzenegger himself perceptively described him in the 1988 election rhetoric of George Bush as a 'kinder, gentler Terminator'.[20] More recently still, the mood-swing towards liberal 'political correctness' which led American voters to reject Bush in favour of Bill Clinton was reflected in Schwarzenegger's own venture *Last Action Hero* (1993) which set out to parody the whole action movie genre through a somewhat laboured attempt at self-referential humour. Whether the film's title was meant to prophesy the demise of the Terminator genre as part of the cult of movie violence remains (at the time of writing) to be seen: it may well be that the unfavourable reaction of critics and audiences alike will bring about this result for quite unintended reasons. In an age when 'self-reinvention' has become almost a cliché of popular culture — and the *sine qua non* of durability from one vogue to the next — Arnold Schwarzenegger must be ranked at least alongside figures such as Jane Fonda and Madonna as a consummate practitioner of the art, and the time is perhaps ripe for a brand new persona to be devised.

BODIES IN COMMAND

The symbolism of the developed body can, as we have seen, be appropriated by a society or its government to reflect the prevailing national self-concept. This tendency may equally be observed within a totalitarian or a liberal-democratic regime, be it Hitler's Germany or contemporary America. In either case, the appeal lies in the imaginative power of the muscular body to suggest a visible embodiment of strength and authority, and to do so in terms which the cultural tradition has enabled the society to read in commonly recognised ways. Not every totalitarian system has used the developed body in this way: Communist China, for instance, does not share the Western cultural tradition of the body and has tended to resort to other imagery, such as the strength derived from the solidarity of the masses. In pluralistic Western societies, the developed body has usually been cultivated as a symbol more by the political Right than by the Left, the capitalist emphasis on individual achievement often being associated with a respect for strong authority figures and a tendency towards military inverventionism (the 'show of strength').

7.15 The Japanese writer Yukio Mishima considered that Eastern religions had undervalued the body. Himself an ardent bodybuilder, he wrote in praise of 'the beauty of symmetry, the splendour and poetry of the male physique'.

The predilection for images of muscularity on the part of a number of right-wing, authoritarian societies must inevitably raise the question of a corresponding social or political outlook on the part of those who pursue such an outward appearance. Is there, in other words, an organic or causative link between the pursuit of muscular development and a (perhaps implicit) social or even political agenda? The question is brought into sharp focus by the high public profile of two of the most fascinating figures of our time, Yukio Mishima and Arnold Schwarzenegger. Despite their very different and even contrasting characters, each of them espoused both the persona of the bodybuilder and the pursuit of socio-political aims emphasising power and dominance.

Yukio Mishima (1925-1970) was probably the best-known Japanese writer —certainly the best-known outside Japan — of the twentieth century, his novels and short stories having been translated into numerous languages. His enthusiastic cult of bodybuilding was the product of an exceptionally complex personality, torn as it was between Western cultural values and an attraction to the militaristic Samurai tradition of old Japan. Believing that Buddhism and Confucianism had undervalued the strength and beauty of the body, leading to the commonly-held view of the modern Japanese as a drooping, bespectacled figure of a small man with a frail body wrapped in Western dress, he pursued 'the beauty of symmetry, all the splendour and the melancholy and, yes, the poetry of the male physique.'[21] Whilst this romanticised, and totally un-Japanese, view owes much to Mishima's own homosexuality, his political agenda was the creation of a new class of Samurai, filled with national pride and promoting traditional Emperor-worship and the restoration of Japan's armed forces — a reactionary attitude which still attracts a small but significant following among the Japanese extreme Right.[22]

The Introduction Mishima wrote for Tamotsu Yato's collection of bodybuilding photographs, *Young Samurai: Bodybuilders of Japan*, is a generally lyrical and traditional Western-type eulogy of the developed male body, rather reminiscent in some ways of Walt Whitman, though some of his other writings and opinions were such a hotchpotch of political zealotry and pathological sado-masochistic fantasy that his sanity was certainly in doubt, and his bizarre death by *seppuku* ('hara-kiri' or ritual self-disembowelling) may confirm such a view. He can hardly be seen as representative figure, and his reputation rests on the remarkable literary quality of his best work rather than on the bizarre eccentricities of his pantheon of social values. What is significant in the present context is that, as a Japanese, he should have chosen from the storehouse of Western culture so strikingly alien an activity as bodybuilding to symbolise the new warrior-class of which he dreamed. Even across the cultural divide, he discerned and sought to develop an organic relationship between the personal pursuit of muscularity and a political outlook in tune with his own right-wing demagoguery.

7.16 Despite the samurai stage-effects, Mishima's fascination with the muscular body (particularly his own) was curiously foreign to the Japanese mind. His success as a writer was, not surprisingly, always greater outside Japan than within it.

The case of Arnold Schwarzenegger is a good deal less extreme or idiosyncratic —and, unlike that of Mishima, spectacularly successful. As one of America's most public figures, he has been the subject of extensive commentary including several books covering both his career and his views, which need only be touched on here.

Schwarzenegger has been disarmingly honest in his account of his reasons for leaving his native Austria and making his home in America. Quite apart from the opportunities offered to a professional bodybuilder, America symbolised to him from his earliest youth a land where one could achieve material success and 'upward mobility' through the exercise of initiative and enterprise. European tradition and its relatively fixed social system meant that the horizons of those who were not part of the 'establishment' must forever be limited by the prejudices of those who were, whereas in the USA the acquisition of obvious wealth was itself a source of power.[23] And America had great wealth and great power, along with the opportunity for successful individuals to share in both. From childhood, Schwarzenegger had recurring dreams about people who were in positions of great power, and even in his mature years his attitude had hardly changed:

> 'My relationship to power and authority', he is quoted as saying, 'is that I'm all for it. People need somebody to watch over them and tell them what to do. Ninety-five percent of the people in the world need to be told what to do and how to behave.'[24]

These sentiments would certainly be re-echoed by most dictators of either the Right or the Left, and Schwarzenegger's public frankness as to his socio-political views, combined with the apparent endorsement of quasi-militaristic violence in some of the films of his middle period (before he turned to comedy and family entertainment movies), has occasionally led to speculation as to possible neo-Nazi sympathies. Wendy Leigh's 'unauthorised biography' (Arnold[25]) made much of his father Gustav's purported membership of the Nazi party from 1938 onwards, and of Arnold's claimed support of the Austrian President Kurt Waldheim who was widely suspected of Nazi sympathies.

Such claims, whether with or without foundation, appear not to have damaged Schwarzenegger's reputation, and in 1991 he was honoured by the Simon Wiesenthal Center, a Jewish foundation dedicated to the study of the holocaust and of which Schwarzenegger had been a supporter in both words and money. Equally importantly, they are peripheral to his real political alignment, which lies squarely with the US political power elite rather than with any residual fringe-group. Married to a member of the Kennedy clan and chosen by George Bush to lead the President's Council on Physical Development and Sports, Schwarzenegger has forged links with both

Democrat and Republican Parties and achieved his ambition to take a leading place in the American political establishment. The earlier prophecies of some commentators — fuelled by Schwarzenegger himself — that he would run for the US Senate (or perhaps even the Presidency) remain, however, unfulfilled. His high profile in Bush's unsuccessful 1992 re-election campaign appears to have marked a turning point, leading to his eventual recognition that the prospect of another actor, particularly a foreign-born one, being elected to high political office in the USA is at best remote.

The fundamental question raised by Schwarzenegger is whether America adopted him or whether he adopted America. The country which, more than any other in the twentieth century, had fostered the cult of muscularity and had used it to symbolise its aspirations had found in him the perfect embodiment of its fantasies. He, for his part, had found in America the land where his bodily development could provide a seemingly endless upward mobility, provided that the attached persona was prepared to re-invent itself periodically to take account of changing social emphases. The need to dominate as an individual, to blitz the opposition — to be the world's best-paid movie star, to make the world's most expensive film, to have the world's most famous body — these are (Hitler notwithstanding) not so much typically Austrian as typically American ideals. It was certainly the need to express this personal dominance that led him to leave his native land, and it is plausible to suggest that it went back to even earlier days — to the decision to take up bodybuilding.

7.17 Power of one kind or another — including political influence — had always been part of Schwarzenegger's personal agenda. Former President George Bush appointed him President of the President's Council on Physical Fitness and Sports, and Arnold reciprocated with campaign support in Bush's unsuccessful re-election bid.

It is apparent that certain individuals who have been personally attracted to the cult of muscularity have embraced a world-view in which the exercise of power has figured prominently. The question still remains whether such social or political tendencies are inherently a part of the pursuit of muscular development itself. Some research studies have claimed to establish such a link, in particular those of Alan Klein who based his findings on observations made in a prominent bodybuilding gym in Venice/Santa Monica, California, between 1979 and 1985.[26] Klein argues that narcissism and fascism are the main elements underlying the bodybuilding sub-culture, whose members relate to the outside world through 'an arrogant veneer of superior fitness' in order to contain a deep-rooted sense of inferiority. In this sense, Klein argues, there are parallels to be drawn between the exaltation of power or physical perfection and the fascist beliefs of Nazism, though he is careful not to extend the parallel to the point of a necessary causal relationship. Indeed, he concludes that the narcissism involved in bodybuilding `compensates for the self-esteem that participants lacked before taking up the sport, and in this sense serves a socially and psychologically therapeutic function.'

Klein's analysis is certainly revealing, though it may suffer from its limitation to the example of the Southern Californian bodybuilding scene. Anyone at all familiar with the USA will recognise this region as *sui generis* and by no means typical, in its culture, of the United States in general. In his popular exposé of the world of bodybuilding (*Muscle*), Sam Fussell has described the typical Southern Californian gym as frequented by 'health fascists' of extreme political views, who wear caps decorated with buttons bearing slogans such as 'Pray for War' and 'I'd rather be killing Communists in Central America'.[27]

It must certainly be acknowledged that the subject of Klein's study (the Venice Beach area) is likely to provide fertile, and informative, ground for any sociological analysis of the bodybuilding culture. This is the site of Gold's Gym, popularly referred to as the 'Mecca of Bodybuilding'. Gymnasiums in this area are likely to attract a clientele more than usually obsessed with the cult of muscular development, and to that extent they may exhibit in extreme form a number of the motivations and attitudes underlying the practice of bodybuilding in general.

On the other hand, whether or not Klein's research findings would be duplicated in other gymnasiums could well depend on the extent to which they cater for would-be (or practising) professional bodybuilders as distinct from those members of the general public whose pursuit of muscularity is far from dominating their lives and is rather a sporting or social interest comparable to other sports or pastimes. Examples of near-neurotic obsession become more common, in the case of many sports, the more closely one approaches the professional ranks — though the bodybuilder's preoccupation with a perfect physique does certainly convey more hints of self-absorption than, say, the snooker-player's obsession with a perfect break.

The element of personal empowerment provided by the physical development of the body is clearly an important, and perhaps widespread, motivation amongst bodybuilders, and may well account for the popularity of bodybuilding in many working-class and socially depressed areas, as well as within the prison population. To that extent, it may well have the function of overcoming feelings of inferiority and thus have the therapeutic value to which Klein refers. The overcoming of inferiority is one thing, however; its replacement by a mystique of superiority and dominance is another.

In some individuals, physical development may be purely a social pastime which at most has the effect of restoring or (in a positive way) enhancing self-esteem. In others, it may show itself in the more extreme form of 'gym politics', where the display of muscular development is aimed at achieving or retaining a dominant position within the hierarchy of one's own tribal group. In yet others, it may be linked to a wider social allegiance in which the values of one's own group must be seen to dominate those of other groups. In the last-named case, the tyranny of the perfectible body can no longer remain a private matter: it becomes a public issue, and its place in the fabric of an enlightened society must at least be open to question.

7.18 T-shirts emblazoned with 'macho' slogans are aimed at reinforcing the status of their wearers within the gym hierarchy. They function as a popular contemporary variation on the muscular Roman breastplate.

8.1 **CHAPTER 8** THE SEXUAL BODY
The use of muscle as a sexual signal is a powerful motivator, successfully exploited by the billion-dollar gym industry.

8

THE SEXUAL BODY

IMPROVE YOUR SEX LIFE

Though it had long been implicit in the artistic depiction of the powerful body, the association between the male sexual drive and the impetus towards the exercise of power (physical or otherwise) was not subjected to scientific scrutiny until the late nineteenth century, when Freud's concept of 'castration anxiety' brought together the fear of sexual impotence and a more generally diffused fear of powerlessness. Various forms of male self-assertion and even aggression were seen as linked to the sexual drive or to men's need to demonstrate their masculinity to themselves and others. More recent scientific research has tended to confirm Freud's hypothesis: though most scientists now consider hormone levels to be less significant than cultural conditioning in fostering aggressive behaviour, there is evidence to show that women who have been injected with testosterone not only develop secondary male sexual characteristics but also tend to become more aggressive, while men injected with female hormones tend to become less aggressive.

It was perhaps not entirely fortuitous that the pioneering work of Freud, Havelock Ellis, Krafft-Ebing and other analysts of male and female sexuality began towards the end of the nineteenth century, amid the first stirrings of female emancipation. Kern (*Anatomy and Destiny*) has suggested a close link between the late nineteenth-century obsession with male physical strength and men's psycho-sexual anxieties arising from the emergence of women's sexual consciousness about that time:

8.2   For over 50 years, the Charles Atlas magazine advertisements held out to the world's adolescents the prospect of becoming sexually potent 'he-men' by following his bodybuilding courses.

'While some literature on gender roles in the late nineteenth century began to consider the advantages of acknowledging, or even cultivating, active female sex roles, a large body of material reveals the traditional man defensive and protesting. One reaction to emergent female sexuality by the men was sexual confusion and sexual failure. The male sexual ego, conditioned as it was to always dominate passive female sexual objects, was for a time paralysed by the new sex roles that accompanied the feminist movement. Of course not all men became impotent, but the literature on manliness reveals an increasingly anxious preoccupation with the causes and treatment of psychic impotence.'[1]

The overcoming of 'weakness' by exercise and the building of the body was, Kern argues, part of a struggle against the insecurities felt by some men who were becoming conscious of their changing sex roles. Any examination of the copious literature on muscular development and physical culture which emerged around the turn of the century will confirm Kern's hypothesis. The constant references to reversal of the 'physical degeneration' of men, to the strengthening of weak and undeveloped physiques and the use of bodybuilding techniques for the promotion of 'manliness' and the formation of 'complete men', can be read as at least implying, if not openly stating, the supposed effectiveness of strength training and muscular development as prophylactics against the widely-feared problem of male sexual impotence.

It took the eccentric but well-attuned Bernarr Macfadden to recognise the nature of this male anxiety and to name it openly. In his 1900 work *The Virile Powers of Superb Manhood*, he took up and enthusiastically bandied about the term 'virility', redolent as it was with suggestions of sexual confidence and energy, and certainly more seemingly scientific in connotation than Walt Whitman's use of terms such as 'amativeness' and 'mettle' to refer to his own identification of physical muscularity with sexual potency. Macfadden's influence on the world of muscular development was of long duration, and for the generations that followed the code-word 'virility' was a feature of advertisements for books, equipment and food supplements aimed at fostering the development of a muscular body. Though given a curious new twist in more recent times, when steroids and other androgenic drugs may have the effect of lowering the body's own testosterone production and causing temporary impotence, the appeal of bodybuilding as a supposed enhancer of sexual prowess has had a powerful effect on many of its adherents and promoters.

The world's largest-selling contemporary bodybuilding magazine, *Muscle and Fitness*, owes much of its circulation success to the association of muscular development with increased sexual potency. Unlike most similar magazines, whose covers usually depict a prominent male bodybuilder exercising or posing for the camera, *Muscle and Fitness* almost invariably has a cover-shot of a male and female bodybuilder, or male bodybuilder and swimsuited female model, posing together; the woman is usually running her hands over the male physique, and on occasion there is a suggestion of an erotic embrace. The cover, as is customary in such publications, is liberally sprinkled with bodybuilding slogans ('king-size delts', 'giant thighs', 'washboard abs'), but included among them are strategically-placed messages such as: 'Hard bodies are sexy', 'Trim, strong, sexy you', 'Strengthen your sexual muscles', 'Shaping a hard, sexy body', 'Stronger is sexier' and even 'Magic sex in muscles'.

These cover-slogans are clearly intended to convey the message of bodybuilding as an enhancer of sexual drive: the recurring word 'sexy' can be understood as referring primarily to sexual potency rather than sexual attractiveness. Occasional slogans make the point more explicitly: 'Don't Droop: Put Virility Power Into Your Body', proclaims the April 1987 cover, just below the caption 'Getting Big!' The cover-phrases often bear no relationship to the articles contained within the magazine itself, though occasional features with titles such as 'Exercise Makes You Sexy', 'Sex and Bodybuilding' or 'So You Want a Hard, Sexy Body' extol the benefits of exercise in hormone production and improved self-confidence. Reassuring or ego-boosting statements ('Our bodybuilding lifestyle puts you in tune with all the sensations and movements of your body that can make the sex act the ultimate thrill') encourage the belief that bodybuilding is 'a short-cut to increased sexuality.'[2]

A not insignificant feature of the *Muscle and Fitness* covers is that they have, in recent years, hardly ever portrayed a black bodybuilder. In a sport as dominated by outstanding black competitors as contemporary bodybuilding, this fact has sometimes led to suggestions of racial bias on the part of the editors, a theory which can hardly be substantiated in view of the extensive coverage given to black (and other non-Caucasian) competitors in the inside pages of the magazine — a coverage considerably higher than the ten per cent of the US population which blacks comprise. A more plausible explanation is that those readers who are attracted to buy *Muscle and Fitness* by its promise of a more vigorous sex life are predominantly middle-class whites, who need to be able to identify (if only in fantasy) with the sexually potent figures shown on the cover. The corollary of this theory — that Afro-Americans are less afflicted by anxiety as to declining libido or sexual impotence than are their white fellow-citizens — may or may not be true in fact. What matters is that the magazine cover (directed at 'casual' rather than subscription buyers) is the product of extensive marketing research aimed at identifying and responding to wish-fulfilment on the part of the largest segment of the potential market.

8.3 The *Muscle and Fitness*
     cover: the white male-
     white female coupling
     has proved a successful
     formula. The
     alternatives (white male-
     black female; black
     male-white female;
     black male-black
     female) would either
     pose difficult socio-
     sexual questions or lose
     their appeal to the wish
     fulfilment of white male
     readers.

8.4   The dominance-display theory
helps explain the interest in muscle-
building developed by many males
at puberty and through
adolescence. Testosterone-driven,
it relates to fantasies of dominance
over competitive males.

The message of improved sexual prowess, whether obliquely hinted-at or openly proclaimed, undoubtedly accounts for much of the fascination of bodybuilding amongst adolescent and young adult males, particularly in the primacy accorded to sheer muscular size over such qualities as proportion, symmetry and balance of development. The obsession with 'twenty-inch arms', for example, which haunts many enthusiastic adherents of the sport, is one of the signs of a more generalised adulation of sheer muscular bulk which perhaps has its origins in that identification of physical dominance with tribal leadership (and sexual rights over female members of the tribe) that can be observed in a number of 'primitive' cultures and among the higher apes. 'The dominant monkey', Desmond Morris has observed in relation to baboon behaviour, 'is always much larger than his underlings. He has only to hold himself erect and his greater body size does the rest.'[3] In human societies, Morris remarks, the creation of specialised sub-cultures provides the needed opportunity for tribal leadership and dominance mimicry: 'A champion canary-breeder or body-builder would, in all probability, have no chance whatsoever of enjoying the heady fruits of dominance, were it not for his involvement in his specialised sub-group.'[4] Such an approach does much to explain the appeal of muscular development within the bodybuilding sub-culture, and in particular to indicate the basically non-erotic nature of the fascination of heterosexual males with the more highly developed bodies of other males. That the response is primitive in nature does not detract from its cultural significance, and indeed would account in large measure for the particular increase of interest in muscle-building developed by many males at the onset of puberty. Viewed in this light, the sexual connotations of the activity are seen to relate to fantasies of social, and particularly sexual, dominance over competitive males in the conquest of available female sex partners.

The ethological theories of Desmond Morris have not met with unqualified acceptance in academic circles — perhaps because, more than other writers on comparative animal behaviour from Konrad Lorenz to Robert Ardrey and, more recently, Jared Diamond,[5] he has committed the intellectual sin of being an unashamedly popular writer. More importantly, there is often a tendency in ethology and sociobiology to undervalue or explain away the role of specifically human behaviour responses (notably language) in both communication and cognition. Nonetheless, such theories do command a certain persuasive force if they can account for patterns of human behaviour which, though not immediately explicable in terms of complex 'evolved' social interaction, become clearly meaningful once they are seen in the context of more primitive social groupings. Whether or not Morris' approach to dominance mimicry and sexual rivalry fits into this latter category, a degree of confirmation of his views can be found in some contemporary psychological and psychoanalytical theories. In his 1980 work *The Masculine Dilemma*[6], Gregory Rochlin drew on psychoanalysis to explore the insecurity and instability of men's hold upon their masculinity. According to Rochlin's theory, this inherent vulnerability and the instability of identity which it entails leads to the constant necessity for men to 'prove themselves'. In this process, the 'defining other' is the homosexual, who has opted out of the competitiveness of male rivalry: heterosexual males are engaged in competitive behaviour with other males in order to assert their maleness, or to re-assure themselves as to their masculine identity. Paradoxically, therefore, the 'arbiters' of what it takes to be a successful male are other males — including, implicitly, homosexuals who are seen as failed males in opposition to whom heterosexuals must define and position themselves. Rochlin's theory has been strongly criticised by Jonathan Dollimore (*Sexual Dissidence*), who rejects the notion of a homosexual 'opting out' derived from a fear of the other sex but does suggest that 'heterosexual masculinity involves at least intense anxieties about, and probably fears of, the same (sex)'.[7]

An example of the male interest in other male bodies can be found in men's common fascination with comparisons of penis size and length. The penis and its operations are a constant source of male anxiety and insecurity: as a 'part of the body' (in John Webb's words) 'over which he has no control, which moves and stirs on a whim and which has intentions of its own'[8], it is the primary focus of sexual uncertainty in a context where the ability to 'perform' is a sign of masculinity and male adequacy. Curiosity about the sexual organs of others can thus be aimed at self-reassurance or a validation of one's own gender identity. Diamond points out that it is a misconception to see penile display as being aimed at women.

'Many women say that they are turned on by a man's voice, legs, and shoulders more than by the sight of his penis. A telling point is that the women's magazine *Viva* initially published photos of nude men but dropped them after surveys showed lack of female interest. When *Viva*'s nude men disappeared, the number of female readers increased, and the number of male readers decreased. Evidently, the male readers were the ones buying *Viva* for its nude photos. While we can agree that the human penis is an organ of display, the display is intended not for women but for fellow men.'[9]

8.5 The penis sheath is a form of sexual dominance-display aimed primarily at other males. Dani native, New Guinea.

As with the penis sheaths worn by some New Guinea tribesmen, the possession and display of a large penis is seen as a sign of sexual prowess or status, aimed (if only implicitly) at other men. Given the well-established symbolism that associates the hard, muscular body with the engorged, erect and potent phallus, the need for reassurance and confirmation of male adequacy (whether of the sexual organs or of the body as a whole) can be seen as grounded not so much in homosexual attraction as in heterosexual status rivalry and its attendant performance anxiety. (This is not, of course, to deny the point overlooked by Diamond, that at least some of *Viva*'s male readership may have been motivated by homosexual voyeurism.)

The phallic symbolism of the male body is most clearly observable in men's use of sport and physical activity as a means of enhancing their body-image and thus gaining status in the eyes of other men. 'The sportsman straining for excellence, the body-builder pumping iron', writes Rosalind Miles, 'is not doing it for a woman.' Miles points out that the organ which is the chief focus of male anxiety, the penis, cannot be enlarged or 'built' by the methods applied to muscular development: the aura of strength, physical potency and masculinity is therefore sought through a process of transference or displacement whereby the body itself becomes the organ of sexual dominance-display. Muscle thus does for the body-image what the young man cannot do for his penis: referring to actors such as Arnold Schwarzenegger and Sylvester Stallone, Miles wryly observes that

'each becomes a public phallus, huge, rock-hard, gleaming and veined with blood. And as the phallus first stirred and came to life in the primeval swamps of the male imagination, so males above all are uniquely alert to its siren call and baleful power. Becoming an athlete, body-builder or 'jock' is therefore a clear and overt statement of manhood and male potency, and the clearest possible message to other men.'[10]

The oft-repeated observation that the classic image of the muscular mesomorph reflects not women's but men's view of desirable manhood — or, as it is sometimes stated, a mistaken male view of what women find attractive[11] — is seen by Miles as confirming men's emotional exclusion of women. Based on an inherent inability to offer warm and intimate relations with other men, the dominance-display becomes a form of aversion therapy for warm and equal male-female relations. Though there is some evidence that women's attitudes to the developed male body may be changing towards acceptance or even attraction (perhaps as a result of women's increased self-confidence and confidence in their own bodies), Rosalind Miles has articulated an important element of the feminist critique of the male body. Her incisive analysis underlines, moreover, the significant contribution which contemporary women's writing is making to the discussion and analysis of the semantics of masculinity.

8.6 Muscle as dominance-display: the body becomes a 'public phallus ... huge, rock-hard, gleaming and veined with blood'.

The grounding of this impetus towards dominance mimicry in deep-seated fears of sexual impotence may help explain the need for its expression through the super-normal visual stimuli of male muscle bulk and masculine body-shape, though there seems little reason to suppose that for most males who pursue the goal of muscular development this basic urge reaches pathological proportions or results in unusually predatory social behaviour. There is a dearth of hard evidence in this area, which does not appear to have attracted much interest among sociologists and social psychologists, and firm conclusions must await future statistical analysis. Anecdotal evidence and personal observation, however, suggest that whilst most men engaged in bodybuilding at the recreational level appear to form equally stable and lasting sexual relationships as occur in the surrounding society as a whole, the incidence of marriage breakdown is somewhat higher than average amongst those engaged in competitive bodybuilding, particularly at the professional level.

8.7   Despite its emergence at
the time of the Women's
Liberation Movement in
the late 1970s, women's
bodybuilding is
generally not
considered 'politically
correct' amongst
ideologically-driven
feminists. Successful and
highly intelligent women
such as Carla Dunlap
have had to combat
image problems not
confronted by other
women athletes.

Though a number of professional (and advanced amateur) bodybuilders do have a reputation as 'super-studs' obsessed with female sexual conquest, many of those experiencing the repeated breakdown of sexual relationships appear to be subject to the pressures of high-level competition which equally affect other sports. They are also exposed to the stress of survival in the artificial world of 'show business', a psychological strain which is also reflected in the marital instability of many film-stars, politicians and other personalities whose lives are the object of constant public scrutiny. To these factors must be added the common use by competitive bodybuilders of anabolic steroids, the psychological effect of which often includes increased aggression and erratic variation in emotional states, neither of which is conducive to stable sexual relationships.

The dominance-display theory of bodybuilding (and of muscular development in general) is a useful approach to understanding its appeal to sexually active males, though as we have suggested this is only a part of the total picture. It does, however, go some way towards explaining the negative reactions of some women who find the super-normal physical stimuli of muscular development intimidating and at times express even more vocal feelings of disgust and revulsion than do men at the sight of the developed male body. It would also help to account for the general rejection of male muscular display which is characteristic of contemporary hard-core feminism. Nor has the entry of women into the world of bodybuilding had a discernible effect in modifying radical feminist attitudes towards the display of muscle, the latter being seen as so inextricably linked with phallic symbolism that a specific language of 'women's muscularity' is inherently contradictory. Women bodybuilders, in this view, can at most incorporate the worst features of sexist stereotyping, combining emulation of the male dominance-display with the erotically-tinged posing of a female sex-object. Notwithstanding the origins of female bodybuilding in the general trend of the 1970s towards women's liberation, the basic socio-sexual orientation of most female bodybuilders, as research studies have indicated, is not generally attuned to feminist goals and tends to be conservative in terms of sexual politics (if not of sexual morality). Based largely on the direct transposition of a male understanding of muscularity into the female domain, the world of women's bodybuilding appears generally uninterested in the radical re-evaluation of male and female gender roles, and most female bodybuilders appear happy with the role of 'sex-object', believing that their training makes them more attractive to men.[12]

It is clear that the sexual drive plays a vitally important role in the pursuit of physical development, and that in at least some cases it is the dominant factor. That an extreme concentration on muscular development can cause a reduction in testosterone and prolactin production (through body fatigue or anabolic steroid use) and thus decrease the male sexual drive, hardly seems to matter. In an age of sex symbols, it is the symbol rather than the reality that counts.

239

BODIES ON THE BORDERLINE

The association of muscular development with heightened sexual capacity goes hand in hand with the image of visible muscularity as an erotically attractive signal. Just as sexual vigour is marketed by magazines and the purveyors of gym equipment and bodybuilding diet supplements, so the promise of sexual desirability is held out to muscle-builders by the manufacturers of designer workout clothing on the implicit premise that appearance in the weight-room is a form of seductive display. Even outside the 'gym culture', the motivation to take up some form of physical exercise is often grounded in the desire to make the body more physically attractive rather than in the quest for better health or improved fitness. In this context, the relationship between heightened muscularity and the transmission of sexually-oriented visual messages becomes so intimate as to raise the question whether the display of the muscular body is primarily, even exclusively, an erotic transaction.

This is, of course, by no means a peculiarly modern issue, and the difficulty of identifying a completely unequivocal significance in the 'messages' of bodily display has haunted the Western consciousness for centuries. Even in a culture where religious belief has waned and secular values predominate, the inheritance of the Christian cultural tradition has invested the body with an ambiguous status. Nowhere is this more apparent than in the world of art, where the nude body was both — and often at one and the same time — the supreme symbol of proportion and reason, and the most effective vehicle for the expression of sexual feeling. Indeed, as Edward Lucie-Smith has pointed out[13], until the scientific writing of the last 150 years, painted nudes were always more candid about sexual feeling than was any written form of communication. It was not, in fact, until the scandalous appearance of works such as D.H. Lawrence's *Lady Chatterly's Lover* (1928) and Henry Miller's *Tropic of Cancer* (1934) that the language of the body was used in Anglo-Saxon literature with the frankness attaching to pictorial art.[14] The whole point of the latter was precisely its capacity for ambiguous messages: unlike the written word, which presupposes a one-to-one relationship between the name of a thing and the thing named, the painting could ostensibly depict one subject and yet evoke vivid images of another. Thus, the human body could be depicted nude in the Western artistic tradition — and even carry more than a hint of eroticism — while the apparent 'subject' of the painting was a moralising scene from mythology or Biblical history. Here as elsewhere, a single image may permit two or more quite different readings, the beholder's particular frame of reference determining which of them prevails.

8.8   For men as well as women, appearance in the weight-room may be a form of seductive display – particularly as more women take up gymnasium training.

The messages emitted by the body, in fact, depend for their significance at least as much on their recipients as on their senders. Without a recipient who reacts to the message, it is not a message at all but merely an unsuccessful attempt at communication. If sender and recipient do not share the same cultural language or the same expectations, then either no message is conveyed or else the message received differs from that which was intended. If we fail to see anything erotic in a Japanese painting of a love-scene, it is because our cultural language differs from that of Japan and we have not learned to read that country's traditional pictorial language. Equally, some early European travellers in the Pacific found the mere sight of bare-breasted island maidens so erotically stimulating that they remained for a time in a state of constant sexual arousal, whereas the local males (scarcely an impotent breed of men) managed to go about their daily work with equanimity. Though the 'senders' emitted similar messages to both groups, the cultural background of the recipients differed markedly and the messages deviated accordingly.

These observations underscore the difficulty of making valid or even moderately defensible statements about the specific messages emitted by the developed body. More particularly, the extent to which the display of a muscular body is an erotic transaction, while it may to some degree depend on its originator's intentions, its specific form, and the context of its presentation, will ultimately be determined by the psycho-sexual make-up of those who are at the viewing end of the display. Some people, we are told, are 'turned on' by Sumo wrestlers, while still others find the sight of nurses in starched uniforms irresistibly erotic. There is simply no accounting for the vast array of human sexual preferences and fantasies, and the message received may bear no relationship to the intrinsic purposes of the sender or the activity in which he or she engages.

With the above provisos, however, some general propositions may be advanced concerning the language of advanced muscularity, and an attempt may usefully be made to explore the at times tenuous lines of demarcation which *in principle* separate the muscular and the erotic modes of bodily display. The issue is posed in acute form in competitive bodybuilding, an activity in which a number of performers appear in public in a near-nude state, and move through a sequence of poses designed for no other purpose than to display their physical attributes to a group of interested spectators. The recipients of the body messages conveyed are in attendance precisely because they derive some form of satisfaction from observing the relatively unclothed bodies of (usually young) athletic men and, in some cases, women. Put in such stark terms, the question of erotic attraction can hardly be avoided.

8.9 '... A near-nude performance, designed to display one's physical attributes to a group of interested spectators who derive satisfaction from observing the relatively unclothed bodies of athletic men ... The question of eroticism can hardly be avoided.'

8.10 The 'posing pouch' photos popular in some physique magazines of the 1950s and 60s pandered to the tastes of homosexual readers who did not yet have access to their own specialised publications.

The issue is further complicated by the visual media which convey to the public the pictorial image of the bodybuilder. Some of the publicity photographs (particularly of female trainers) found in bodybuilding journals are hard to distinguish from those in soft-core erotic magazines, and indeed some erotic publications specialise in photographs of bodybuilders. In particular, there is a well-established section of the market aimed at the homosexual community which concentrates on photographs of well-muscled young men[15]. Even well-known and successful professional bodybuilders, including the 1982 Mr Olympia Chris Dickerson and internationally-placed professionals such as Bill Grant and Tony Pearson, have posed for nude photographs or videos targeted primarily at the gay community. A nude photograph of Arnold Schwarzenegger in bodybuilding pose, taken in the 1970s by an anonymous photographer, was recently published by *Spy* magazine and has since been widely reproduced, prompting discussion as to Arnold's willingness to pander to homosexual tastes even though it may have been originally intended for publication in *Cosmopolitan* (Arnold subsequently withdrew his permission).[16] It is clear that there is a recognisable market-segment which finds muscular development erotically stimulating: while the 'legitimate' bodybuilding magazines pander mainly to the sexual response of heterosexual males through mildly erotic photographs of female bodybuilders, the alternative market catering for homosexual readers and viewers is a good deal more explicit.

The use of muscularity as an erotic signal is not of recent origin. Eugen Sandow was not averse to displaying his body for the purpose of exciting an overtly sexual response, and although in his public appearances this took a heterosexual form (in the performances billed as 'for ladies only', where he would pose dressed only in a silk posing-strap) it is probable that photographs of the classical poses in which he appeared clad in a false fig-leaf were being circulated in the English homosexual community towards the turn of the century[17]. It is also worthy of note that the three main periods in which the portrayal of the nude male body in Western art was pursued with most vigour — the age of classical Greece, the Renaissance and the latter part of the nineteenth century — were periods in which homosexuality had a more than usually observable profile in public life.

The overtones of homoerotic display which had dogged bodybuilding since its inception were magnified in the period from the late 1940s to the late 1960s, owing largely to the images conveyed by photographs of 'artistic' male posing following the work of Townsend and others. The most successful bodybuilding photographer of this period was Alonzo Hannagan, known as 'Lon'. In the late 1940s, his work was appearing in physique photo albums with titles such as *Masculine Perfection*, where well-known bodybuilders of the time such as John Grimek were shown in aesthetic poses. Other bodybuilders were even described, without apparent irony, as master *poseurs*, and their photographs were for sale as 'athletic poses' or

8.11 Masquerading as 'art studies', the physiques in some of the pseudo-bodybuilding magazines were of models who had, to all appearance, never been near a barbell in their lives.

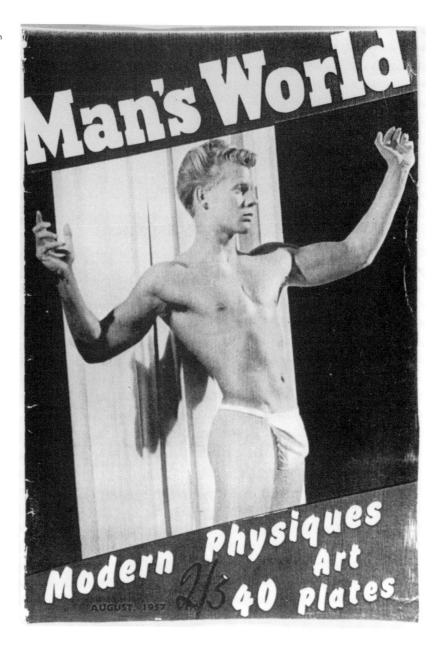

'artistic pose arrangements'. Lon was the chief exponent of this type of photography, and by the 1960s he had opened studios in London and several cities in the USA[18]. Occasionally, two bodybuilders were photographed together in dual poses, perhaps in mock combat or wrestling, as if to stress the element of homosexual attraction.

Even mainstream bodybuilding magazines such as the *British Amateur Weightlifter and Body-Builder* and the *Reg Park Journal* carried such material, which along with photographs of recognised and professional bodybuilders included 'studies' of nude or near-nude young men who had visibly never been near a barbell in their lives.

On the basis of this evidence, it is tempting to conclude with Margaret Walters that (male) bodybuilding is essentially a form of erotic display, directed chiefly if not exclusively at other males. In her feminist critique of the male body, *The Nude Male*, Walters places her analysis of bodybuilding in the section entitled 'Men for Men', alongside homoerotic art and photography[19]. Walters' book is one of the most serious and thought-provoking treatments of the male body ever to appear in print, and her understanding of bodybuilding as primarily a voyeuristic homosexual activity is therefore worthy of attention.

In evaluating Walters' views, it is important to recognise her avowedly feminist perspective and the element of personal taste inherent in her critique. 'Could anyone,' she asks, 'seriously want to look like one of Michelangelo's expressively distorted nudes? Or like the Farnese Hercules, if it comes to that?'[20] These are of course rhetorical questions, to which the implicit answer is: 'Of course not'. Such an answer, however, manifestly ignores the evidence that there are (not inconsiderable) numbers of men who, to all appearance, seriously *do* want to look like these heavily-muscled exemplars. Whether such extreme muscularity is found attractive or grotesque is no doubt a matter of personal taste. It is perhaps worth noting in this context that some psychologists have found that men tend to react more favourably (and, in the case of homosexual men, to react more positively in erotic terms) to muscularity than do women, many of whom find extreme muscularity more threatening than attractive[21]. Gender differences, in this case, may well affect the taste of the beholder, and in Margaret Walters' case it is possible to argue that the 'distancing' provided by artistic treatment (of which she generally approves) confers upon the muscular body a degree of acceptability not echoed in its live display.

The problem of interpretation often resides in an over-preoccupation with the recipients of bodily messages rather than the messages themselves. If some homosexuals are attracted by the sight of muscular male bodies, it is concluded, then the point of bodybuilding must be homosexual voyeurism. This is rather like arguing that if some men are sexually aroused by the sight of women such as nurses in starched uniforms, then the point of nursing is sado-masochistic sexual arousal. While the analogy is far from perfect — bodybuilding, unlike nursing, is essentially a form of sarcous display — it nonetheless serves to shift our attention away from the assumption that the message received by some is a key to the nature of the message itself.

8.12 Bob Paris is the first, and to date the only, major international bodybuilding champion to have proclaimed his homosexuality openly.

Finally, it is relevant to point out (even in the absence of hard statistical evidence) that the opinion of those involved in the administration and practice of contemporary bodybuilding is overwhelmingly to the effect that homosexuality is no more prevalent in the bodybuilding world than in the community at large. The great majority of bodybuilders and their audiences are visibly heterosexual in orientation, at times even aggressively so. In the top professional ranks, a few bodybuilders have been known to be gay, though to date only one internationally-placed competitor (Bob Paris) has openly admitted his homosexuality. Schwarzenegger, who deliberately set out to eradicate the presumed association between bodybuiding and homosexuality, has perceptively referred to the need to distinguish between bodybuilders themselves and their audiences. Claiming (somewhat unimaginably) not to know of any competition bodybuilders who were gay, he has agreed that there is a not inconsiderable homosexual following of the sport — though adding that it also attracts younger women, older women and heterosexual men.[22]

To disagree with Margaret Walters' thesis is not to deny either the importance of her critique or the issues to which it draws attention. In the first place, although a distinction can be drawn in principle between the public display of muscularity and the erotic stimulation it may evoke in some individual spectators, the fact remains that the line between erotic and non-erotic display of the body is always, at best, tenuous. In the world of high art where the distinction cannot always readily be drawn between erotic and non-erotic nudes, as in the world of nudism where the limits of propriety are an ever-present issue, the sexual messages of the disclosed body are so potent that they can never be entirely denied[23].

Secondly, and importantly, Margaret Walters tends to concentrate on what she calls the 'overlap' between bodybuilding and overtly homosexual pinups, to the exclusion of the difference in codes of presentation which separates the 'straight' bodybuilding magazines from the homosexual 'physique' publications. In the latter, which Mark Gabor correctly describes as 'transitional' publications (the link between early homoerotic photography and the overtly gay magazines of the 1970s and later years), the instrumental use of bodybuilders for erotic purposes was as much a subterfuge as the portrayal of naturists and sun-worshippers in nudist publications. Gabor points out that the physique magazines of the 50s and 60s

8.13 The physique magazine used coded references ('magnificent art plates', 'virile manhood') to indicate the inclusion of homoerotic photography.

'are ambiguously titled; references are made to the "philosophy" of the physical culturist; the editors feel called upon to state such purposes as "aiding the artist, sculptor, photographer, and model"; no copyright is claimed; sets of photographs are offered for sale; one or two dull, poorly illustrated articles may appear on judo or karate, evidently so the magazine can claim another "instructional" function.'[24]

There is, he notes, a world of difference between these publications and the mainstream bodybuilding magazines:

'The advertisements in the "straight" muscleman magazines are for body-building equipment, vitamin products, and other musclemen publications. Feature articles and illustrations stress physical fitness, competition, growing from weakling to superman, and attracting women. The principal readers are young men, from the age of puberty to the mid-thirties, interested mainly in building their bodies in a quest for self-confidence and admiration by their buddies and girl friends.'[25]

The change in legal regulations and censorship requirements which took place in the 1970s brought about the demise of the pseudo-art magazine and helped clarify the difference in principle which separates the bodybuilding and the erotic display, as well as the audiences at which they are directed.

To draw this distinction of principle may appear over-defensive, and it must be conceded that it does not always apply in practice. Indeed, there is a sense in which Margaret Walters is justified in including her discussion of bodybuilding under the heading 'Men for Men'. Although we have attempted to analyse the male bodybuilder —male audience relationship primarily in terms of the dominance-display theory of behaviour, the gradations of human sexuality are such that it makes little sense in practice to divide responses into two entirely discrete categories (homosexual/ non-homosexual). It is manifestly not the case that predominantly homosexual males can respond to the bodybuilding display only in erotic terms, totally different from those in which it is viewed by predominantly heterosexual males. The corollary of this proposition would suggest that, even for the latter group, it is difficult to separate out an element of repressed or sublimated sexual interest from the total spectrum of imaginative constructs, fantasies and personal obsessions of which their interest in muscular development is composed.

One of the most revealing aspects of the implicitly erotic content of highly developed muscularity is the phenomenon popularly known as 'musclephobia'. This relates to the extreme negative reaction experienced by some people at the sight of a minimally-clad muscular body, a reaction often described by those who experience it as 'disgust' or 'revulsion'. Few other forms of bodily display, body decoration or even mutilation produce such violent reactions or so potent a need for those who experience them to proclaim publicly their distaste or disapproval. Individuals who are deeply affected in this way are not merely indifferent to muscularity and its overtones, and are thus to be distinguished from those members (possibly a majority) of the community who have no appreciable interest in muscular display. The 'musclephobe', on the contrary, experiences an irrepressible urge to affirm his or her normality while denouncing as socially or sexually deviant those who exhibit any form of hyper-muscularity[26]. As a species of psychological repression, this phenomenon reveals by its very intensity at least as strong a reaction to the sight of muscularity as is found in those who respond favourably to it or even find it sexually arousing.

The Freudian understanding of repression is commonly accepted in contemporary psychological theory, even among those who would not see themselves as belonging to the Freudian school. In simplified terms, repression is a form of subconscious attraction, usually of a sexual nature, but that attraction is perceived (often because of upbringing or early childhood experience) as taboo: the conscious

8.14 Despite a number of differences of principle between the bodybuilding display and the erotic display, it is doubtful that the element of sublimated sexual interest can ever be divorced from the appreciation of muscular development.

8.15 'Sport allows men to gaze on and devour the male form without homosexuality being alleged or feared.' Surf carnival (Australia): iron man event.

mind therefore intervenes to deny the presence of such feelings, and forces them, as it were, underground. The more vocal the outward denial — in reality an attempt at self-persuasion or self-reassurance — the greater the extent of the repression involved. In the present instance, what is perceived as taboo and thus vociferously denied is a deep-seated tendency towards voyeurism.

In its more extreme forms, voyeurism (sometimes technically referred to as 'scopophilia') takes the form of a pathological interest, usually of a prurient nature, in viewing the unclad bodies of others. It can be a defence mechanism covering up a degree of sexual inadequacy, such that sexual arousal is obtained from the viewing of people either naked or undressing, rather than from conventional human sexual contact. Like many other 'abnormal' states, this is an extreme version of a phenomenon which in most people is present only in a latent form and is kept in balance or under control. It needs to be acknowledged, for instance, that attraction to bodybuilding display depends upon a certain element of voyeurism, though socially acceptable and even (as in the case of sport in general) legitimised by the public context of the display.

> 'Sport', writes Toby Miller, 'allows men to dissect other men's bodies in fetishistic (yet sporting) detail. It proffers a legitimate space within which men can gaze on and devour the male form without homosexuality being either alleged or feared. The fetish of admiring individual bodily components ('look at those triceps') gives a scientistic pleasure.'[27]

Whether tacitly repressed or vehemently denied, the 'devouring gaze' has an undoubted place in the total spectrum of visual transactions of which the public exhibition of muscularity is constituted.

There is some evidence to suggest that the contemporary re-appraisal of gender-roles following the Women's Liberation movement is significantly altering the context of erotic or quasi-erotic display of the male body. The traditional distinction — men are 'the sex that looks' whereas women are 'the sex that is looked at' — no longer appears to hold true in liberal Western cultures. The first stirrings of a change in attitude can be traced back to Sandow, whose 'ladies only' posing sessions (significantly contemporaneous with the age of women's emancipation) first established the unclad male figure as an object of public female scrutiny. The double legitimation involved (for women, the legitimacy of looking; for men, the legitimacy of being looked at) meant a profound change in socio-sexual expectations, though not till more recent times has the shift in general social values given widespread currency to the newer understanding.

8.16 The 'hunk' photograph: symbols of undoubted masculinity now have no hesitation in being photographed in various states of undress for posters or calendars.

Since the mid-1980s, the concept of 'Men for Women' has gained increasing acceptance in the presentation of the sexually attractive male body. The popularity of male stripping with female audiences, and particularly with younger women[28], has become well established, while symbols of undoubted masculinity such as football players now have no hesitation about being photographed in various states of undress for pin-up 'hunk' calendars, no longer inhibited by the suggestion that such photography is aimed at homophile audiences. The male strip-show and the 'hunk' calendar have their antecedents in the two traditional forms of expression of bodybuilding (the live display and the photographed pose), and it may well be that the renewed popularity of bodybuilding in the later 1970s, associated with the rise of the super-masculine Arnold Schwarzenegger, is equally related to the re-appraisal of gender-roles which occurred at that time.

In no field has this shift in attitude been more noticeable than that of advertising. In the print media, the initiator of the male-sex-object genre was the (US) series of Calvin Klein 'Obsession' underpants advertisements, which featured Bruce Weber's erotically-tinged photographs of bronzed, well-toned male models clad only in the maker's product. Weber's photos of 'virile muscular beach-boys', says Emmanuel Cooper, 'created a powerful, squeaky-clean eroticisation of the male body':

'Whether promoting the Calvin Klein perfume 'Obsession' or underpants, Weber's authoritative images combine elements of neo-classicism with a contemporary sense of sexual expression and vitality. Bodies are hard and perfectly formed, achieved by models spending many hours each week in the gym keeping in good shape. By implication the product is one which relates to and reflects classic, enduring qualities; they suggest a state of emotional and physical equilibrium, which is rationally rather than intuitively constructed. These are cool, laid-back figures who are totally in control. The models both offer and deny sex.'[29]

Other underwear makers (Hom, Fruit of the Loom) followed suit, and were soon emulated by jeans manufacturers (Levis, Guess) and makers of men's toiletries. Such was the popular appeal of these mildly erotic images that a number of them were enlarged and sold commercially in poster-shops. Television advertising has more recently ventured into this field, notably in the celebrated jeans commercial where a well-muscled young man enters a laundromat and proceeds to strip to his underpants whilst admiring young females (and shocked older ones) look on. By a scenario (a man doing his own washing) which suggests either that he is a 'sensitive, new-age guy' or that he is temporarily unattached and therefore sexually available, or both, the commercial effectively reinforces the bodily image of a well-built and desirable sex-object while maintaining an unambiguously heterosexual social context.

Because you'd like him to know you care

Baron

8.17 Like other commercial images, the men's underwear advertisement may use attractive features and lithe musculature to widen its appeal across the gender divide.

Advertisers claim that the success of these campaigns rested on the fact that women typically purchase such items for their male partners (as opposed, for instance, to electronic products and automobiles, where a predominantly male market is still wooed by the more traditional images of attractive female models). It seems likely, however, that the appeal is also to the not inconsiderable gay market in which male consumers buy for themselves or their partners: though explicitly homosexual messages are obviously to be avoided, the ambiguous sexuality projected by the lithe musculature of the male models (heavily muscled bodies are not generally used) is seen as appealing to both women and gay males.

The issue is further complicated by the emergence, in recent years, of the distinctively modern breed of female pop star and sexual icon exemplified by Madonna and Cher. Independent, assertive and sexually highly charged, such figures define themselves as being manifestly women in control — in particular, in control of their own sexual engagement. In videoclips and other media images, the new figure of the dominant female is often surrounded by muscular men, here reduced to the status of sexual toys, in a role-reversal reminiscent of that more discreetly hinted-at in the celebrated swimming pool sequence of *Gentlemen Prefer Blondes*, where Jane Russell sang 'Ain't There Anyone Here for Love?' to a chorus-line of preening swimsuited male athletes. Unlike the earlier movie, there is less appearance of a send-up in the contemporary performance or videoclip, where certain images verge on the mildly (or even explicitly) pornographic without being generally regarded as exploitative or sexist since the chief protagonist is female. The sexual imagery here is explicitly subversive of traditional gender-roles, whether the purely decorative male appears as suggestive background (in a beefcake version of the male vocalist's traditionally female chorus-line) or whether his sensuously glistening body is the focus of more overt erotic attention on the part of the singer-seductress. The power-symbolism of the muscular male body is here contradicted or denied, not by the presence of attenuating features in the physique itself or its pose, but by the dominant role of the empowered woman. It is perhaps not surprising that the implicit transmutation of the traditionally super-masculine 'hunk' into a sexual plaything has turned stars such as Madonna and Cher into highly popular icons of gay culture.

In both advertising and other areas of popular media such as the videoclip, images which a generation earlier would have been perceived as unambiguously homoerotic have today acquired a more universal socio-sexual currency. As John Leland and others have put it:

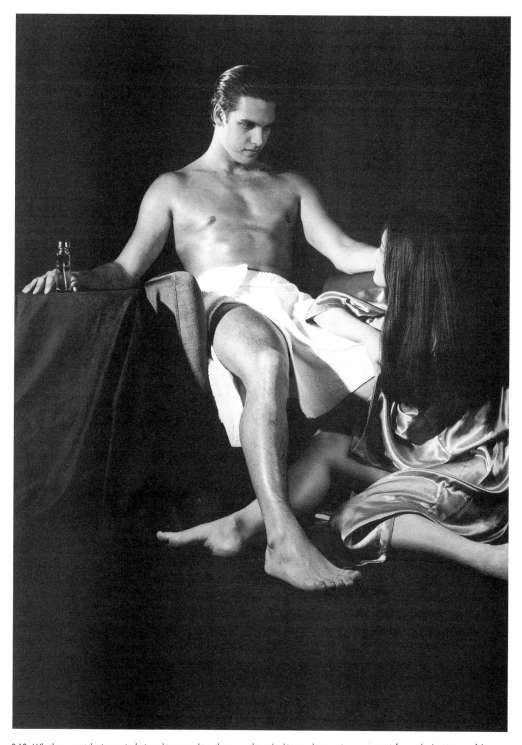

8.18 Whether or not the image is designed to appeal to other men, the onlooking and approving woman reinforces the legitimacy of the male body as object of the gaze.

'What's new about the [Calvin] Klein ads, as well as most of Madonna's recent work, is that they flaunt specifically homoerotic imagery. As gay-bashing has become one of the most common hate crimes in America, gay iconography is bubbling up defiantly in mainstream media ... [Madonna has] raided gay subculture's closet for the best of her ideas. Like Klein, she isn't just taking explicit sex mainstream; she's taking explicit homosex mainstream.'[30]

How far the homoerotic tradition has succeeded in deconstructing stereotypical constructions of maleness and created a non-aggressive and pro-feminist (even androgynous) imagery of the male body is a question to which we shall later turn. For the moment, it is worth noting that a reading of men's bodies first developed in the context of a specific (gay) sub-culture has been increasingly appropriated by the popular media and is now routinely aimed at an audience not explicitly defined in terms of any particular sexual preference.

The display of the developed male body appears, in some Western cultures at least, uncertainly poised on the borderline between curiosity and desire, between fascination and seduction, between fetish and phobia. If feminism has changed women's perceptions of themselves, definitions of masculinity have also changed in the process. Female empowerment has entailed a radical re-evaluation of the male body as object of the 'devouring gaze', and as if to highlight the completeness of the reversal of gender-roles, the images chosen to represent the newly-objectified male have been those most suggestive of male power and dominance — the muscular male body. We can understand in this context John Webb's observation that 'if fat is a feminist issue, then muscle is a masculine issue'.[31] That we shall ever see the definition of pornography extended to include women's sexual exploitation of the male physique seems highly doubtful, however logical such a culmination of modern trends might appear. The messages of muscularity cover such a range of human aspirations and reactions that their content in any individual act of communication will to some extent move beyond the control of their originator and depend in large measure on the personal, sexual and social preconceptions of their recipient.

Sex Show or Sport?

For most of its hundred years of history, the bodybuilding exhibition — the chief forum for the public demonstration of muscular development — has occupied a curiously uncertain zone lying somewhere between sporting activity, entertainment and erotic display. For the last fifty of those years, sporadic attempts have been made at the organisational level to dissipate some of the aura of ambiguity, notably by emphasising the sporting character of organised competition. The recognition of bodybuilding by the US Amateur Athletic Union in 1940 was accompanied by the formulation of competition rules which remain basically similar from one organisation to another, those laid down by the International Federation of Bodybuilders (IFBB) being the most commonly applied.

In addition to an extensive set of rules covering judging criteria and procedures and the accreditation of official judges, an important factor in the attempt to classify bodybuilding as a respectable sporting activity was the regulation of acceptable costume. In earlier years, male competitors had at times appeared in states of semi-undress which were to say the least questionable: underpants, jock-straps and G-strings had all made their appearance on the contest stage, to the delight or outrage of audiences depending on individual taste. The IFBB rules set out to abolish such aberrant practices: 'Men competitors', they stated, 'must wear trunks which are clean and decent. Men are not allowed to wear bikini-type trunks'; in the later rules for women the costume 'must conform to accepted standards of taste and decency.'[32] Over the last twenty years, costumes for men and women have tended to become briefer and higher-cut at the rear, a fact which officials might well put down to a change in 'acceptable standards' over that time.

A further, and highly significant, move on the part of officials was aimed to establish the bodybuilder as a 'sporting' figure rather than an object of erotic interest. The bodybuilder was given the earnest moral advice that he or she was 'expected to serve as an example, both morally and physically, in order to inspire other young people to participate in our sport.' In support of this exhortation, the IFBB stipulated that

'It is a serious offence for any bodybuilder to allow themselves to be photographed in the nude, or show any genitalia. Any bodybuilders (men or women) found guilty of such an offence will be suspended from the IFBB for a period of time to be determined by the Disciplinary Committee.'[33]

The rule appears not to have always been applied in practice, or at least not to have adversely affected the careers of a number of male and female bodybuilders who have posed for nude photographs or even made erotic videos ranging from nude posing to various forms of soft-core pornography. Whether a blind eye was turned by officials or whether such activities did not come to their attention, the existence of the rule is a significant reminder of the peculiar susceptibility of bodybuilding to turn into a form of erotic exhibition and of the obvious sensitivity of officials and organisers on this score. It is hard to think of any other sporting activity in which such a rule would be conceivable, let alone necessary.

8.19 The 'moon shot' or display of the partly-bared buttocks has been barred from some bodybuilding competitions.

Similar concerns regarding propriety were to lead the IFBB in more recent years to outlaw certain poses which were considered suggestive or potentially indecent. Notable among these was the so-called 'moon shot' in which the competitor touches his toes with back turned to the audience. The pose is still permitted by a number of (non-IFBB) organisations, on the ground that it permits competitors to display their hamstring and calf development, though it is easy to understand why the pose (particularly when performed in trunks cut high across the buttocks) might cause concern among an official body anxious to promote the image of the bodybuilder as a 'moral and physical example' to youth.

While official vigilance had some effect in minimising or at least reducing the erotic overtones of muscle display at the organised competitive level, perhaps a more significant development in the overall image of bodybuilding lay in the greater liberty of social expression and open publication which was becoming accepted by the 1970s, especially in relation to sexually-oriented material. Magazines intended for erotic interest could now be published for what they in fact were, and it was no longer necessary for them to masquerade as collections of 'physique studies' of bodybuilders — or, for that matter, publications intended for dedicated naturists or sun-lovers. Whatever one's judgment on the emergence of this specialised literature, we have already noted its effect in separating out the serious market for bodybuilding publications from that aimed purely at sexual gratification. From the 1970s onwards, any sexual (and particularly homosexual) overtones in mainstream bodybuilding magazines would at most be implicit, and the 'athletic young models' had disappeared from their pages, though an element of homosexual voyeurism is still evident in some men's 'lifestyle' and fitness magazines.[34]

In varying degrees, the above developments have reduced the aura of uncertainty surrounding bodybuilding and in particular its identification as a form of conspicuous erotic display. They have not, however, been entirely successful in freeing it from its traditional representation as an abnormal mode of quasi-sexual behaviour or enabled it to achieve an undisputed status as a sporting activity.

'A big contest like Mr Olympia or Mr Universe,' writes Margaret Walters, '[is] a beauty pageant ..., with the strongman, just like the beauty queen, offering up his body as an object to be admired. He deforms his body even more than she does; the irony is that those grotesquely developed muscles are for display, not use ... Weight-lifting as such is no longer even part of the contest ritual, which centers on a series of pseudo-classical poses in which one set of muscles after another is — literally — erected.'[35]

8.20 Men's lifestyle and fitness magazines sometimes include 'hunk' shots aimed at male readers, though explicitly homoerotic photos are now generally confined to the overtly gay publications.

These views would probably be echoed by most of those observers of the world of competitive bodybuilding who are not attracted towards its cultural paradigms. Even more than for most sports (assuming that the term 'sport' is justified), it is a world apart, a world of its own. Anne Honer has described it as 'an intersubjectively transmitted, extraordinary world of meaning with its own criteria of relevance'[36], while others have characterised it as an autonomous subculture with its own status hierarchy, rituals and specific system of language and demeanour[37]. It is a world in which arcane terms of jargon such as striated glutes, diamond calves, abdominal vacuums and pumped lats all have meaning and significance, and where the relative merits of high reps, pre-exhaustion, staggered sets, split routines and a multitude of other techniques are eagerly debated by insiders while to those outside they seem meaningless or futile. Bodybuilding contests and works on bodybuilding are generally considered 'fair game' for TV commentators, newspaper journalists and reviewers who traditionally grasp the opportunity to indicate their personal distaste and thus implicit normality by holding up the activity to mild ridicule.[38]

In attempting some kind of objective appraisal of bodybuilding as an autonomous activity, it is useful to refer to the terms of Margaret Walters' illuminating if critical analysis quoted above. Her comparison with weightlifting (the 'muscles are for display, not use') implies that the move from instrumental to representational muscularity which marked the birth of bodybuilding underlines the 'uselessness' of muscular display, a view often advanced in order to contest the sporting status of bodybuilding. As Johan Huizinga's authoritative study of games and sport (*Homo Ludens*) has argued, the very 'uselessness' of all sporting activity — from golf to pigeon-racing — is precisely what constitutes them as sports or pastimes[39]. Christopher Lasch, who disputes a number of Huizinga's conclusions, agrees that the point of sporting mastery is

> '... to ratify a supremely difficult accomplishment, to give pleasure; to forge a bond between [the sportsman] and his audience, which consists in a shared appreciation of a ritual executed flawlessly, with deep feeling and a sense of style and appreciation.'[40]

The element of display and representation, Lasch argues (in a passage which has particular relevance to bodybuilding) is a vitally important reminder of the former connections between play, ritual and drama. Ceremony requires witnesses (in this case spectators), who are conversant with the rules of the performance and its underlying meaning — a point which, as we have observed, was also made by Barthes in his essay on all-in wrestling.

The suggestion that bodybuilding competition is a form of beauty pageant has rather more substance. Women's bodybuilding competitions do at times tend to elicit from male members of the audience a form of quasi-erotic response, though this has undoubtedly much to do with the still-uncertain status of women's bodybuilding, in which the 'Playboy bunny' image sometimes vies with that of a 'man in a bikini top'. Such a response appears less common at the higher levels of women's competition, and is not paralleled in the case of female (and, for obvious reasons, male) audience reaction at the men's contests. The women's beauty pageant, on the other hand, is overtly to do with (appropriately sanitised) sexual messages, and its otherwise unlikely combination of swimming costumes and high heels — the latter being intended to accentuate the movement of the buttocks[41] and suggest sexual vulnerability[42] — makes clear the overtones of erotic voyeurism which have led to the vocal denunciation and even disruption of pageants such as the Miss World Contest by feminist groups.

8.21 Like other forms of sporting mastery, the bodybuilding contest aims 'to ratify a supremely difficult accomplishment, to forge a shared appreciation of a ritual executed flawlessly.'

The element of sexual voyeurism is, as we have seen, always implicit in bodybuilding, and is demonstrably more overt in the case of women's competition. Some women competitors openly pander to this response, and it is not always obvious that judges (particularly at the lower levels of competition) are anxious to discourage the deliberate provocation of such audience reaction on the part of competitors. Though audience response is largely beyond the control of officials, it is sometimes evident that the latter's attempts to eliminate the sub-text of sexual display — at least in women's, and sometimes in couples', competition — have been far from successful.

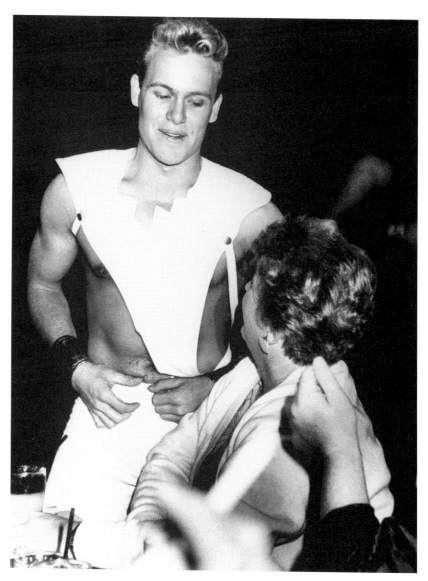

8.22 Male strippers now routinely perform to audiences such as women's social clubs, sports clubs and even old-age pensioner groups.

In respect of men's competition — the subject of Walters' categorisation of bodybuilding as a beauty pageant — the lines of demarcation have been somewhat more successfully drawn by contest organisers. The emergence of the male stripper in the 1980s may provide a more relevant analogy than the beauty pageant, particularly as in most male stripping the final state of undress of the performer approximates closely to that of the bodybuilder. A comparison of the two forms of activity helps us to clarify further the contextual (if not always actual) difference of bodybuilding display and erotic display.

Male strip shows, originally restricted to the seedier clubs and cabarets and intended largely for homosexual audiences, were to see a significant rise in popularity in the 1980s, and leading groups of strippers such as the 'Chippendales' currently attract audiences (mainly female) of over 50,000 per week in appearances throughout the world. No longer restricted to back-street clubs and gay bars, they perform before women's tennis-clubs, social and recreational clubs, charity organisations and even old-age pensioner groups. Male stripping has been the subject of movies (*For Ladies Only*) and stage-plays (*Ladies' Night Out*), and can now be seen regularly on American TV; even in relatively small provincial centres it can provide a lucrative source of income for those adept at it. At least in those cases where it stops short of total nudity, it has become a socially acceptable form of display in liberal Western cultures.

Like bodybuilding, the male strip show often (if not always) employs muscularity as a form of expression, and many male strippers are also enthusiastic bodybuilders. The body symbolisn of both forms of display is also similar: the strippers in one group (*Manpower*), says Greg Callaghan,

> 'go to hell and back to win their Adonis-like physiques. Each goes to the gym six days a week, for grinding two-hour workouts that presumably strain every muscle in their perfect pecs and washboard stomachs. There are other tortures: a couple of the more hirsute of the members need to have their bodies waxed every four to six weeks; then there is the matter of the all-over tan, which requires countless hours lying in solariums and rubbing in fake tanning solution.'[43]

What distinguishes the male bodybuilding display from the male stripshow is primarily the context of display. It is an understood convention that mild (and thus, nowadays, acceptable) sexual titillation is the purpose of the stripper's activity and that this is the expectation of the audience as well as the aim of the performers; the gestures, attitudes and activity are all designed to suggest or mimic sexual attraction and desire, and the 'bumps and grinds' are directed to that purpose. The journalist Zak Jane Keir describes an act by the Dreamboys:

8.23 Male stripping requires a less massive musculature than competitive bodybuilding, but most successful strippers work long hours in the gym to refine their physiques.

'The third item is the Dreamboys' song, *Talk Dirty*. Bare to the waist, glistening under the lights, they carry on ecstatic conversations with white plastic telephones, sliding their hands suggestively into their waistbands until the crowd can hold back no longer. 'Off! *Off!* OFF!' they scream, and the Dreamboys oblige. Down to their G-strings, they pose and spin and twirl, occasionally slipping the garments down to reveal irresistible pert buttocks.'[44]

The unambiguous nature of the messages emitted, conveyed and received by the stripper's form of bodily disclosure bring into sharp contrast the more elusive and ill-defined act of communication involved in the bodybuilder's 'pseudo-classical posing'.

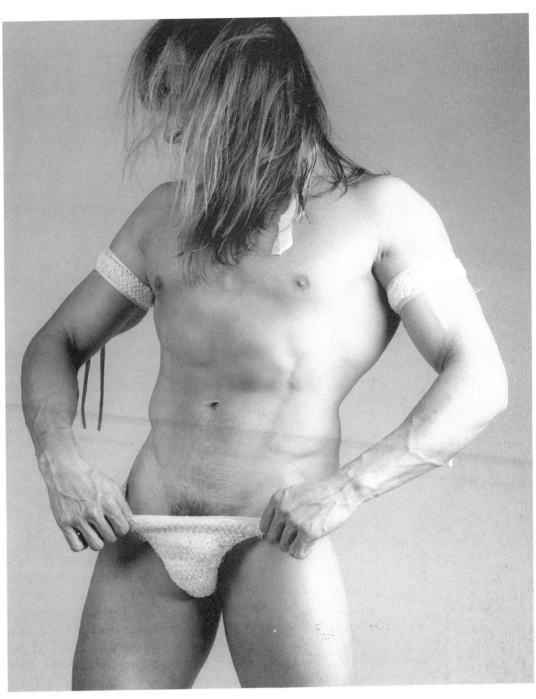

8.24 The stripper's gestures mimic eroticism, offering the audience an implicit invitation to sexual contact or congress.

If the bodybuilder (like the stripper) offers himself to the audience, he equally offers himself to the judges who separate him both physically and symbolically from that audience. He is literally 'distanced' from the spectators, and never leaves the podium to strut around the auditorium. He is never touched, and no-one throws money or under-garments at him. He enters and leaves the stage as directed by the officials. Whatever the implicit suggestions of his choreographed routine, its aim is not to evoke desire; it is to lose fewer points than his opponents. The contextual signs of competition bodybuilding are modelled on those of individual competitive sport, bearing some similarity to gymnastics, diving and other forms of sporting activity in which the language of subjective aesthetic appreciation is applied by judges with a dispassionate, almost clinical technicality.

> 'The judge', says IFBB Rule 6 for compulsory poses, 'will first survey the triceps display and then conclude with the head to foot examination. In this pose and in the side chest pose, the judge will be able to survey the thigh and calf muscles in profile, which will help him to grade their comparative development more accurately.'

Neither strength display nor beauty contest — though often understood as a failed attempt at one or the other, or both — bodybuilding is still seeking its identity as a sport. Whether it will ever gain widespread public acceptance in these terms seems at least open to doubt, notwithstanding the efforts of official organisations. As long as the body remains both the focus and the organ of human sexual desire, no activity which focuses so intently upon the body itself can ever achieve the degree of social legitimation accorded to sporting activity in general.

The attempted 'de-sexualisation' of bodybuilding has distanced it from the more overt forms of erotic display by providing it with a degree of contextual autonomy. To do more would be impossible, since it would be to deny one of the most fundamental components of our fascination with the body and its enduring power over us. The developed body may speak to the mind, but it speaks in the language of the senses.

8.25 The bodybuilder's posing is removed both physically and contextually from the overt sexual suggestivity of the stripper's erotic mime.

9.1   **CHAPTER 9**   THE SELF-ABSORBED BODY
In an age when the visible self is the leading constituent of our identity, an obsession with the self tends to become an obsession with the body.

9

THE SELF-ABSORBED BODY

OBSESSIVE BODIES

Susan Sontag in her groundbreaking book *Photography* was one of the first to note our increasing reliance on photographic images to verify the reality of our existence in a world where the self seems fleeting and existence groundless. The camera, she argued, renders the sense of selfhood dependent on the consumption of images of the self[1]. In a society as dominated by the visual dimension as our own, the visible self becomes in fact the leading constituent of our personal identity. In an equally influential study (*The Culture of Narcissism*), Christopher Lasch pointed to the role of visual images in projecting desirable or ideal states of being in our society[2]; these, he stated, were organically related to the individual psychological self-absorption, or 'narcissism', which he saw as characterising contemporary America — and, by implication, contemporary Western culture as a whole. Though targeting the social values of the 1960s and 70s, Lasch's central thesis remains in many respects applicable to the equally (if at times differently) narcissistic generation which followed in the 1980s and early 90s.

One of the dominant forms in which these desirable or ideal states of being are held up to our society is that of the fit or healthy body. We referred to this phenomenon earlier as 'healthism' — a particular form of 'bodyism' in which a hedonistic lifestyle is (paradoxically) combined with a preoccupation with ascetic practices aimed at the achievement or maintenance of an appearance of health, fitness and youthfulness. Appearance (the visual image) having often become a more important motivation than reality, simplistic equations are formulated and are purveyed by the media and the manufacturers of products and services aimed at producing this appearance. Fat is bad, therefore thin is good — and thus the thinner you are the better. Exercise promotes fitness — therefore the more you exercise the fitter you will be. Muscularity enhances the look of the male body — therefore the bigger your muscles the more attractive you become. Goals which may in themselves be harmless or even beneficial can take such a hold of the individual that they dominate, and even to some extent define, the personality.

9.2 Though in themselves beneficial, various forms of physical exercise (aerobics, running, weight training) can become psychological fixations, leading to dependency, obsession or addiction. It is not so much the underlying aspiration, as its escape from rational control, which is the problem.

This is not to suggest that all who engage in the pursuit of fitness or physical development fall victim to such extremism. In most cases, a sense of proportion and the need to get on with the ordinary business of living prevent their quest for the physical ideal from escaping rational control. In any of its manifestations, however, physical perfectibilism can become so powerful an influence on certain individuals that it assumes obsessive proportions and turns into an addiction.

The most characteristic forms of this disorder, which tend to affect women in particular, are the so-called 'slimmer's diseases' anorexia nervosa and bulimia. Though not restricted to women who take up aerobics or weight training in pursuit of a more lithe or slender appearance, they have a relatively high incidence among this group. Since the average mature female body contains 25 per cent body fat (compared to 15 per cent in mature males), the preponderance of anorexia and bulimia amongst this group of women is not altogether surprising, given the simplistic view which equates the presence of excessive fat — and thus *all* body fat — with an unsightly or unhealthy body. In an allusively autobiographical public reference to these disorders, the Princess of Wales has described them as grounded in 'the quest for perfection'.[3] While this description bears a substantial element of truth, the crucial factor is not so much the quest for bodily perfection itself (an aspiration which may remain within rational voluntary control) as its co-incidence with an obsessive personality syndrome based on a distorted self-image, a psychological disturbance which is all the harder to correct as it has escaped the control of the reasoning mind and conscious will.

Like anorexia, an excessive need to exercise is a form of compulsive behaviour which affects a number of individuals. In this case, the behaviour is associated with a fixation on 'fitness' and especially the cardiovascular fitness promoted by bodily exertion in the form of jogging, running or aerobics. Just as the anorexic can never be sufficiently thin, so the chronic exerciser can never get enough exercise; case studies have revealed instances of individuals experiencing a pathological need to exercise six hours a day or more. Undeterred by the fact that this practice makes them especially prone to injuries, they continue to exercise despite their strains and sprains, being unable to bear the thought of others exercising more than themselves. Exercise takes precedence over other people in their lives, and the maintenance of stable personal relationships is threatened or even becomes impossible.

Though restricted to a relatively small proportion of exercisers, exercise addiction affects so many individuals in absolute terms that a number of hospitals and health foundations have been obliged to establish units aimed at helping compulsive exercisers to exercise less. As with the eating disorders mentioned above, treatment is not straightforward. It is unlikely that the obsessive exerciser will respond to logical argument and simply come to recognise that, if some exercise is 'good for you', it does not follow that more exercise must be 'very good for you'. In some instances, an effective treatment — as in drug rehabilitation — may consist in reducing or eliminating the dependence on the 'exercise high' which is believed to result from the secretion of endorphins, a group of hormone-like substances manufactured in the brain which tend to act as opiates and have psychoactive properties. In most cases, however, the chief condition requiring treatment is neither intellectual nor physiological but psychological: it lies in the dependence on exercise for self-esteem, on the need to over-achieve as a form of compensation for deep-seated feelings of insecurity. Uncertain as to who I really 'am', I seek an identity and find it in my self-presentation as a person who exercises, a person who is fit: with no other self-concept to fall back on, my fitness — my exercise — becomes the sole constituent of my identity, and I come to rely on it (in existentialist terms) to 'prove to myself that I exist'.

9.3 'No pain, no gain': as with other forms of physical exertion, the pain of weight training can itself become a form of masochistic pleasure which is then sought for its own sake.

Like other forms of exercise, weight training can become an addictive or compulsive form of behaviour. The bodybuilder is frequently afflicted by the 'more is better' syndrome — the need to spend more and more hours in the gym — and almost every training manual describes at length the phenomenon of overtraining or the repetition of exercises to the point at which muscular response diminishes. The recommended answer to this problem is to train less; the addict, however, simply trains more. As in other modes of exercise, the pain of exertion tends to become a kind of masochistic pleasure: as with the compulsive jogger, covered in sweat, gasping for air and face contorted in agony, so the compulsive bodybuilder seeks heavier and heavier poundages, until his body eventually gives way under the strain. 'No pain, no gain' here becomes a self-destructive creed, in which the pain becomes a kind of value in itself: 'I hurt, therefore I am'.

Physiological dependency can also be a factor in obsessive weight training, in the form of the exercise high known to the bodybuilder as the 'pump'. Arnold Schwarzenegger has described the sensation as follows:

> 'It is the greatest feeling I get. I search for this pump because it means that my muscles will grow when I get it. I get a pump when the blood is running into my muscles. They become really tight with blood. Like the skin is going to explode any minute. It's like someone putting air in my muscles. It blows up. It feels fantastic.'[4]

The pump is the normal physiological indicator of maximal muscle tension, the sign that all muscle fibres have reached the point known as complete tetanus. In his most celebrated reference to this sensation — 'a good pump is better than coming, ... the best feeling you can have'[5] — Schwarzenegger accounts for both the experiential pleasure of the process and its dominance of the bodybuilder's psyche as a state of semi-erotic arousal which can be produced at will and constantly renewed. The pump can become a self-sustaining experience: no longer an incidental by-product of muscular exercise, it becomes the goal of the exercise itself. Just as, for the addicted runner, the experience of the runner's high can take on more importance than the cardiovascular benefit of the exercise, so for the 'gym junkie' the sensual pleasure of the workout becomes its main point. Hedonism and asceticism no longer co-exist in a state of tension; they become indistinguishable, and it is in this sense that we can understand (even if we do not necessarily share) Clive James' view that bodybuilding is merely 'self-indulgence as a form of self-discipline'[6].

9.4 'It is the greatest feeling I get ... like the skin is going to explode any minute ... It feels fantastic ... A good pump is better than coming.' (Arnold Schwarzenegger.)

The most common form of obsession among bodybuilders has to do with sheer muscular bulk. The public statements of official organisations to the effect that the aim of competitive bodybuilding is the development of balance, proportion and harmony in the physique are of no interest to the bodybuilding 'size freak'. The scales loom as large as the mirror as his point of reference and judgment. His catchcry is 'Big, big, big!' and his heroes are the super-heavyweight champions. If his obsession is the opposite of the anorexic's, it is just as different from that of the health addict: health and fitness are willingly sacrificed in the compulsive battle to 'put on size'. High-cholesterol diets, unnecessary protein supplements and amino acids, and a variety of tailor-made 'miracle' muscle-building substances are devoured with reckless abandon.

The size fixation has undoubtedly to do with overcoming deep-seated feelings of insecurity. While it may be associated with a desire to increase effective physical strength, it is conceptually different, and the size-fixated trainer is less concerned by a drop in the poundages he can lift than by a drop in the poundage his body carries. Though associated also with the visibility of muscular development, the quest for 'bigness' may actually render visible muscularity less evident because of the loss of definition in the muscles resulting from a higher percentage of body fat. The process of 'bulking up' is thus a more satisfying experience than the subsequent 'cutting up' required for competition, and it is common for would-be competitors to drop out of a contest because they are unable to cope psychologically with the prospect of 'losing size'. Dependence on the maximum physical bulk for a positive self-image has its roots in a profound anxiety related to feelings of personal inferiority, which may equally (and more dangerously) have their outcome in aggressive modes of behaviour.

The psychologist Ronald Conway has characterised the obsessive-compulsive cultivation of the physical body as merely a part of a more pervasive malaise within Western society, in which the self tends to be construed as a purely sensual phenomenon. In societies where nothing is believed to succeed like excess, says Conway, an otherwise laudable concern for health and physical development may be exaggerated to the point of becoming a self-justifying activity:

'Certainly there is nothing wrong with the regular gym 'workout' in crowded cities where millions normally sit upon spreading backsides in driving seats. But the balanced, smoothly Grecian bulking-out of male bodies, fashionable in the days of bodybuilding idols such as Steve Reeves and Gordon Scott, has given way to straining, fleshless monsters with ugly knotted and veined torsos, suggesting nothing so much as flayed animals in an abattoir; and female bodybuilders whose breasts are reduced by steroids to mere extruded nipples. How remote such Western grotesqueries seem from the classical ideal of "a sound mind in a sound body"!'[7]

Conway sees the 'macho cult' of largeness, hardness and muscular force in Western nations as linked to an increasing emphasis on sex-role specialisation over the past two or three centuries, and argues that this tendency has robbed the male body of much of its potential to convey sensuous beauty and tactile pleasure.[8] Though I have suggested in the present study the abiding influence of a stronger alternative tradition in the Western approach to the male body than Conway allows, one can certainly acknowledge the force of his attack on the extremism to which the Western cult of the physical self has so frequently led. Yet it is important to recognise that personality disorders occur in all societies, and to distinguish between the obsessive manifestation of a social tendency within certain individuals or groups and its (potentially more benign) effect within the society as a whole. The existence of sick individuals does not necessarily mean a sick society.

The forms of obsession described above all relate in various degrees to a preoccupation with the self, in its visible embodiment or in the pleasurable feelings associated with certain bodily states. As such, they can be seen as extreme manifestations of that contemporary narcissism or tendency towards self-preoccupation to which Christopher Lasch and Ronald Conway have referred. Inward rather than outward-looking, they centre upon the physical self as the chief, or even the exclusive, determinant of the identity we assume in our own eyes. The perfectible body can make us its prisoner.

9.5 '... straining, fleshless monsters with ugly knotted and veined torsos, suggesting nothing so much as flayed animals in an abattoir ...'

UNNATURAL BODIES

Bodybuilders are the chief consumers of anabolic steroids, a form of organic compound which stimulates the production of cellular protein and can aid remarkably in muscle growth. The effect of most of these substances is both anabolic ('growth producing') and androgenic ('male-producing'). The most potent of the body's natural androgenic hormones is testosterone: in the transition from the pre-pubescent to the pubescent stage in males, the production of testosterone increases 20-fold and muscle weight is increased 14-fold. Like naturally produced testosterone, synthetic anabolic steroid tends to accentuate 'masculine' characteristics, with the result that female steroid users often develop a marked increase in body and facial hair, a lowering of the vocal register and a disruption in the menstrual cycle. Increased aggressiveness can also be a side-effect in both sexes[9].

The manipulation of the structure of the testosterone molecule increases the likelihood that synthetic steroid will cause imbalances in the body's assimilation patterns, particularly in the glands and organs which assist anabolic processes. Anabolic steroid use is therefore considered a potentially dangerous practice, especially if not carried out under strict medical control: kidney and liver dysfunction may result, and secondary effects can range from an increased strain on the heart to the incidence of skin problems such as acne. Steroid abuse can result in serious injury and even death.

Neither the well-publicised health hazards nor the banning of steroids by official sporting bodies are of concern to the obsessive bodybuilder, who is prepared to endanger his (or her) life for the sake of putting another inch of muscle on the arms or legs. If the regular 'steroid fix' cannot be obtained from medical sources, there is always the black market or direct importation from countries which do not regulate the sale of such substances; in some cases, resort can be had to veterinary steroids, with the obvious unpredictable results. In a 'pill-popping' culture which craves instant satisfaction and maximum achievement with minimum effort, the attraction of the 'quick-fix' is as great in bodybuilding as it is in any other area of drug-taking.

The widespread use of anabolic steroids is an open secret in the world of competitive bodybuilding. Open, because everyone who moves in this world is aware that practically all top competitors, for the last twenty years or more, have been steroid-users; a secret, because almost all have publicly denied the fact. The occasional bodybuilder does 'come out', admitting to having used steroids in the past, though this most frequently occurs only after serious health problems have obliged the person concerned to retire from the ranks of competition or from bodybuilding in general[10]. Some (though by no means all) official bodybuilding organisations run sporadic drug tests, and bodybuilders who test positive are subjected to a (usually relatively brief) ban from competition. They are generally apologetic, not for steroid use but for their foolishness in not having taken the usual pre-contest precautions to render the presence of the drug undetectable in the body system.

The dilemma confronting bodybuilders is heightened by the undoubted effectiveness of anabolic steroids in promoting muscular growth. In a world where the leading competitors are steroid-users, aspiring champions must either join their ranks in order to compete on a basis of equality, or else shun steroid use and enter competition knowing that they will not achieve a placing. The use of steroids has so changed the image of the top bodybuilder that 'natural' (non steroid-using) competitors tend to look undeveloped by comparison. A number of drug-free or 'natural' bodybuilding associations have been formed, but their ability to attract only a small minority of competitors is testimony to the hold which the steroid culture has taken in the major organisations. It is no longer a problem restricted to 'obsessive' or addictive bodybuilders, but affects all those with ambition to rise to the top in their chosen sport.

Steroid use is of course not restricted to bodybuilding, as a number of well-publicised expulsions from Olympic and other international athletic competitions have shown. Sprinters, cyclists, weightlifters and competitors in various other sports including football have used steroids to enhance their explosive muscular power. Only in bodybuilding, however, has the use of steroids become endemic at the competition level. Though usually monitored by medical advisers in the case of top professionals, it poses very real problems lower down the line, particularly in cases where bodybuilding is a compulsive neurotic activity from which any concept of 'excess' has been abolished.

9.6 John Bubb, a former top British bodybuilder who once placed second to Arnold Schwarzenegger, is one of a number who have made a public admission of earlier anabolic steroid use, once having abandoned the contest platform.

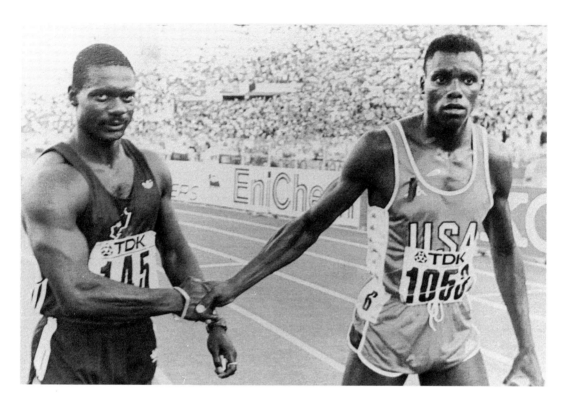

9.7   Sprinters Ben Johnson and Carl Lewis shake hands at the 100 metre event of the 1987 World Track and Field Championship. Johnson's later positive testing for the presence of anabolic steroids was to create a furore in the world of athletics.

The most graphic and frank account of bodybuilding neurosis and the resort to anabolic steroids is that given by Sam Fussell in his autobiographical account *Muscle: Confessions of an Unlikely Bodybuilder.* An 'unlikely' participant in the world of competitive bodybuilding in view of his university education, Fussell has shown that an obsessive involvement in such activity is not necessarily the sign of an inferior intellect. The important factor, in his as in many other cases of compulsive physical behaviour or exercise addiction, is the low self-esteem or sense of insecurity which leads to a fanatical degree of involvement in an activity that offers a refuge against the exposure of the vulnerable self in conventional social intercourse. 'The attempt at physical perfection', he candidly admits, 'grew from self-disgust.'[11]

In the aimlessness which not uncommonly marks the years between the completion of formal study and the prospect of settling down to employment, Fussell was like many other young men ripe for an obsession. In the threatening world of urban New York, he found his in the apparent invulnerability afforded by building a physique like that of Arnold Schwarzenegger. In pursuit of his 'disease', he moved to the hub of obsessive bodybuilding, the Southern Californian muscle-shrines which tend to attract the craziest of fanatics. From this base, he risked his mental and physical health in a frenetic, almost manic, steroid-boosted attempt to break into the world of competitive bodybuilding. Following his disappointing second placing in a local contest, he at last became fully conscious of his obsession and its basis in an underlying psychological disorder. Having abandoned the world of bodybuilding, he determined to expose it in a chronicle of his experiences.

Fussell's book is an important and intensely revealing study of the obsessive, all-consuming pursuit of muscular development, and in particular of the cult of 'bigness'. In the process of self-disclosure, he unmasks the hypocrisy and blatant profiteering of many of those involved in, or at the fringes of, the world of organised bodybuilding in the United States — the steroid pushers, magazine proprietors and supplement salesmen who pander to muscular obsession and help to create it. He writes graphically of the effects of steroid use, and successfully de-mythologises a number of well-known figures of the bodybuilding world.

The main weakness of Fussell's book lies in its suggestion that all who pursue bodybuilding share his degree of neurotic addiction or personal insecurity — or worse, resemble the freaks and crazies whom he meets in the course of his all-consuming quest. Like a modern-day Candide, he wanders naively into the company of an assortment of junkies, nymphomaniacs and air-heads, each of whom is skilfully characterised. The role of *ingénu* is highly effective and only rarely overplayed

9.8 '... dumbbells of flat, ugly, black iron ...' Sam Fussell's bitter attack on the world of weight training and bodybuilding tends to extrapolate rather too freely from his experience of the establishments he frequented during his obsessive personal quest. The ambience of most commercial gymnasia is very different from the picture he paints.

9.9   The well publicised health hazards associated with anabolic steroid use are often ignored, or are accepted as a necessary risk, by bodybuilders: once the cult of bigness has become an obsession or a prophylactic against deep-seated feelings of inferiority, rational argument is of no effect.

('That doesn't seem very natural' is the unbelievably wide-eyed response of this Oxford graduate when informed after months of training that some bodybuilders actually use steroids![12]). Its use as a literary device, however, enables the author to suggest more than he actually says. The dumbbells of 'flat, ugly, black iron' are not the stuff of a factual account but have the symbolic value of a literary conceit. 'Is this a gay gym?' he asks of an effeminate trainer; 'Look, honey', is the reply, 'all gyms are gay.'[13] That the quip is manifestly untrue does not rob it of its shock-value as a piece of literary dialogue, but the lack of authorial commentary must (or is perhaps even intended to) leave the untutored reader with an assumption of its factual accuracy. The first-person narrative is peculiarly suited to the sub-conscious persuasion of the reader to the writer's point of view: the author-as-narrator (theoretically omniscient and all-revealing) is doubled by the author-as-character (who can be as selective as he likes in what he observes and shows us). Thus, all the non-bodybuilding characters in Fussell's book appear normal; all the bodybuilders appear in some degree demented. We are left to draw the obvious conclusion, without any need for the narrator to hazard the implied proposition.

Muscle remains the most important contribution yet made to our understanding of bodybuilding as an obsession, once allowance is made for the book's nature as a personal apologia or a polemic directed against a world once enthusiastically embraced and now vehemently rejected. Like other forms of obsessive 'bodyism', the cult of physical development can pass outside the control of the rational mind and take exclusive possession of our fantasies. As with religious or political fanaticism, all-consuming devotion to an ideal tends to reveal more about the behaviour of the human personality than about the inherent value (or otherwise) of the ideal itself. What it does reveal about the latter is its power to capture the imagination, even at times to dominate it.

The pursuit of physical development need not be an obsession, and for most people — even those who embrace it with enthusiasm — it is kept in proportion and under control by the rational consciousness and a relatively stable personality. That it can assume the dimensions of a mania is further proof of the pervasive imaginative power of the perfectible body.

10.1 **CHAPTER 10** THE SELF-CONTAINED BODY
Like a work of art, the developed body can open up a world rich in imaginative associations, which may include simply its own existence as an expressive object.

10

THE SELF-CONTAINED BODY

BODIES BOLD AND BEAUTIFUL

Human beings are more than bodies, and a preoccupation with the world of physicality or outward appearance to the exclusion of deeper and ultimately more meaningful concerns can turn the pursuit of the developed body from an engrossing imaginative exercise into a futile obsession with the shallow surface of existence or a narcissistic cult of the self. More dangerously still, the distortion of physical development from a subjective means of personal expression into an ideological programme is to pervert its creativeness and reduce it to the crudest form of physical suprematism and social intolerance. The bigotry of the body can take possession of an individual, a group, a society or a regime. Only when the quest for physical perfectibility is held in balance with a desire for the general good of our fellow man and woman can it ever be a fully, and admirably, human aspiration.

Yet to those who have learned to read the language of the developed body, it can open up a world rich in imaginative associations. At the purely representational level, freed from the accretions of higher or lower purpose, the heavily codified display of the bodybuilder is a unique expressive exercise, all the more inexhaustible in its allusive suggestions because of that absence of utilitarian aims which is the mark of pure play as it is of art. It gives concrete form to one of the limits of our potentiality as physical beings, and explores the symbolic and expressive capacity with which the developed body has been endowed by the inventive imagination of Western civilisation.

10.2 Erotic numbness: '... the mythological statuary that is incapable of arousing sensuous pleasure.' José Alvarez Cubero, *The Defence of Saragossa*, 1823. (Madrid, Museo de Arte Moderno.)

The bodybuilding display is, in a peculiarly twentieth-century form, the inheritor of what we have called the 'heroic' tradition in Western art. Its inception coincided almost exactly with the final abandonment of the heroic style of representation of the body as a leading theme of high art, and the conventions of one medium of expression passed with little modification into another. Since the time of the early bodybuilders and their mock-classical poses and accoutrements, the convention has undergone further evolution in conformity with the changing tastes of successive generations, but its basis in the metaphorical language of its beginnings remains clearly in evidence.

The heroic figure in Western art is often referred to as 'self-contained'[1]: that is, it is seen as an end in itself and not as reaching out to us to seek, or produce, gratification. We admire it because of the fascination that a human physical structure can hold on account of its perfection of purpose and function — a perfection found in harmony and proportion, in the muscle and sinew which indicate the discipline of control and mastery, in the classical attitudes which convey an inner energy and a striving towards ideal form. As Rudofsky puts it:

> 'The erotic numbness that emanates from a perfectly proportioned body assured generations of city fathers that all the mythological statuary that clings to public fountains or dots a town's parks, and the caryatids and atlases carrying sham loads of palace porticos, are incapable of arousing sensuous pleasure.'[2]

This is not to deny the presence, even the importance, of the erotic element in high art. It is to distinguish a particular tradition in the depiction of the body, in which the self-containment of the representation restrains any overt sexual response.

The heroic tradition can be distinguished in principle from what might be called the 'aesthetic' tradition in the rendering of the muscular male body. Both conventions use muscularity as an important element of the visual message, though in the aesthetic convention the muscularity tends to be subordinated to the overall impression of physical beauty — whether of the body itself, the facial features, or the graceful elegance of the pose. The aesthetic tradition has always co-existed alongside the heroic: the commanding statues of Greek gods stand alongside the vase paintings of lithe young athletes; the herculean giants of Michelangelo alongside the coltish *David* of Donatello; the chiselled muscularity of Sandow alongside the burnished grace of Sansone; the imperturbable body-landscape of George Butler's photographs of Schwarzenegger, alongside the lingering curiosity of Robert Mapplethorpe's photographs of muscular nudes.

The distinction being proposed here is one of principle. In practice, an individual representation or display of the developed body may contain elements of both traditions; one or the other may predominate, or both may be present in more or less equal measure. While in general the aesthetic tradition has favoured a more lithesome, less massive muscularity than the heroic tradition (bodybuilders are generally not sought as male models, even for beachwear or in advertisements requiring a sexually attractive male physique), only the context can determine which if any of the two traditions is dominant in a particular instance. The aesthetic tradition can never be divorced from a hint of mild eroticism, and while the overtly erotic (or pornographic) representation of the body may appear to eliminate any traces of 'aesthetic' appeal, it is best seen as an extreme or (in some cases) perverted instance of the aesthetic as opposed to the heroic mode of depiction.

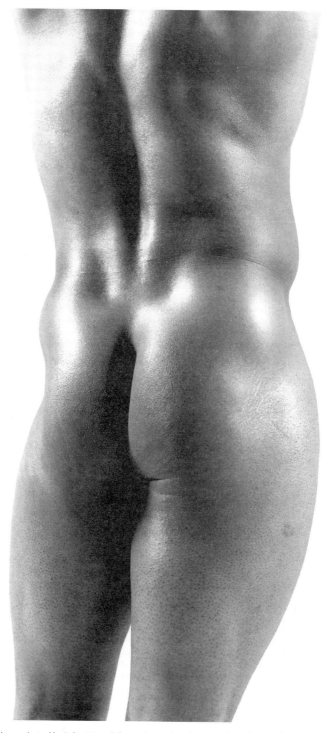

10.3 As with the idealised blacks popularised by Robert Mapplethorpe, the aesthetic/erotic mode in photography is characterised by a lingering
      attention to sensuous detail, a hestitation between formal detachment and tactile intimacy. (John Freund, *Back*.)

A telling illustration of the distance which separates the heroic and aesthetic/ erotic modes of representing the muscular body can be found in a comparison between the bodybuilding magazine photograph and the 'art' photograph. As examples of the latter medium we can take the studies of muscular black nudes made by one of the most original and gifted of late twentieth-century photographers, Robert Mapplethorpe (1946-89).[3] The very ambiguity of Mapplethorpe's portrayals of these lithe and well-developed bodies — enigmatically caught at mid-point between what Hollinghurst calls the 'intensely sexy silkiness' of their skin texture and the 'aestheticizing into sculpture' of their body outline[4] — serves to bring more clearly into focus the extent to which the world of bodybuilding as sport has established its distance from the world of eroticism. It is true, for example, that in Mapplethorpe's photographs we are in a sense looking at bodybuilders, but what is significant about them is precisely what makes them different from the conventional bodybuilding photographs which fill the pages of the popular monthly bodybuilding magazines. It is not simply a matter of the nudity of Mapplethorpe's figures (actually a very chaste nudity by his standards), though this clearly marks an important difference in convention and overtones. It is rather the hesitancy between detached and formal appreciation on the one hand, and on the other the lingering attention to sensuous detail in the curve of a buttock or the glint of light on a nipple, which not only characterise Mapplethorpe's work but give it an unforgettable beauty. His attempt in these photographs to prevail over the sexual seductiveness of the physique by the sheer sculptural beauty of line and texture has divided critical opinion —some believing that formal elements dominate emotional involvement while others consider that the two are inextricably intertwined — but what is clear is that they never leave the world of aesthetic for that of purely heroic depiction.

If the equally meticulously photographed physiques in the quality muscle magazines seem totally uninspired by comparison, it is precisely because they are lacking in mystery and desire, directing our attention immediately and unambiguously to the formal quality of the body and the technical criteria of the judging panel. It is not the beauty of Lee Haney's body but its awesomeness of development, not the sensuousness of Schwarzenegger's physique but its perfection of balance and proportion, that is the message intended and, for most people, the message received. The role of the camera here is purely to record, to reproduce in minute detail the physical presence of the body itself. It is not the photographer who has taken over the role of artist as author of the 'heroic' message: it is the subject of the technically flawless but neutral photograph — the bodybuilder as author of his own muscularity, as sculptor of his own body. He speaks to us without the intermediary of art, even of photographic art: the only transcendence involved is that of the body's capacity for self-transcendence.

10.4 The meticulously photographed physique of the muscle magazine, reproducing in minute detail the physical presence of the body itself, without any sense of emotional involvement. Kevin Levrone (Joe Weider's *Flex*.)

THE ALL-INCLUSIVE BODY

The term 'erotic numbness' used by Rudofsky to characterise our response to heroic art applies equally well (but for different reasons) to the effect produced by the bodybuilding display. In both cases, this observation must obviously be confined to 'typical' responses, since as we have already noted the possible range of human reactions to the sight of the body, whether in art or in real life, is determined by the psychological disposition of the individual at the viewing end of the transaction. Though the Laocoön, the Farnese Hercules or Michelangelo's David can in no meaningful sense of the term be considered erotic art, it is at least conceivable — and probably factually the case — that some people would find these statues irresistibly exciting in sexual terms. So too with the bodybuilding display: the phenomenon of 'muscle eroticism' is well known to psychologists dealing in the area of psycho-sexual fantasy, and such a disposition makes the very sight of muscularity a powerful source of sexual arousal. In this area, any general propositions that one may advance will apply only within the bounds of what can be considered typical or 'normal' human reaction.

With this caveat, it is possible to suggest that there is a curiously asexual quality discernible in the advanced muscularity of the bodybuilder's physique, and it could be argued that this is a central element in the symbolic language of the developed body. It is not so much that the body is here devoid of sexual connotations, as that it combines in a unique fashion elements of both male and female sexuality, or that by simultaneously affirming and denying male and female sexual messages it manages to escape or even transcend the male-female duality and attain a symbolic completeness which comprehends them both. Implausible though such a theory may at first seem, it not only accounts for some of the particular conventions of bodybuilding display which defy explanation on other grounds, but also corresponds to a deep-seated aspiration towards sexual unification which has found expression in various forms since antiquity.

It should be noted that this is a somewhat different concept from that of unisexuality or the elimination of visible differences between the sexes, a tendency which has been found in certain idealistic movements from the apocryphal writings of the 1st century A.D., through medieval and Renaissance mysticism to modern incarnations as disparate as the rock musical *Hair* and Maoist China[4]. It differs also, at least in mode of presentation, from the androgynous or sexually ambivalent characteristics and mannerisms adopted by a number of male pop performers from David Bowie in the 1970s to Prince and Michael Jackson in the 1980s and 90s. What is suggested by the bodybuilder's physique is not a diminution or denial of

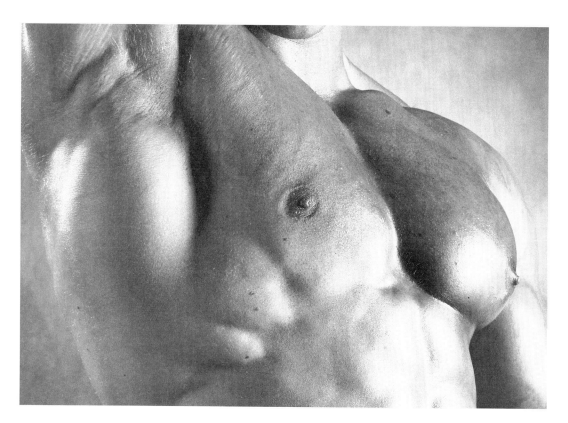

10.5 The bodybuilder's physique – not so much devoid of sexual connotations, as simultaneously affirming and denying male and female sexual messages.

masculine qualities, so much as their explicit affirmation in a context which simultaneously suggests complementary messages associated with opposite qualities. There is a basic principle of selective perception involved here, one long recognised by traditional scholastic philosophy which neatly encapsulated it in the maxim *expressio unius rei est exclusio alterius*: the presence of a characteristic or quality implies the absence of an opposite quality (hardness implies the absence of softness and vice versa) and thus suggests incompleteness of being. Conversely, the reconciliation of opposing characteristics can lead to our apprehension of a sense of completeness or self-sufficiency. Kenneth Clark, for instance, has observed that 'the disposition of areas in the torso is related to our most vivid experiences, so that abstract shapes, the square and the circle, seem to us male and female'[6]; in this context, 'the old endeavour of magical mathematics to square the circle' is related to the ancient cosmology which saw the union of opposites as a restoration of primordial harmony and perfection.

The combination of male and female characteristics has been noted by a number of observers of the bodybuilding display. George Butler has vividly described one of his photographs of Arnold Schwarzenegger as follows:

'He seems to float, suspending himself palms down on the rails of two back-to-back chairs... His upper body — trapezius flexed, deltoids rolled forward, abdomen vacuumed into a small shadow — is an accumulation of striking details. The pectoral muscles beneath are large and sweeping. They glisten so shockingly in the air of the shabby room that the figure who bears them seems neither man nor woman ...'[7]

Equally, Lisa Lyon has characterised the image projected by the female bodybuilder as 'neither masculine nor feminine but feline'[8]. Margaret Walters has commented that 'for all his super-masculinity the bodybuilder's exaggerated breast development, as well as his dedicated self-absorption, can make him look unexpectedly, surreally feminine.'[9] Whilst the latter comment is part of Walters' dismissal of bodybuilding which she sees as 'the most purely narcissistic and, in that sense, most feminine, of pastimes', it is nonetheless possible to endorse her perceptive identification of the crucially suggestive elements of the bodybuilder's physique without sharing her distaste for this form of bodily manifestation.

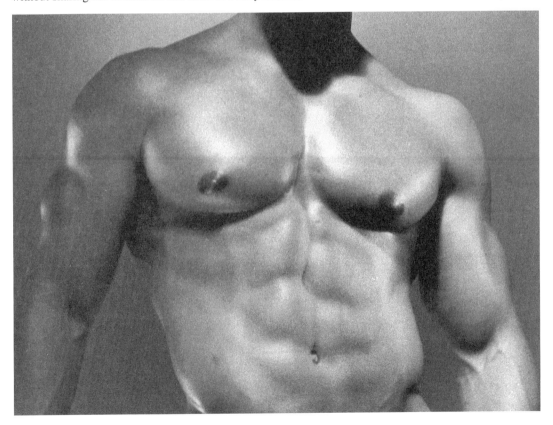

10.6 '... unexpectedly, surreally feminine': the bodybuilder's 'exaggerated breast development' (Margaret Walters). Yet this is hardly a man trying to look like a woman: there are too many messages to the contrary.

The three elements identified here are the basic shape or outline of the body ('super-masculinity'), the modelling of the body's surface ('unexpectedly ... feminine'), and an overall air of self-absorption (characterised as 'narcissistic'). With regard to the last-named characteristic, it is no doubt possible to draw different conclusions as to the extent to which it is a universal trait of bodybuilding performance. For one thing, there are considerable individual differences between bodybuilders in the degree to which they seek to interact with their audience, and in any case the extent to which such interaction is possible differs in the 'compulsory' and 'free' posing of which competition is made up. The extreme concentration required by any high-level competitive sport is here directed towards the body itself, in maintaining the 'pump' and flexion of the muscles; in this sense, the self-absorption of the bodybuilder may not differ greatly from that of the diver standing on the platform and mentally rehearsing the movement of his body in a high-dive.

If the term 'self-absorption' accurately conveys the self-directed concentration of the posing display, a more revealing indication of its distinctive and perhaps unique character as a form of spectacle is the alternative term 'self-containment'. The pose does not look beyond itself; it is meaningful only in terms of the body's ability to suggest, by its inherent expressivity of mass and gesture, the exaltation of physical existence.

10.7 The 'archer' pose: it may appear to mimic the drawing of a long bow but it is not 'about' archery or anything else outside itself. Its aim is purely to exhibit a potentiality of the body.

10.8 Three views of a familiar pose which highlights the latissimus dorsi muscle of the back: (a) Apollonios, son of Nestoros, *Boxer*, mid-1st century A.D. (Rome, Museo delle Terme); (b) Michelangelo, *Ignudo* known as 'The Athlete', 1511. (Vatican, Sistine Chapel); (c) The 'three-quarters twisting back shot' of the bodybuilder.

In this sense, the bodybuilding display can be compared to ballet, not to those scenes in which the performers advance the action by way of a superior and aesthetic mime related to the events of the plot, but to those in which the action is halted and a dancer performs a bravura solo in which the body expresses nothing beyond an inner mood. Even here the analogy falters, however, because what the bodybuilder seeks to express has about it nothing cerebral, no reflection of an interior life, but the evocative power of the body itself, the ability of visible form to conjure up in the minds of those who understand its language deep-seated images and fantasies of perfection and completeness. There is little difference in principle between such a form of contemplation and the delight of the mathematician confronted by a 'perfect' theoretical equation, the rapt wonderment of a musicologist studying a Bach fugue, or the intent admiration of an art-lover standing before an abstract sculpture by Brancusi. In each case, the intimation of formal perfection is real, though it can be appreciated only by those who have learned the language of the medium by which it is conveyed. In each case, as in the so-called classical ideal of art, form takes precedence over content; in one sense, indeed, the form *is* the content.

The posing display suggests self-containment because it is not 'about' anything other than itself. The so-called 'archer' pose for example, mimics the bodily attitude of a person drawing a long-bow in a lunging position; its reference, however, is not in any sense to the sport of archery but purely to the muscular configuration and line of the body which can be displayed in that particular position. The 'three-quarters twisting back pose' is precisely that of the antique *Torso Belvedere* and of one of the *ignudi* (sometimes known as 'The Athlete') from Michelangelo's

Sistine Chapel ceiling. Once again, there is no sense in which the pose 'refers' to these artistic works, of which the bodybuilder (and no doubt most of his audience) are very likely unaware given their cultural background; it is rather that the bodybuilder, like the artist, has chosen that pose because it expresses a potentiality of the body. Handed down to the contemporary poser by his predecessors (the art-studio models), it reveals in Clark's words 'a compelling rhythmic force [which] drives every inflection of the human body before it.'[10] Like its artistic forerunners, the pose indicates nothing beyond the power of human anatomy to transform itself into an instrument of expression.

Pursuing the terms of Margaret Walters' analysis, we can discuss in closer detail her reference to the co-existence of 'super-masculine' and 'surreally feminine' characteristics in the bodybuilder's physique. In its fundamental shape and outline, the latter is unmistakably, even aggressively, masculine, emitting precisely those super-normal stimuli of masculinity to which we referred in an earlier chapter. The ideal bodybuilding physique, says Robert Kennedy,

> 'should have wide shoulders, trim hips, a small waist, arms with balanced development from the wrist to the shoulders, legs that flow aesthetically from the hips to the knees, and then into a full calf development. The lats should be wide, but not too much at the lower lats. The neck should be developed equally on all sides. Pectoral muscles should be built up in all aspects, especially the upper and outer chest region. The glutes should be rounded but not overly heavy in appearance. The overall muscle separation and definition should be clearly visible when contracted or flexed.'[11]

The broad shoulders, trim hips, wide latissimus dorsi, small buttocks and relatively thick neck are all super-normal masculine stimuli. All of them, it will be noted, are characteristics of body shape and are visible features of the body when seen in silhouette. The development of the pectoral muscles, on the other hand — what Walters refers to as the 'exaggerated breast development' of the male bodybuilder — seems somehow to be of a different order, having more to do with the modelling of the skin surface and the tactile quality of body-texture than with the outline of the body. It is here that we enter into a world of body-imagery strangely different from that of masculine stimuli.

The tactile quality of the body's surface is clearly an important component of the messages emitted by the bodybuilder's physique. The skin, as psychologists have recognised, has a vital role in erogenic stimulation, related as it is to the considerable suggestive power of the sense of touch. Physical love-making is

10.9 The skin has such a vital role in erogenic stimulation that the mere sight of bare skin can act as an erotic stimulus.

intensely reliant on touching, and certain parts of the body (the so-called 'erogenous zones') are especially sensitive to erotic messages conveyed by stroking, kissing, fondling or other forms of skin-to-skin contact. The powerful imaginative force of tactile messages is so great that the mere sight of bare skin can act as an erotic stimulus, without the need for actual touching to take place[12]. (The same applies, it should be noted, to tactile experiences involving non-human objects: fur, leather, silk and velvet, as well as garments associated with another person, can all act as erotic agents and take on the pathological dimensions of fetishism.) The erotic role of the skin itself is intimately associated with the polarised attitudes towards the display of nakedness which we saw above to be characteristic of Western society.

While skin is not of itself a purely female characteristic, as a mode of conveying bodily messages it belongs to a different order from that of super-masculine stimuli. The latter are all related to the outline of the body, and are observable even when the body is clothed; indeed, some male clothing (from padded shoulders to tight-fitting jeans) is designed to accentuate the super-masculine body-shape. Bare skin, however — endowed with all the erotic overtones mentioned above — is suggestive of the body-as-object rather than the body-as-agent, of the 'sex that is looked at' rather than the 'sex that looks'. To present the skin-surface as 'object of the gaze' is not a traditional male dominance-signal, but on the contrary a sign of submissiveness or seductiveness. Not for nothing did the erotic tradition in art, from the seventeenth to the nineteenth century, typically depict a clothed male in the presence of a nude female — never the other way round.

That a man should bare his body for presentation to the objectifying or fantasising gaze of others — whether women or (even more) other men — is so signal a departure from Western sexual convention that it would almost be unthinkable as a public spectacle but for the simultaneous display of super-masculine stimuli which obliterate or even deny any suggestions of female role-play and provide a sexual 'neutral ground'. The legitimising context of the posing display leaves the spectator's mind, if not 'erotically numb' at any rate erotically uncertain. Not so much transcending sexuality as rendering it illegible, the bodybuilder's performance aims at a kind of sexual self-containment which subliminates desire.

THE TRANSFIGURED BODY

Over the years of its evolution, bodybuilding has adopted a set of conventions related to the grooming and attiring of the body for competition and public display. Designed to enhance the visible muscularity of the physique, these measures have an obvious cosmetic purpose and can readily be understood in terms which apply also to other types of public spectacle: the bodybuilder, like other performers, must appear 'in character'. Like stage make-up and costume, these are part of the accepted practice of theatrical presentation and are aimed at the improvement of the performer's appearance. At a deeper level, however, the conventions of presentation can be related to the implicit metaphorical language of the developed body, and can be read in symbolic terms as significant (if subliminal) elements of the message it transmits. Some of these practices have subsequently been transposed from the specific context of competitive bodybuilding into other, more general spheres (such as film and advertising) which make use of the expressive character of muscular development.

The shaving of body-hair is a case in point. Since the super-normal stimuli of masculinity are to be found in those characteristics by which male and female bodies are most sharply differentiated, one would expect that the presence of male body-hair would be an important component of the messages of the muscular body. Yet the reverse is the case. Competition bodybuilders shave all exposed parts of the body, including the chest (where necessary), legs and armpits. The common and most obvious explanation of this practice is that body-hair tends to conceal muscular shape, so that the definition and striation of muscles are not visible. In this and a number of other aspects of body-presentation, however, the obvious practical explanation, while entirely valid so far as it goes, is only a part of the total picture. If its practical purpose were accepted as the complete explanation of the practice of body-shaving, there would be no reason why the underarm should be shaved, since it is not the site of a muscle-group. The practice of body-shaving, in both men and women, clearly has an additional set of connotations connected with the heightened messages conveyed by hairless skin.

In this respect as in several others, the conventions of bodybuilding have merely articulated in somewhat exaggerated form a set of widely held, if latent, cultural attitudes towards the body. Given the significance of facial and bodily hair as biological markers of masculinity, the male ideal might logically be the figure of a hirsute, bearded he-man; yet in fact the masculine images portrayed in Western media as ideal models are those of lithe, smooth-bodied youths. Only by reference to the symbolic language by which the body has been interpreted in the Western cultural tradition can we understand the conventions underlying this shift.

10.10 Though not the site of a muscle-group, the underarm is always shaved in bodybuilding competition, for reasons connected with the messages conveyed by hairless skin.

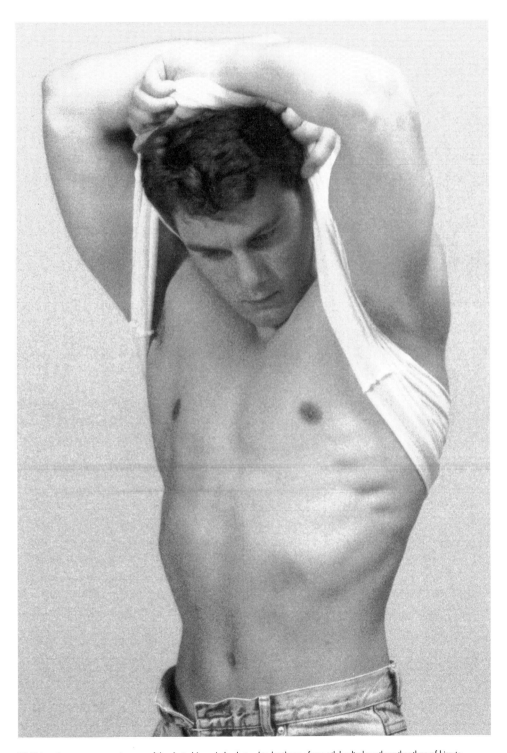

10.11 Popular contemporary images of the desirable male body tend to be those of smooth-bodied youths rather than of hirsute, bearded he-men.

The shaving of the whole or parts of the body has been practised in human societies since primitive times, sharpened stones having originally been used as a form of neolithic razor. The practice has possessed various kinds of significance — religious, political, social or sexual — from one culture to another. In ancient Egypt, both men and women commonly shaved their heads and bodies, possibly as a matter of hygiene[13]; in ancient Greece, the athletes who appeared naked in the gymnasium or arena were known to go so far as to shave (or pluck out) their pubic hair[14]. In contemporary Western society, certain parts of the body only (the face for men, the legs and underarm for women) are commonly shaved. The wearing of a beard is more frequent amongst certain male groups — academics and students, for instance — just as unshaven legs among women may be a social sign of feminism. The shaving of the head has often been required by authorities as a mark of submission: prisoners of war have had their heads shaved to humiliate them, and men and women who join religious orders have traditionally received the tonsure as a sign of humility and devotion[15].

Although the various messages involved in shaving are complex and disparate, it is possible to hazard some suggestions as to those connected with the modern bodybuilding display. The anthropologist Robert Brain has suggested that the shaving of body hair is associated with man's desire to make 'cultural' human qualities prevail over 'natural' beastly attributes, to distinguish us as humans from brute creation around us: 'A hairy body is an animal body. Wild men, like Esau the hunter, are hairy. Body hair is beastly and has to go in the interests of humanity.'[16] This distinction appears to have prevailed in fifth century Greece, where (as we have noted) the civilised, 'Apollonian' bodies of gods and athletes were hairless while those of more elemental, 'Dionysiac' figures were often misshapen and hairy. Other ancient cultures used a somewhat different symbolism: R.D. Guthrie notes, for instance, that in earlier and more authoritarian Western societies 'full beards, woolly chests, and rancid odours reinforced the lines of authority by giving a rather awesome or even fearsome visage.'

> 'Hairiness,' says Guthrie, 'is associated with most of the more important components of status — sex, age and size. It is easy to see why, in the locker room, a hairy body is nothing to be ashamed of. In a society that must emphasise co-operation and de-emphasise direct serious competition, excess hair may be too gross for most tastes, because it is a symbol for rough masculinity. If the best key to physical prowess among humans is the amount of body hair, the corollary is the more body hair, the greater the intimidation.'[17]

10.12 The smooth, hairless skin surface tends to contradict and thus neutralise the potentially intimidating messages of the muscular body.

In relation to facial hair, Guthrie's observation certainly accords with a number of social practices, from that of the heavily-bearded kings of Persia and the Pharaohs of Egypt (who wore false beards on ceremonial occasions to emphasise their power and authority) to that of the bikie-gangs of today who often cultivate beards as part of the image of fearsomeness.

In the case of the bodybuilder's shaven body it is doubtful that the message has directly to do with co-operation as the opposite of intimidation. On the other hand, it could have a good deal to do with a slightly different antithesis proposed by Guthrie: that between the older male and the baby or new-born, baby skin being 'our standard of inoffensive child-like beauty.'[18] He suggests a variant form of the behaviour known as *neoteny* — the reversion to an earlier state of evolution or life-cycle — which he calls 'social neoteny'[19]: this is a particular means of reducing the messages of intimidation by reverting to a more childlike appearance. Nakedness, a hairless body and smooth skin texture are all forms of social neoteny, signalling a childlike non-threatening quality and thus denying messages of aggression. In the light of such suggestive (if not conclusive) evidence, it could be argued that the point of shaving the body is to contradict, and thus neutralise, the aggressive or intimidating message of the super-normal adult male body-shape: to demonstrate, in other words, that this is not a body to be feared on account of its dominance, but rather to be looked at or touched — a body that places itself in the submissive role of 'object'.

The distinction being made here has been closely paralleled in the film world by the distinction which Michael Malone has noted between the dark-haired and blond-haired male movie star. Here, says Malone,

'the blond is the more spiritual, more "feminized", more childlike half. The male's blondness gives him an iconographic chastity. He seems more vulnerable, more fragile...... He lacks the self-protective (because conventional) camouflage of dark virility, and so he is visually connected, probably on a subliminal level, to the female sex role, with its cultural cognates — among them passive desirability'[20].

Malone contrasts the 'wholesome boyishness' of the blond Hollywood pin-up (such as Tab Hunter and later Jan-Michael Vincent) with the dark, moustached, macho star (Clark Gable, Burt Reynolds), who is always the seducer, never the seduced[21]. That many dark-haired film stars are hairy-chested and most blond stars smooth-chested may suggest a link with the messages of the hairless body, particularly as the removal of male body-hair was insisted upon by some film directors for actors who appeared with bare torsos. Some stars have even presented themselves in both guises: William Holden appeared with shaven chest in 1957 (*The Bridge on the River Kwai*) but with chest-hair in 1958 (*The Key*)[22], and the naturally hairy John Travolta has also 'shaved down' for the photographer. There has been only one hairy-chested Tarzan (Mike Henry), while Stallone and Schwarzenegger have very obviously been influenced by the bodybuilding convention and always appear with shaven bodies.

It is clear, then, that the hairless body conveys a particular message or set of messages, possibly related to the attenuation of hyper-masculinity by the enhancing of those submissive tactile qualities associated with the skin of the infant. So pervasive has the association become that body waxing and electrolysis for men is becoming increasingly common in some Western societies. The proprietor of a firm specialising in men's skin care has reported a marked trend towards hair-free torsos and limbs:

10.13 John Travolta is one of many male film stars who have on occasion shaved off their natural chest-hair for the camera.

'....the increase in hair removal for men [she says] reflected a reversal of roles. While women had undergone treatment for years, men were following suit. Women's aesthetic expectations of men were such that many gave their husbands or boyfriends gift cards for treatment. "A lot of the women tend to send the guys to have it done."'[23]

It would appear that the influence of bodybuilding on the presentation of the male body has extended, possibly by way of the film and television screen, into the wider world of social fashion, and that it has been affected at least to some extent by the increasing acceptance of the male body as an object of aesthetic or erotic contemplation.

10.14 The only hairy-chested screen Tarzan, Mike Henry (*Tarzan and the Valley of Gold*, 1966). From Elmo Lincoln onwards, all other actors have where necessary 'shaved down' for the role.

In a number of its manifestations — from heroic art to the erotic pin-up — the history of muscular body-display has been that of the nude male body. On the other hand, the one part of the bodybuilder's physique that is always kept covered is the genital region. Again, the most obvious explanation — social mores, the need for decency and a respectable sporting image, the avoidance of erotic overtones — is entirely correct but not entirely complete. It is well known, for instance, that penile display is an important part of the intimidation behaviour of primates other than man, and it would follow that it, like hairiness, must be reduced to the minimum if the messages of sexual (or other) aggression are to be neutralised. We noted earlier the unusually small size of the penis in many nude sculptures of the Classical period, and more than one commentator has pointed to the apparent discrepancy between the bulging muscles of the bodybuilder and the apparent tininess of the male organ hidden beneath the posing trunks[24]. Those who have seen professional bodybuilders naked will attest, not only to the unfoundedness of this assumption, but also to the remarkable adaptability of the male sexual organs and the compressive powers of Lycra. According to the interpretation proposed here, this is precisely the point of the exercise: once again, it is to neutralise the aggressive sexual message of the male body, in this case by giving the genital region the inoffensive and undeveloped appearance of the baby or pre-pubertal youth. In contemporary bodybuilding practice, posing trunks are worn as brief as possible, as if to reinforce the neutralising message.

In the ancient world, the diminutive and almost childlike penises of Greek vase paintings (and, to a lesser extent, the often disproportionately small sexual organs of heroic statuary) contrasted markedly with the exaggerated phalluses seen on satyrs, in pornographic figures and in Dionysiac celebration. The latter tradition is still reflected in homosexual toilet graffiti, of which Delph writes:

10.15 The bodybuilder's
posing trunks are
designed to minimise the
apparent size of the
genital area. Even in
Schwarzenegger's day,
the miniaturising trunks
of today's contests
would have been
considered
unacceptably brief.

'if one compares the proportions of the penis and testes to the rest of the torso in these drawings, they assume enormous size.... the larger the penis, the more virile the individual is thought to be, enhancing the amount of attention he receives.'[25]

At a more generally acceptable level of eroticism, it is a fact well attested by those 'in the business' — though seldom publicly admitted — that the G-strings and posing trunks worn by male strippers are commonly padded so as to give the genital region an appearance of greater size. This practice, which is often the source of fascinated speculation by viewers ('What do they keep down there?' asked one TV host, 'their lunch?'), is a further illustration of the contrast between the conventions of erotic display and the more complex messages of bodybuilding. As distinct from the bodybuilder's miniaturising trunks, the 'posing pouch' favoured in the sexually provocative physique magazines of the 1960s tends to draw attention to the genital area, often revealing a few tufts of pubic hair. The subsequent banning of this form of dress in competition bodybuilding may have had less to do with what it actually revealed (modern posing trunks are practically just as abbreviated, and any visible pubic hair is shaved) than with the extent to which it accentuated the bulge of the genitals.

10.16 Male strippers (the Australian group *Manpower*): 'What do they keep down there — their lunch?' asked a TV commentator. As well as being often padded to suggest a copious genital endowment, the stripper's trunks may sometimes be the recipients of financial contributions from the audience.

10.17 It has become increasingly acceptable in contemporary bodybuilding practice to leave part of the buttocks exposed, permitting the display of gluteal striation. The next logical development – the G-string – has not yet gained official acceptance.

Over the last ten years or so, male posing trunks have tended to be cut higher at the rear, exposing at least the lower half of the buttocks. This practice has become more common since a number of leading bodybuilders, beginning with Richard Gaspari, have made a feature of their impressive gluteal striation (the visible separation of muscle-bands in the gluteus maximus or large muscle of the buttocks). As in previous instances, however, there are perhaps more latent suggestions underlying the development in fashion. Unlike the male sexual organs, the buttocks are seen as non-intimidating, a symbol of passivity associated with infancy or childhood: a baby's bottom can be patted, smacked or even admired for its 'dimples'. Women's bodybuilding costume (like some women's beachwear) is often cut so as to leave some, if not all, of the buttocks exposed; the recent adoption of this fashion for men, as in the G-strings or 'thongs' which are now worn on some beaches, can here be seen as a further shift in gender-roles which has rendered the male body an acceptable object of aesthetic or erotic curiosity.

The skin which the bodybuilder exposes to our gaze is hardly ever the 'natural' skin, but rather a skin-surface which has been subjected to processes designed to enhance the message of muscular development. In Sandow's generation, the practice was to cover the already pale skin with a coating of white powder, in order to stress its resemblance to marble statuary. By the 1930s, however, social customs had undergone considerable change as the leisured classes had both the time and the means to take summer holidays, usually in a sunny climate[26]. This meant a complete reversal in fashion as compared with earlier generations in which tanned skin was the mark of the peasant or the outdoor labourer: the tan now became the badge of the upper classes, as the French Riviera and the beaches of Rio became the favourite resorts of the wealthy. Pale skin was the sign of the lowly office or factory worker, whose long working day was spent entirely indoors. The association with leisure and exercise gave rise to the notion of the 'healthy tan', which soon took over from the earlier pale skin as the new bodybuilding convention. By the time of the leading American bodybuilder of the 1940s, John Grimek, it had established itself completely and has since become almost mandatory.

Even in the present age, where the dangers of exposure to ultra-violet light are well publicised and the medical profession issues frequent warnings of the risk of melanoma or skin-cancer, there is no sign of a change in the convention of bodybuilding, and the tanned body is the universal norm. This being the case, it is probably fortunate from the medical point of view that those who do not tan easily have access to a wide range of chemical body dyes, tanning lotions, vegetable-based 'body-stains', canthaxanthin (or Vitamin A) tablets and a host of other artificial means of producing the desired colour. That the tan is 'fake' is unimportant: it is essentially a form of stage make-up. The skin need not *be* tanned, but it must *look* tanned.

10.18 The bodybuilder's tan, whether natural or not, is basically a form of stage make-up aimed at making the body look harder – at giving it the appearance of burnished bronze.

10.19 The deeply coloured and polished skin of the black bodybuilder creates naturally the effect that pale-skinned competitors can achieve only by tanning or artificial skin-colouring.

The metaphorical meaning of the convention is not far to seek, and is even clearer when seen in conjunction with the other chief mode of skin-preparation, the oiling of the body. Though much disputed as late as the 1960s, the coating of the skin with a light layer of oil is now standard practice. If inexperienced bodybuilders tend to overdo the effect and present the glistening spectacle of a body which appears to be wrapped in cellophane, more seasoned competitors seek the effect of a low sheen rather than a high gloss.

The tanned and oiled body replaces the symbolic associations of marble with those of polished bronze: the glint of light on the rounded muscle-surface contrasts with the deep colour of the depressions, so that the musculature stands out in dramatic and highly tactile contrast, a dark and polished surface which emphasises the rises and hollows of the muscles more vividly than can be achieved by the pale, matt texture of marble. The association is even more obvious in French, where the terms *bronzé* and *bronzage* are used to refer to tanned skin. The rise to eminence of a number of black bodybuilders in recent years, though mainly attributable to their genetic endowment and often formidable muscularity, has no doubt been assisted by the fact that their deeply coloured and naturally polished skin allows them to achieve the sought-after effect without resort to artificial means.

The visual effect in question is often described by bodybuilders themselves as 'looking hard', an optical impression which suggests the tactile firmness of the flexed muscle. At the level of metaphorical suggestion, however, the aim is not simply to resemble the appearance of burnished bronze, but to convey what the bronze statue and the bronze-like body alike suggest to us. No art-form, not even sculpture, is more purely concerned than the bronze with the visible *surface* of things: it is in its surface, says Jennifer Montagu, that the supreme quality of bronze resides, its particular effect being chiefly dependent on 'the interplay of its shapes and the movement of light and shade on its modelling.'[27] The frequently-made bronze copies of marble statues seem to speak a different language from that of their originals, the translation of light-absorbing stone into light-reflecting metal concentrating all attention on the outward play of highlights and shadows. Its dark, gleaming surface is suggestive of impenetrability or even invulnerability, as Jean-Paul Sartre recognised when he made the bronze statue in his play *Huis Clos* ('In Camera') the symbol of the inanimate world of fixed being as distinct from the human world of shifting inner consciousness.

Yet the body we see on the stage is not a statue, an attitude captured at a moment of time. We are in fact conscious of opposing and neutralising messages: this medium of representation is not impenetrable metal, but living and resilient flesh. The body moves, it breathes; it is part of our human world of mutability and transience. The muscles flex and unflex, limbs are extended and retracted, the abdominals turn suddenly from a cavernous vacuum into a glistening washboard,

10.20 The bodybuilder on
stage: not just an
inanimate object or
bronze statue, but a
living and breathing
human being who
inhabits the world of
subjectivity and
feeling.

the pectoral muscles are bounced up and down. The performer's face is at one moment serene and smiling, at the next contorted with effort; the body is now a road-map of vascularity, an anatomical drawing, now a series of soft and rounded planes, as sweeping as though drawn with a compass. At once aloof and intensely present, the body we see before us belongs to both the world of inanimate objects and the world of subjectivity and feeling, to the world of fixed being and the world of becoming.

It is obvious that this sophisticated array of self-cancelling messages of affirmation and denial could never have been designed or introduced as a pre-planned system. Despite its relatively recent origin, bodybuilding (like most sports) has evolved over the years more by experimentation and the processes of trial and error than by deliberate design. As innovations were introduced, they would either be adopted because they seemed somehow 'right' or would be abandoned. As with any internally consistent but outwardly hermetic code, the elements can be developed and elaborated only by those who speak and understand the symbolic language by which it operates. Had anyone set out in advance to devise a means whereby the human body could suggest, purely by its own visible configuration and presentation, a totality of physical being which by subsuming and reconciling opposing qualities both completes and somehow transcends them, one may well doubt that such an enterprise could ever have been successfully achieved. Only the accumulated and refined perceptions wrought by centuries of cultural tradition could have endowed the developed body with such imaginative potential.

PART III

THE CONTEMPORARY BODY

11.1 **CHAPTER 11** THE BODY OBSERVED
The male body as object of the female gaze is one of the more hotly debated issues of socio-sexual politics.

11

THE BODY OBSERVED

THE BODY'S IMAGE

The most characteristic means by which the twentieth century has filtered
the visual world and rendered it intelligible has been the photographed image. To
explore the contemporary social significance of the developed body is thus above all
to examine the ways in which it presents itself through the eye of the camera. At a
deeper level, since such images differ from those of the 'real' (non-photographed)
world in that they are seen through two pairs of eyes — our own and those of the
photographer — it is to ask how far they reflect a common social perception of the
body and how far they serve to 'construct', or at least to modify, that perception.

From the time of its origins, photography appropriated the human body as its
subject par excellence. Although the nude is only one of the forms in which the
camera has sought to capture, confront or express what it means to be human,
photographers have constantly seen the depiction of the body, free of the camouflage
of clothing, as in some way revealing the essential dimension of humanity. At some
time in their careers, most of the important photographers have turned to the nude as
though it represented the yardstick by which photographic talent was to be measured;
a number of them, indeed, have sought to define their individual talent by their
particular way of presenting the unclothed body. Although the nude appears to depict
the body as immediately accessible to our scrutiny, free of artifice and accretions —
or perhaps because it merely *appears* to do so — its political and sexual ramifications
are constantly open to changing ideological interpretation. How is it to be 'read',
and why? Can it ever be understood in purely formal terms, as mere shape and
texture filling a space, or does it necessarily entail an engagement (or disengagement)
which defines an attitude — social, sexual or even political? Such questions apply
equally to the female and the male body, but their relation to photographed images
of the developed male body has particular significance for our central theme.

11.2 Tom Bianchi, *Carl on a Pedestal*. The pedestal is the classical prop *par excellence*. Often used to decontextualise the human
subject and suggest a classical fixity, it here belongs to a landscape of dead objects which throw into relief the living human
form.

Even if we accept the style of depiction of the objectified body as to some extent conditioning our interpretation of its 'meaning', there remains the issue of how far any single interpretation can exhaust the total reservoir of possible readings of which the displayed body may be capable. Some viewers will consider the photographer's intentions relevant to their own appreciation of the work, while others, more alert to the 'intentional fallacy', will see the work as inescapably incorporating a set of attitudes of which the photographer may well have been unaware. While it is obviously important to distinguish between the photographer's intentions and the reading (or readings) which the viewer may derive from any actual photograph, this does not mean that these two ways of seeing are mutually exclusive or that we are obliged to choose between them. As we have observed in relation to the world of high art, a work may operate at several levels, at one of which it may be interpreted in terms of purely formal qualities (treatment of light and shade, composition, colour, texture, etc.) whilst at others it may be understood as reflecting a social attitude — from voluptuous eroticism or tender affection to savage irony. The very openness of non-verbal modes of communication to a range of interpretative possibilities means that an individual work can be 'read' simultaneously in a number of ways. In relation to the nude, it is precisely because the contextual signs of 'meaning' are to be found in the body itself (or, implicitly, in its pose or setting) rather than in the more variable clues provided by the artist's treatment of 'conventional', i.e. clothed, reality, that the social meanings we can derive from the nude are so elusive and potentially so heterogeneous.

While questions of this nature are central to the serious discussion of photography, such discussion tends for this very reason to relate chiefly to what is thought of as 'serious' (or 'art') photography — exhibited in either small and specialised galleries or art museums, reproduced in limited-number catalogues and analysed in magazines and journals aimed at sophisticated or academic audiences. In relation to popular, commercially-oriented photography, on the other hand, such questions are less frequently posed, save perhaps in the context of the sociological analysis of commercially-driven media in general.

In the case of the unclad male body, however, the neat division into 'serious' and 'popular' photography has become a good deal more tenuous with the increasing vogue of 'upmarket' photography of the male body which has been current (especially in the USA) since the early 1980s. Typically, it has been associated with the work of 'name' photographers whose portraits of the rich and famous have brought them both celebrity and professional respectability, not least through establishing their work at the upper end of the lucrative commercial market. Photographers such as Robert Mapplethorpe, Bruce Weber and Herb Ritts have taken the muscular male body (whether nude or minimally clad) as a dominant theme of their work alongside the portraiture of the international glitterati and political celebrities which appears to be a requirement for superstar status within the photographic profession. In the

11.3 Tom Bianchi's photographic series *Deserts and Hot Springs* is a re-working of the Adam myth. Though it can be appreciated as a purely formal study in contrasting shapes and textures, this photo from early in the series can also be understood in the context of the myth — man, newly-emerged from the primeval dark, offers himself to the sun which is the source of life and light. (Tom Bianchi, *Natural Bridge*.)

process, they have achieved such stature as contemporary iconographers of the developed body that their work has moved well beyond the sphere of 'art photography' and into that of popular culture. Mapplethorpe calendars, Weber wall-posters and Ritts postcards are now high-volume sellers in stationery outlets around the world, having become equally familiar as items of trendy domestic decor as the ubiquitous images of Madonna or Bruce Springsteen. Almost as much as the torsos of Schwarzenegger or Stallone, these photos have come to define the popular image of male muscularity, and at the same time underscored the difficulty of achieving a single, unequivocal reading of their status as artistic objects.

The notoriety attaching to Robert Mapplethorpe's openly pornographic studies[1] has to some extent distracted public attention from his crucial formative role in this group. Quite apart from his portraits of celebrities, his classicising studies of black nudes — notably Derrick Cross, 'Ajitto' and 'Thomas' (gay porn-star Joe Simmons) — had an important role in popularising the muscular male nude as an object of public attention.[2] While most media debate on Mapplethorpe has revolved around the artistic value (or lack of it) of his pornographic work, a more interesting

— because less predictable — argument has taken place concerning the interpretation of these highly sculptural, idealised black bodies. Though most early criticism praised the extraordinary beauty of line, texture and finish of Mapplethorpe's pseudo-classical studies,[3] recent commentary has often been less inclined to dwell on these formal elements and has condemned Mapplethorpe's view of black 'otherness' as decadent, imperialist or even racist. Melody Davis, for instance, has accused Mapplethorpe of hypocrisy, of purporting to compliment blacks while wiping out their identity under muscular physiques whose sole sign is sexual agency[4]; and Allen Ellenzweig has denounced him for pandering, even posthumously, to a commercial art market all too ready to accept slickly-packaged and beautifully sculpted sex as yet another expensive commodity to be hung on the wall.[5] Davis' criticism is rejected by those who do not share her view of looking-as-power and who recognise in Mapplethorpe a genuine empathy with his black subjects as fellow-outsiders, while Ellenzweig's attack is seen by some as simply misplaced — justified perhaps in relation to the art-market but not in respect of a photographer who set out (successfully) to subvert its values.

11.4 'A study in dualities, contrasting not only formal but human qualities: shade and light, faces and no faces, the natural and the posed, human emotion and classical fixity, real people and anonymous sculptural figures.' (Tom Bianchi, *Two Men/Two Statues*.)

11.5 The photograph can often be read at a multiplicity of levels. In Tom Bianchi's, *Victor's Solo Flight*, the composition at first appears paramount, belying the complex set of allusions – mythological, literary, artistic –which give it a semantic content beyond its purely visual appeal.

Reaction to the work of Bruce Weber has been equally divided. Here, here we move from the world of Mapplethorpe's blacks to that of muscular and wholesome 'all-American boys', virile college athletes or marines. Weber's domain is the exclusive advertising market (*Gentlemen's Quarterly*, *Per Lui*, *L'Uomo Vogue*) and the deluxe coffee-table volume[6] rather than the art photography exhibition, while his more popular Calvin Klein *Obsessions* series gave him international exposure as a purveyor of 'squeaky clean' icons of self-possessed, youthful beauty. Yet this uncomplicated world of physical perfection has not been without its detractors, not only on account of its subservience to desirable advertising images aimed at seducing consumers into purchasing a product and, implicitly, the 'look' that goes with it, but even more damningly because of the underlying utopian aesthetics which makes his photography so reminiscent of fascist art. Good-looking and well developed, these racially superior Aryan specimens cavorting or exercising in the open air bear an unmistakable resemblance to the German athletes of the 1930s who inspired Leni Riefenstahl, Arno Breker and Hans Surén, so much so that E. Roger Denson can refer to Weber's photography as suggesting 'the restitution of Nazi metaphors and the perverse recharge of their power as sexual and emotional fetishes'.[7]

Herb Ritts, whose reputation was built on the twin bases of regulation portraits of the rich and famous, and the seminal and much-reproduced 'hunk' photo *Fred With Tires* (1984), has continued in both veins, his physique photography moving first to the nude (the 'Man in a Bubble' series) and subsequently to the homoerotic with his studies of bodybuilder Bob Paris making love on the beach with his marriage partner Rod Jackson.[8] So great has been Ritts' popular success in the field of male eroticism that it has added further to his celebrity as a 'name' photographer of the famous, rather than the other way around.

Ritts' increasingly daring forays into homoeroticism have not only done no harm to his professional reputation, but can in some ways be seen as reflecting the growing acceptability — at least in more sophisticated or 'trendy' circles — of the openly erotic photograph as an object of public taste. It may at first seem surprising that a master of the contemporary image such as Victor Skrebneski, whose dramatic chiaroscuro transforms his own muscular nudes into formal studies of detached anatomical observation, should praise the suggestively erotic images of soft-porn gay iconographer Jim French for their controlled intensity and passion.[9] Yet in so doing he underlines even further the impossibility of isolating the body as pure visual object from its latent overtones of sensual desire. Ever since Susan Sontag advanced her persuasive thesis that the act of photography is by its nature a surrogate possession of the object, no attempt to capture the human body through the lens of the camera has been exempt from interpretation as an act of sublimated eroticism, and it is not for nothing that one leading international photographer of the male body has been described to the author by a colleague as 'photographing the men he cannot have'.

But the popular status of the male body-cult in contemporary photography cannot be understood in purely artistic or even erotic terms, divorced from its commercial and marketing overtones. Indeed, the leading figures in this popularising movement seem to constitute a relatively small and exclusive group clustering around the commercial fashion industry and the style-houses of New York. There even seems at times a kind of incestuous aspect to their mutual interaction: Herb Ritts takes a series of TV and magazine shots of dancer/rapper/model Marky Mark, to whose body Annie Leibovitz had already devoted a coffee-table pictorial volume; Mark is modelling the very same brand of underwear (Calvin Klein) on which Bruce Weber had made his popular reputation; and so it goes on. Yet this tightly-knit little world of expensive 'name' photographers, precisely because of its intimate links to the commercial world of glossy magazines and fashion houses, is uniquely in a position to dictate 'The Look' which is held up to mass consumers in search of those images of perfection which contemporary Western society has come to see as attainable commodities.

The above discussion has focused on photographers whose work has had a significant impact on popular images of the male body, as distinct from those who have concentrated on experimental work or who have had relatively little public exposure. It is precisely because of their huge commercial success that the images of a Mapplethorpe or a Weber cannot be construed merely as examples of form-as-content, however skilful their technical use of line, mass, light and surface. There is something about Mapplethorpe's sculpturally decontextualised (and thus 'safe') blacks and Weber's uncomplicatedly heterosexual (and thus 'safe') athletic demigods which compels a deeper, even a darker, reading, even if the latter never rises from the subconscious to reach the seductive physical surface at which these photographs exercise a popular appeal as the mirror-images of materialistic desire.

Outside the lucrative but compromised world of commercial image-making, the work of Tom Bianchi[10] has taken a more straightforward and in many ways more honest approach to the use of the developed male physique as a photographic object. Not constrained by commercial pressure to avoid or conceal messages of homoerotic desire, the photographer's unashamed delight in the physical beauty of his muscular subjects is at once evident and attenuated by other points of interest in the photograph which endow it with a visual and referential complexity — even at times a certain humour — rarely found in this genre. Bianchi's aim is to challenge the conventions of 'high art' — the legitimising conceits which permit us to gaze upon the naked body but, in so doing, rob it of warmth, tenderness, affection or delight. Many of his photographs thus depend on our first recognising the high art convention in order to understand the point of his departure from it.

At once evoking and rejecting the decontextualisation of Mapplethorpe's *Ajitto* series (the idealised black body on its classical pedestal), Bianchi's *Carl on a Pedestal* takes us back to the natural setting of the original painting by Hippolyte Flandrin (*Jeune homme nu assis au bord de la mer*), but replaces the romantic seascape by arid dunes among which man is the only living thing. *Two Men/Two Statues* is a study in dualities, contrasting not only formal but human qualities: shade and light, faces and no faces, the natural and the posed, human emotion and classical fixity, real people and anonymous sculptural figures. At the most complex referential level of all, *Victor's Solo Flight* supposes a cultural background including painting, poetry and mythology. The 'solo flight' here is not only a reference to the figure of Icarus, but more particularly to W.H. Auden's poem *Musée des Beaux-Arts*, with its evocation of the Brueghel painting in which 'everything turns away/Quite leisurely' from what is going on elsewhere in the scene — 'Something amazing, a boy falling out of the sky.' Whereas Auden leaves the reader caught between human grandeur and the everyday triviality of living, Bianchi reverses the metaphor: his suspended flyer, classically sculpted and isolated, is contrasted with the world of human dialogue in which the foreground figures engage with each other or (implicitly) the viewer.

If, as seems likely, Bianchi's work achieves a wider circulation, particularly outside the gay community, it may well mark a new phase in the re-establishment of the muscular male nude in serious photography. His best works demand to be approached not as icons but as commentaries, as requiring of intellectual reflection as Dureau's nude cripples but here asserting the shared celebration of the physical self in a world where the fear of AIDS has led to its denial or displacement. Calling upon the suggestive overtones of physical perfection which have become deeply ingrained in our Western consciousness and our common visual language, he has sought to endow them with contemporary meaning and relevance, and above all with humanity.

11.6 Can the nude ever be understood in purely formal terms, as mere shape and texture filling a space, or does it necessarily entail an engagement or disengagement which defines an attitude? (John Freund, *Four Studies of Chuck*.)

MEN'S BODIES, WOMEN'S EYES

In the world of European high art, women were (with rare exceptions) denied a place in the ateliers where male models posed in classical attitudes. Women artists usually found themselves restricted to still life or natural history painting, their eventual admission to the life-class in the late nineteenth century being a sign of their incipient sexual as well as social emancipation. The romantic notion of a 'world of art', removed from and more morally elevated than that of everyday reality, gave a degree of social and ideological acceptability to the role of women as observers of the male body. Even this advance was not without its setbacks, as witness the demand by the Pennsylvania Academy of Fine Arts in 1876 that Eakins resign his teaching position for allowing his women students to draw from nude male models in defiance of 'maidenly decency'.[11] With the photographic studies of nude males by Imogen Cunningham in the 1920s (and later, those by the 'new realists' Yvonne Gregory and Hedda Walther), the overtones of erotic suggestion could no longer be overlooked, but the formal and technical excellence of these women's treatment of their male subjects was sufficient, at least in the eyes of the art establishment, to place their work in the morally exempt category of 'art photography', which had taken on a status earlier reserved for traditional painting and sculpture.

The Women's Liberation Movement, however, was to change the social mood entirely, and from the 1970s onwards sporadic attempts would be made in various media to publish representations of the male body aimed specifically at female audiences. More significantly, these moves were to take place, not under the banner of artistic licence or higher purpose, but with the avowed intention of presenting the male body as an object of desire. In popular women's magazines and in advertising images aimed at women, men now routinely appear in various stages of undress and engage the (implicitly female) viewer in a frankly erotic visual exchange.

The emergence of the well-developed male body as the object of the female gaze has created an unusual dilemma for those who hold to a radical feminist position, since it cuts across traditional gender-based stereotypes. Indeed, within the spectrum of socio-sexual viewpoints broadly labelled feminist, it is possible to discern at least two quite different attitudes towards the male body as erotic public object. On the one side, its display is welcomed as a sign of sexual equality for women, whose long-denied role as spectators or observers is thereby legitimised; equally, by placing men in the subservient or submissive category of object of the gaze, it tends to restore the politics of sexual interaction to a position of balance or equality. This is avowedly the motivation behind the growing visibility of the unclad or semi-clad male as background decoration in magazine advertisements promoting clothes or accessories for 'liberated' women, and the re-introduction (after a shaky start in *Viva*,

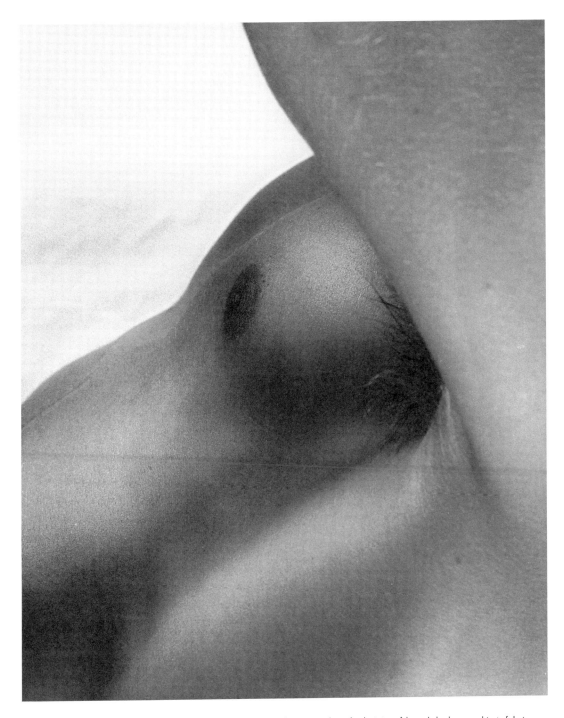

11.7 Women photographers might be expected to have a distinctive contribution to make to the depiction of the male body as an object of desire. Some commentators have seen women's images of the male body as less preoccupied with the language of muscularity and dominance than are the images photographed by men. (Liane Audrins and Toni Shuker, *Robert 3.*)

11.8 'Women now say: "God, see the buns on that guy."' The male physique as an object of erotic contemplation for women is now a feature of a number of popular women's magazines.

Cosmopolitan and the like in the late 70s) of the nude male centrefold, now a regular feature of women's magazines such as *Interlude* (USA), *For Women* (UK) and *Australian Women's Forum*. As the (female) creative director of a firm producing male 'hunk' calendars puts it:

> 'Women now say: "God, see the buns on that guy." We're coming out of the closet, we're allowed to feel free about our sexuality. It's about time we're allowed to have a good perv. Guys have been able to do it for centuries.'[12]

The journalist Deirdre Macken has commented in similar vein:

> 'If you dare, pick up a women's magazine. There is man in full glory. You don't even have to cut along the dotted line to get to him. Rows of penises; nude men reclining on bunny rugs ... The album of today's man is beginning to resemble *Cosmopolitan*-in-drag.'[13]

This relatively recent development, as we noted earlier, borrows heavily from the depiction of the male nude in gay iconography, to the point where articles on the male body in some contemporary women's magazines — and the accompanying photographs —are at times reprinted directly from the pages of male-oriented journals such as *Gentlemen's Quarterly* and various other men's publications catering directly or indirectly to a homosexual readership.

By the same token, however, such role-reversal sits uneasily with the widely-held feminist notion that the erotically-tinged display of the body in commercial media is a form of exploitation directed against women. The feminist author Beatrice Faust has pointed out that 'feminists who claim that the subtext, or indeed the text, of pornography is violence against women, fail to examine homophile pornography, art and erotica.'[14] Such an observation, whilst undermining the traditional hard-core feminist line (men as aggressors, women as victims), is by no means an argument for the acceptance of men's portrayal as sex-objects on the grounds of re-establishing sexual equality; rather, it suggests that the use of the male as well as the female body purely as an erotic object (whether for voyeuristic or commercial exploitation) may now be included in the radical feminist demonology. The otherwise unlikely alignment of certain sections of the feminist movement with the so-called 'moral Right' in the attack on soft-core popular magazines as well as X-rated or hard-core pornography tends to be founded on a convergence of moral, social and (in some cases) religious grounds rather than on the more restricted issue of male-female sexual politics. Not for the first time, and not in this field only, do the social Left and Right come together in ideological coalition to oppose a liberalising tendency which both perceive as gaining untoward social acceptance.

11.9 '... Rows of penises; nude men reclining ...' The relatively recent depiction of male nudity in some women's magazines borrows from the much longer tradition of gay iconography.

Some social commentators have attributed this divergence of attitude within feminism to broadly evolutionary or generational factors in the Women's Movement. Andrew Wernick, for example, argues that the initial stage in the attack on sexual stereotyping, characterised by Betty Friedan's salvos against the depiction of women purely as mothers and housewives, was succeeded by a shift of target to the objectification of women as sexual objects or decorative symbols of desire, particularly in advertising photography but also in more specific instances such as

11.10 Whether portrayed as sexual object or sexual agent, the exposed male body is seen by some social commentators as inescapably phallic.

the celebrated disruption of the 1968 Miss World Contest. In a third and more recent phase, says Wernick, the attack has widened to include all forms of 'visual porn' or sexual objectification, whether relating to men or women.[15] In addition to the already well established historical classification of the Women's Movement into 'First Wave' (equity-based) and 'Second Wave' (gender-based or 'gynocentric') feminism, Wernick can be understood as proposing a third and more recent historical category — no doubt equally grounded in a critique of androcentric or patriarchal assumptions but of more general application across the gender-divide (even if more closely targeted in social terms).

It is certainly the case that the above three areas of concern within the Women's Movement have followed one upon another chronologically, though it would be incorrect to conclude that they therefore represent the attitudes of successive generations of feminists — let alone the views of women generally in bourgeois Western societies. Indeed, it could be argued that the so-called 'post-feminist' movement has radically modified certain of the assumptions underlying the second and third of the phases identified above, whilst the current vogue of male erotic images in some sections of women's media suggests that the third phase (at least) is far from being a general trend, even amongst women who perceive themselves as sexually emancipated. Australian feminists who in early 1993 threw paint bombs at a Melbourne billboard depicting a young woman wearing black lingerie were curiously silent when, a few weeks later, another hoarding in the same city featured the apparently naked body of a seventeen-year-old male with underpants dropped to his feet and a provocative sexual slogan strategically covering his genital area. A few months later, when a well-known surfing 'ironman' appeared on a billboard clad only in his running shoes, prominent feminists were actually quoted as approving the portrayal, while criticism was left to a spokesman for the group Men Against Sexual Violence.

It is clear that there is a marked divergence of attitude between 'popular' feminism (that of the mass-circulation women's magazines) and the more ideologically-driven movement grounded in a serious social critique. The latter, branded as 'academic feminism', has been the subject of well-publicised attacks by the author Camille Paglia (*Sexual Personae; Sex, Art and American Culture*), but the quirkiness both of Paglia herself and of her social analysis, while cleverly serving the cause of her high media profile, seems unlikely to give her a wide following amongst the very audience for which she writes. The most revealing indicator of changing values amongst Western women may, in any case, be found in the mass-circulation magazines and TV talk-shows rather than in the writings of academics on one side or the other of the intellectual debate. The emergence of such groups as Feminists Against Censorship has further complicated the picture, suggesting a move within intellectually serious feminism itself to deflect the focus of attack away from phallocentric conspiracy and towards a less judgmental, categorising approach to male (and female) sexual expression. This move, which tends to affirm sexual iconography (and even pornography), both male and female, post-dates the third of the phases listed by Wernick, against which it represents a backlash bitterly contested by other sections of the feminist movement.

The question remains, then, whether the concept of 'Men for Women' can ever re-establish a balance or equality in the perception of gender-roles or the power relations between the sexes. Images of men that are offered to women as sexual spectacle may indeed, at a superficial level, reverse the traditional roles of spectator and object, but it has been questioned whether this reversal reflects a shift in the fundamental power-politics of sexuality. Rather, it has been argued, the notion of staring as-power and of being looked at as powerlessness (or at least passivity) undergoes a significant modification when gender-roles are reversed so that it is the male who becomes the object of the gaze. In this view, the male body's symbolic status as phallus is inescapable whatever the apparent context of display. Even when portrayed as sexual object rather than sexual agent, the exposed male body is seen as an inescapable affirmation of male identity and thus an implicit assertion of the (hidden, disguised or sanitised) celebration of masculinity and patriarchy. A variant form of this view is applied by radical feminists to the pop-star Madonna, whose indiscriminate portrayal of men and women as both sexual agents and sexual objects is seen as a sign, not of women's equality, but of women's complicity in the politics of sexual dominance, of the star herself as 'female phallus'. Like the feminist debate about the male body, this is only one facet of a wider socio-sexual rather than generational difference in perspective within the women's movement. To at least some extent, it reflects the divergence of attitude between those who cling to a traditional romantic view of sexual love, particularly in the sanitised and idealised form in which it continues to be purveyed by some sections of the popular media, and those (perhaps an increasing number in our society) who hold the more cynical view that sexual relations are ultimately about the physical and emotional power of one person over another.

The approach one takes to the depiction of men's (and women's) bodies in commercial and other public media will depend in large measure on whether one assumes a purely reductionist viewpoint — feminist or otherwise — which interprets all such portrayals according to a single frame of reference, or alternatively whether one accepts contextual factors as defining or modifying one's perception of visual images. These contextual factors will include such variables as explicit or implicit intention (humour, fantasy or parody), cultural conditioning (reflected in historical or stylistic convention) and, perhaps most importantly, the emotional, sexual and social values of the individual observer or viewer. More than one commentator has pointed out that the depiction of a woman's body as the object of sexual aggression may provoke very different interpretations according to whether it appears in a men's 'girlie' magazine or a lesbian S & M publication — a reminder, if one were needed, of the nature of visual images as imaginative constructs rather than 'raw' information. While this is not to deny that the presentation of men's bodies as objects of the female gaze creates its own definable context, it does suggest that the scope left open for women's interpretation of such images is considerably wider than some feminist ideologies have proposed.

It might have been expected that women photographers would have a distinctive contribution to make to the depiction of the male body as the object of desire, but in general their role as 'authors' of such images has not paralleled their role as consumers. Though women photographers have long held an established place as interpreters of the male body, most have preferred experimental modes to the 'idealised realism' of their male contemporaries, or else have concentrated on the vulnerability or pathos of the male body rather than the metaphoric possibilities of muscularity. Melody Davis has pointed out that women's images of male nudity often relay signs pointing more to personal or social relation than to the body as abstracted form or ideological symbol. Though she recognises that none of the issues raised by the male photograph — including narcissism, fetishization and phallocentrism — are gender specific (indeed, to label them as such 'would no doubt engage stereotype'), nonetheless she agrees that there is generally a disinclination on the part of women photographers to move beyond the sphere of 'relational' images (often of husbands, fathers or children) and into that of the nude as an idea.[16]

Of those women who have actually ventured into 'hunk' territory, disappointingly few have added significantly to the photographic language, though one of the more gifted, Grace Lau, has attempted to inject a certain humour even into the women's magazine centrefold by wrapping her models in cling film or various kinds of fantasy garb.[17] The (female) Japanese critic Hiromi Nakamura has suggested that there is open to women a particular way of viewing the male body which builds upon seeing it through female eyes and at the same time, imaginatively, through the eyes of the male models themselves. Through this dialectic, she believes, can be constructed yet a third way of seeing the body — through neutral eyes — leading to a new recognition of what she calls 'the latent plurality of gender'.[18] It is difficult to

11.11 Setting, symbolism, attitude, expression — the visual image of the displayed body is an imaginative exercise rather than 'raw' information.

know quite how such an enterprise might be realised, and it appears likely to remain, at least for the time being, an aspiration of the photographic theorist rather than a visible actuality.

The de-coding of the muscular male body is one of the more problematic issues in the analysis of contemporary imagery, whether serious or popular. In the case of the presentation of the male body to the female gaze, the issue is further complicated by the socio-sexual perspective of the viewer. It is clear that the debate as to the implicit symbolism of the objectified male body is far from resolved within the women's movement, and there seems little prospect that a consensus will emerge. Part, at least, of the problem of interpretation resides in the very metaphoric power of the body itself, its capacity to symbolise and incorporate the often ambiguous and even contradictory social messages which modern Western societies send to themselves in an attempt to establish their own meaning and identity.

THE OBJECTIFIED BODY

In his influential analysis of the image of the male pin-up, Richard Dyer makes the point that the crucial issue of interpretation is not whether the model looks at his spectator(s), but how he does or does not — 'where and how he is looking in relation to the woman looking at him, in the audience or as she leafs through the fan or women's magazine.' Whereas the female model, says Dyer, typically averts her eyes — the normal social reaction of women, based on a tradition of male dominance — the male model tends to look off or up. Unlike the averted eyes, which implicitly acknowledge the viewer, the male model's look suggests a lack of interest in the viewer: it implies rather that 'his mind is on higher things', an attitude reflected in the pose of the body which equally suggests a 'straining and striving upward'. Even when looking at the camera, the male convention tends to be the serious look ('the stare') rather than the inviting smile of the female pin-up. In this way, Dyer argues, the male model disavows the superficial appearance of passivity associated with the fact of being situated as object of the gaze.[19]

11.12 The stare: 'disavowing the superficial appearance of passivity associated with being situated as object of the gaze.'

Dyer cites the typical portrayal of men — whether as pin-ups or other objects of the fantasising gaze — as images of men doing something; 'caught in the middle of an action, or associated, through images in the pictures, with activity'. Importantly, this suggestion is maintained even when the male figure is not seen in action:

> 'Even in an apparently relaxed, supine pose, the model tightens and
> tautens his body so that the muscles are emphasised, hence drawing
> attention to the body's potential for action. More often, the male pin-up
> is not supine anyhow, but standing taut ready for action.'[20]

It is for this reason, Dyer argues, that the body quality most promoted in the objectified male body is muscularity. The copy accompanying these photos typically calls on readers to 'getta load of his muscles', that is, to use muscularity as a key term in appraising men's bodies. Returning to the symbolism which has become a leitmotif of our analysis, Dyer points to the *hardness* of muscle as bespeaking phallic power and dominance. 'The clenched fists, the bulging muscles, the hardened jaws, the proliferation of phallic symbols — they are all straining after what can hardly ever be achieved, the embodiment of the phallic mystique.' While it may be objected that the potential for muscularity is a biological, and thus natural, quality of the male body, the fact is that 'developed muscularity — muscles that *show* — is not in truth natural at all, but is rather achieved. The muscle man is the end product of his own activity of muscle building.'[21] The legitimation of male power and domination, already implicit in the idea of the biological 'naturalness' of male muscle, is further accentuated by the suggestion of achievement implicit in the display of developed muscularity.

Dyer's analysis provides a useful insight into much of the covert imagery of the muscular male physique as presented in contemporary media. One may wonder, however, whether the deconstruction of such images purely in terms of hidden power relationships does sufficient justice to the variety of forms in which the male body presents itself to the objectifying gaze. In particular, one might take issue with Dyer's suggestion that the presentation of the male body as object must always be read in terms of phallic power and dominance regardless of the apparent context of display. This is not to deny the latent phallic allusiveness of the muscular body, however it presents itself: as we have noted in a number of other contexts where muscle functions as an aspirational image — from the pursuit of political dominance to the dream of enhanced sexual potency — the 'body-as-phallus' construct is always an implicit possibility in our understanding of muscular development or display. To that extent, the TV critic Clive James showed acute (if perhaps unconscious) insight in describing Schwarzenegger's pumped and oiled body as looking like 'a condom filled with walnuts', and the popular designation of *Conan the Barbarian* as 'Condom the Vulgarian' can be interpreted as more than word-play. The point needs to be

11.13 'There's a cutting up of men's bodies. We're being shown just bottoms or just thighs ... When you present people as just hunks of meat, it disempowers them.'

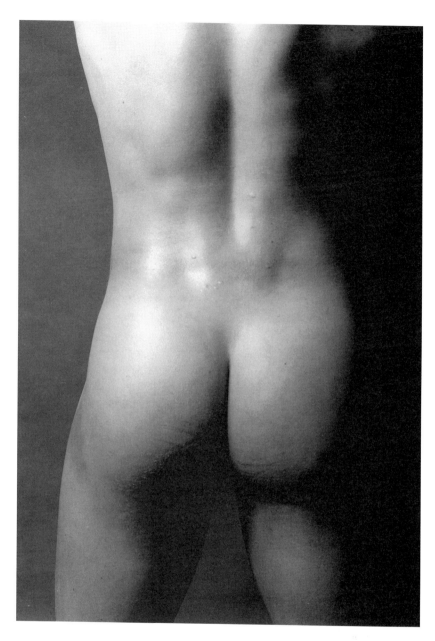

made, however, that the publicly displayed body may be capable of more than one reading, so that simultaneous, alternative or even contradictory readings may be possible. I have sought to argue that the attenuation of the hyper-masculine (phallic) image by a number of contradictory signs can significantly alter the message of the displayed body in such a way as to neutralise — or at least render highly ambiguous —the suggestion of untrammelled male dominance or sexual aggressivity.

The distinction made earlier between the bodybuilder's posing and the male striptease underlined the difference in contextual signs between two modes of muscular display despite their apparent similarities. A major limitation of Dyer's thesis is that, by assuming that the underlying agenda (male power and domination) is always the same whatever the context in which the muscular male body is presented to the gaze, he is obliged to restrict his analysis to those examples which suit his purpose and to ignore those which do not. The non-engagement of the male pin-up with the viewer (the looking off or up, the serious stare at or through the camera) is seen as a denial of being looked at and thus a hidden affirmation of dominant male sexuality. This is a plausible interpretation (though not universally applicable, even to the male pin-up — each woman's journal has its own house-style, and eye contact by the objectified male is employed in the 'hunk' shots used in some of them); but it manifestly does not apply to the much more overt display of muscular machismo often found in the male stripper's routine, where the female viewer's gaze is often met by an unambiguously inviting smile and bodily gestures to match. Are we to conclude that two such contradictory modes of presentation are actually conveying the same message (one overtly and one covertly, perhaps), or may we not equally conclude that the studied non-engagement of the muscular pin-up is an implicit invitation to view his body in more exclusively objective terms — literally, as an *object* — without the suggestion of active sexual desire (and particularly sexual dominance) on his part?

In any case, not every portrayal of the objectified male body (even of the muscular body) uses muscle, as Dyer intimates, to suggest 'striving' and 'straining': a languid or recumbent pose, as we have seen, can effectively contradict the symbolism of phallic power implicit in the tautness of contracted muscle, and this convention is sometimes used in the male pin-up or centrefold. To this may be added the increasingly common depiction of a single part of the male body rather than the body as a whole, a style of representation already familiar in images of women and serving here to undermine the stereotype of male dominance. The sociologist Diana Shaw has commented critically on this practice:

'There's ... a cutting up of men's bodies. We're being shown just bottoms or just thighs. When you present people — whether men or women — as just hunks of meat, it strips them of identity and disempowers them.'[22]

Webb's analysis of this more passive style of depiction accounts for a number of contextual signs which Dyer's hypothesis leaves unexamined: 'For a man to be relaxed and inert and passive is a source of massive anxiety, for what might then enter his body? It means identification with the feminine, and that he is to be *worked upon*, rather than *working*.'[23] Though the visual language of denial is quite different here from the case of the bodybuilder — it transposes eroticism rather than neutralising it — the fact remains that in both cases the reading of the body is less straightforward than the simple phallic power hypothesis would suggest.

Notwithstanding the uncertainties and ambiguities of its contemporary status as a social phenomenon — even, perhaps, because of them — I believe it is still possible to read the developed body in a coherent way, by reference to the conventions embedded in the Western tradition of high art and worked out over the centuries of its evolution. I have argued that there are, broadly, two prototypes for the traditional

11.14 'The Look': a preference for neotenic youth, a lithe body and regular facial features is characteristic of the contemporary male icon.

11.15 Even the heavily-muscled heroic style of the 'hunk' calendar owes to the aesthetic/ erotic tradition elements of a visual language first developed for the gaze of other men.

depiction of the male body-as-object — one of them stressing its heroic, super-masculine traits, the other presenting features associated with the passive object of desire. Heavy muscularity in the 'heroic' mode is conceptually quite distinct from the muscularity associated with youthful neoteny and the lithe and slender physique of the 'aesthetic' mode. Though conceding that there is no accounting for tastes and that the heroic body might appeal to the sexual imagination of some spectators, I believe that the convention is strong enough to maintain this distinction of principle. It can be argued, I think, that most female (and gay male) viewers of the *Farnese*

Hercules would find its exaggerated muscularity as sexually unexciting as the spindly ectomorphism of the puny 'seven-stone weakling'. The popular image of male desirability is of a trim muscularity (commonly characterised as 'well-proportioned' or 'well-developed' but 'not too muscly'): 'the Look', says a gay magazine, 'is now definitely athletic and not overgrown muscle: tight abdomens and buns [and] V-shaped torsos ... While traditional bodybuilding was preoccupied with bulk (the "more muscles the merrier") the new "body sculpting" concentrates on tightness and symmetry of form.'[24] In popular media images designed to appeal to both female and gay male viewers, a lithe athleticism is combined with regular facial features bordering on the neotenic or 'pretty' rather than the rugged or mature, and adolescent girls classify their fantasised idols as either 'spunks' or 'hunks'.

The predilection for the 'erotic/aesthetic' mode of depiction (whether in art, photography or live display) has always been at least tinged with homoeroticism, and often openly homoerotic: this has been the case since its earliest formulation in ancient Greek art, and it remains so today in the visual language of gay culture. What distinguishes its contemporary manifestation is its extension to the gaze of female viewers and thus its appropriation by the sexual mainstream. From 'hunk' calendars and nude centrefolds to male strippers and erotic advertising images, the depiction of the muscular male body as object of desire has used a visual language first developed for the devouring gaze of other men; its recent emergence into the public domain and its growing social acceptability owe much to the current re-evaluation of appropriate gender-roles and in particular to the sexual emancipation of women. If it was gay iconography that first extended to men the role of object and not merely author of the erotic gaze, it was the women's movement that extended to women the role of author and not merely object of that gaze. Whether or not this role-reversal has been accompanied by a shift in the fundamental power-relations between men and women is a crucial (and unresolved) issue within feminist polemics.

11.16 At a far remove from the bodybuilding display with its elaborate confusion of sexual signals, the aesthetic/erotic mode proclaims an unequivocal sexual semantics.

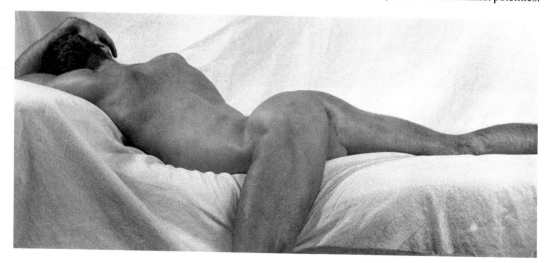

The relatively unclothed male body having taken on such public status and open visibility within Western society as a whole, it has become necessary to devise a code of presentation whereby the messages it emits may become readable. In particular, since many of the messages of the unclad body (at least in the West) are of an erotic nature, the mode of presentation needs to make clear how far eroticism is intended. In presenting the male body as object of the gaze, particularly for other (heterosexual) men, any overtones of homosexual attraction need to be minimised in order to confer social legitimacy on the display. I have suggested that the 'heroic' super-mesomorph body is primarily a form of dominance-display aimed at other men, or at least intended to present the body in such a way that its phallic power-imagery remains latent, repressing overt sexual meanings by rendering them, at most, implicit in the body as a whole. In the case of bodybuilding, this purpose has been addressed by a series of conflicting and self-cancelling messages in which eroticism becomes confused and overt sexuality transcended.

Though the pursuit of competitive bodybuilding is confined to a relatively small circle of devotees, it has articulated what I have called an exemplary (or paradigmatic) language of the male body, by reference to which other modes and levels of presentation become readable. Departures from the elaborate and carefully regulated bodybuilding canon (the modern inheritor, in popular culture, of the heroic tradition in high art) can be interpreted to indicate how far the alternative, aesthetic/erotic convention is intended. In this case, the visible signs of 'denial' are themselves 'denied': those clues which the heroic nude body holds out to us in order to provoke a non-sexual (or a-sexual) reading are in one degree or another eliminated, in such a way that the ambiguities of the heroic body give way to the unequivocal semantics of eroticism. The attenuation of hyper-masculine body outline by a recumbent or submissive posture, the visibility and prominence of the genital area, the stress on facial features and the direction of the model's gaze, the suggestion of supple elasticity rather than hardness of flexion in the musculature and skin-surface — any or all of these semantic units in our visual language can be seen as a departure from the tenuous equilibrium of conflicting sexual signals which neutralises the erotic messages of the bodybuilding display. That most of the contexts in which the male body presents itself for our visual approbation fall somewhere between the heroic and erotic extremes, or that the same body may speak a different language from one representation to another, does not alter the overall framework within which the messages of the developed body are transmitted.

THE AMBIVALENT BODY

Given the capacity of the natural body itself — let alone that of the body as artificially 'constructed' in any individual image (photographic or otherwise) — to be read in a multiplicity of ways, it is perhaps not surprising that social theorists and social critics, each working within his or her own frame of reference, can arrive at sharply differing conclusions as to the deeper significance of the contemporary interest in images of male muscularity.

At one end of the interpretative spectrum, Marc Mishkind and colleagues have set out to explore the social dimensions of the mesomorphic and hypermesomorphic male body, characterised by well-developed chest and arm muscles and wide shoulders tapering down to a narrow waist. In particular, they address the question: 'why do men at this time in history appear to be pursuing the muscular mesomorphic ideal to a greater extent than ever before?'[25] Apart from the obvious contemporary interest in health-promoting activity and its reflection in the look of the body, they point to the current confusion in Western society as to appropriate gender-roles and in particular to the roles expected of men in a world where many activities formerly considered exclusively male-based are being taken over by women. Of the five traditional archetypes of masculinity —soldier, frontiersman, expert, breadwinner, and lord — only the first has not become an archaic artefact. Men, the authors argue, 'may be grasping for the soldier archetype —that is, building up their bodies — in an exaggerated attempt to incorporate what possible options remain of the male images they have held since youth.' The maleness-as-soldier ideal is seen as a reflection of the conservative militaristic trends in contemporary (particularly US) society — trends which are equally reflected in the 'overly muscled mesomorph' Rambo and his imitators.

This theory, to which we have referred earlier, is corroborated, the authors believe, by what they call its 'flip side': the current ideal of thinness for women, connoting the stereotypically feminine traits of smallness, weakness and fragility which are 'the mirror opposite of the strength and power represented by the muscular male body'. On this basis, the authors are led to what they call a polarisation hypothesis:

> 'The male and female body ideals, which are physically and symbolically opposite extremes, may be a reaction against sexual equality, an expression of a wish to preserve some semblance of traditional male-female differences.'[26]

11.17 'Why do men appear to be pursuing the muscular mesomorphic ideal to a greater extent than ever before ...?'

This theory adds to the conventional 'muscle as phallic power' notion the interesting suggestion that the modern blurring of gender-roles following the successive stages of women's sexual and social emancipation has created a climate of insecurity for both men and women, thus paradoxically encouraging them to cling to and exaggerate the few remaining gender-markers available to them. Fundamental biology here makes its last-ditch stand against sexual egalitarianism.

At the other end of the spectrum of interpretation lies Andrew Wernick's analysis of contemporary advertising images which depict men as sexual objects. Apart from the appeal to the specialised gay market, in which the male is unequivocally the centre of interest, much of this advertising also features sexually attractive women, whose eyes 'at once judge and condone the male physique.' But it is not simply, Wernick argues, that the roles have been reversed so that the woman is now the observer and the man the observed: it is rather that two constructions of masculinity (observer/observed) have come to co-exist and that, by implication, the same is true of the observed-observing woman — such that 'promotional images are becoming flexible enough to allow men and women to appear, with increasingly equal plausibility, at either end of the objectified-objectifying sexual scale'. Wernick's highly provocative conclusion is worth quoting here:

11.18 The male-female grouping typical of some contemporary advertising: '... the sexual meaning of the scene is completely ambiguous.'

'In extreme cases, particularly in ads aimed at both sexes, such male-female interchangeability is emphasized for its own sake. And in the androgynous imagery that often results, even the sexual orientation of the figures depicted may then be left up in the air. A 1985 ad for Lee jeans shows two males and one female draped around a bicycle, all wearing the hip-hugging product, each in physical and visual contact with the other two. Like the demure orgies shown in Calvin Klein's famous Obsession campaign, the sexual meaning of the scene is completely ambiguous. The reading it permits is male as well as female, gay as well as straight; beyond which, indeed, can be discerned yet a fifth possibility —bisexual and of indeterminate gender — which synthesizes the others by emphasizing the very principle of gender equivalence that keeps them all in play.'[27]

What is going on in such depictions? The underlying message is to be seen, Wernick argues, not in the narrowly sexual terms of gay/straight/bisexual, but rather in the suggestion that male and female, for all their traditional differences, are to be conceived of as fluid categories — 'what structural linguists would call floating signifiers, free within any given promotional context to swirl around and substitute for one another at will.'[28] In the commercial world which these images are aimed at reflecting and promoting, both men and women have become the mere stuff of cultural coinage, mere tokens of exchange in competitive circulation like the consumer goods they advertise. For men to be depicted as women's equivalents reflects (and naturalises) not only the equal sociosexual roles but — at a more hidden level — the equal socioeconomic roles they occupy in a consumer society.

Wernick's penetrating article takes us beyond the simplistic categories of observer/observed, and explores some of the more ambiguous and disturbing overtones of the fluidity attaching to depictions of the male (and female) body in contemporary media. The notion of the body-as-commodity is as discernible in certain advertising images, even if at a less overt level, as it is in health faddism or the cosmetic surgery industry. It needs to be kept in mind, however, that the advertising image is only one of the forms in which the male body is presented to the fantasising gaze of women (and other men) in contemporary Western society: the image aimed at inducing men (or their partners) to buy a particular brand of after-shave, or at promoting a brand of jeans or underwear amongst potential purchasers, whether male or female, must capture as large a segment of the market as can be reached, and the conventions it uses must be as imaginatively inclusive as possible in order to cater for a wide variety of customers —male and female, gay and straight. It does not follow that the same conventions will apply in the case of, say, the male centrefold, where the equally ambiguous image of a strong and powerful male who is nonetheless vulnerable to the erotic response of the female viewer may require an entirely different visual language.

The aims of the women's magazine publisher or the strip-show promoter may well be as unashamedly commercial as those of the advertiser, but the appeal of the bodily images they present is based on different forms of fantasy. It is as rare for an advertiser to use an explicitly full-frontal centrefold-type image to promote a product as it is for the heterosexual grouping to be used in the 'hunk-of-the-month' feature. It is not simply that, in the latter case, the suggestion of anticipated sexual congress would move too close to the overtly pornographic; it is also, and perhaps more importantly, that the female model would be too intrusive — taking the place of the fantasising female viewer who imagines the male body as exclusively available to her. Mick Carter has argued that the early *Cosmopolitan* male centrefold experiment was a failure precisely because the attempt to provide liberated women with 'a packageable masturbatory landscape' drew attention to itself and away from the main task of the magazine, that of selling. Only when advertisers had developed 'a fully coded erotic male image that was capable of selling commodities as efficiently as the female figure' could it achieve its purpose — a purpose achieved by the presence of a legitimising female figure, so that a possible reading becomes: 'He's the sort of man who gets that sort of woman.'[29] This is an important, and legitimate, distinction between the two modes (or codes) of display, though it does not account for the recent re-emergence of the nude male photo-feature; nor, in its stress upon the body as commodity, does it explain why commercial aims (i.e., the sales of magazines)

11.19 Strong and powerful, yet vulnerable to the viewer's erotic response — the visual language of the 'packageable masturbatory landscape'.

11.20 'Muscular but boyish, with none of the heaviness of the mature man ... The sexy body became the young body.'

have been boosted more effectively by the presence of the solitary male centrefold than by that of the 'polymorphous set of sexual exchanges'[30] suggested by the heterosexual groupings in the advertising image. The two codes are certainly distinct, and, as I have argued, incompatible; yet the (masturbatory) fantasies engendered by the first may well prove an effective enticement to readers to engage in the (commercially pitched) fantasies purveyed by the second.

A somewhat different perspective on the contemporary portrayal of the male body has been adopted by Colin McDowell (*Dressed to Kill*). He points out that since the sixties, and more particularly throughout the eighties, it is the youthful body that has gained the greatest public approbation. In relation to men, he writes,

> 'The sexy body — and men's bodies were increasingly paraded in advertisements and actuality as sex objects — became the young body. Muscular but boyish, whippet-thin but tough, the male icon was allowed none of the heaviness of the mature man. That they were not yet men was acknowledged in their titles: Toy Boy and Rent Boy passed into the language and, indeed, into society. The first were wanted as sexual playthings for women, the second for men.'[31]

Associated with the contemporary cult of slimness in both men and women, this predilection for neotenic youth is of course irresistibly reminiscent of the urban culture of ancient Greece which was discussed in an earlier chapter. As such, it represents a striking contemporary extension of what I have called the 'aesthetic/erotic' tradition in the depiction of the body. A series of 1980s advertisements for Levi jeans, says McDowell, 'captured the sexual power of the pretty young man — still half boy — whilst allowing the shadow of his vulnerability in a corrupt and adult world.'[32] The lithe young models of these advertisements (like those of the Calvin Klein series) are in many ways the modern heirs of the Greek vase athletes, with whom they share many of the contextual signs of depiction. The presence of the 'legitimating' female in such portrayals is not seen by McDowell in Wernick's terms as merely another sexual 'floating signifier', but rather as representing 'an adoring handmaiden to the young man, watching from the sidelines'[33] and thus implicitly confirming the male domination of the sexual world.

Paradoxically, however, this mode of male depiction has come about at the same time as the outward signs of homosexuality have undergone radical change. 'The eighties', says McDowell, 'saw the virtual demise of the mincing pansy.' Homosexuals swung to the other extreme from the 'limp-wristed falsetto "screaming queen"' and began to dress tough in jeans and leather jackets, cropping their hair and wearing 'macho' Mexican moustaches.[34] The new gay icon was now the super-masculine image:

11.21 'Homosexuals began to dress tough in leather jackets, cropping their hair and wearing "macho" Mexican moustaches.' Sydney's Gay and Lesbian Mardi Gras.

'Tough and hard, with firm pectorals and tight muscles, he stared challengingly from the pages of *The Face* and *iD*, the very antithesis of the pansy and the poofter. He was not effeminate. That his narcissistic love of the male body frequently found expression in homosexual activity was unimportant. Working-out and body building are essentially homo-centric occupations. Gymnasiums are centres of sublimated homosexual desire.'[35]

Though the last two sentences sit uneasily with McDowell's recognition of the recent popularity of weight training among women, they serve to underline the confusion which surrounds the sexual messages emitted by the body in contemporary society: 'With young men increasingly proud to be considered pretty and young women happy to be physically strong — even muscled — there has been a change in the equation of attractiveness.'[36] McDowell is thus forced to the conclusion that in today's society 'semiotic signals no longer mean anything'.[37]

Such a conclusion seems not only unnecessarily defeatist, but also to run counter to the obvious fact that semiotic signals are manifestly as abundant in today's society as ever before, and are adopted precisely because they do have a meaning and a purpose in social transactions. Moreover, any analysis which leads to the classification of such notorious heterosexuals as Schwarzenegger or Stallone as closet homosexuals on account of their muscle-building proclivities is surely flying in the face of reality. A more helpful construction of the examples quoted by McDowell would be to suggest that the range of visual modes in which the male body may present itself is only partially congruent with the issue of sexual preference or orientation and may have more to do with social expectation. It is noteworthy, for instance, that the emergence of the 'macho' image of the homosexual has been contemporaneous with the age of 'gay liberation'; in a new climate more favourable to gay self-assertion (even aggressive self-proclamation), the adoption of the symbolic body-language of empowerment and dominance — i.e. the muscular or 'phallic' body — may well be less paradoxical than McDowell suggests. The Co-ordinator of an AIDS project has even proposed the disturbing suggestion that the contemporary cult of muscular 'body fascism' in the gay community is a reaction to the fact that extreme slimness may be taken as a sign that a man is HIV-positive — a reaction which, for all its distasteful overtones, reflects the modern tendency to express the self primarily in terms of outward appearance.[38] Conversely, the visual language of the aesthetic/erotic tradition may well have a particular attraction in a society seeking to affirm a less dominant or threatening image of male heterosexuality, and may serve to indicate this symbolically by the use of an inoffensive and even vulnerable neoteny.

The social critiques which have been applied to the display of male muscularity in popular media and performance tend to reflect the commentator's point of view and socio-sexual agenda, and thus to be highly selective in the examples they cite. Much of the contemporary analysis of the male body, however illuminating in its exploration of the hidden agenda of masculinity, is inescapably limited by the tendency of writers to bring to the subject their own particular bias or to examine it within a frame of social reference defined *a priori*. Only by reference to the whole range of images and overtones conjured up by the sight of the powerful (muscular, dominant, phallic) body when it subjects itself to scrutiny and symbolic availability can we begin to understand the totality of its imaginative potential. While the social critic or polemicist can often provide important insights into the implications for personal and group relationships of a particular mode of presentation of the embodied self, the approach of the social anthropologist or human social anatomist is perhaps more likely to account for the total spectrum of at times confused and often multiple contexts within which such transactions take place. Though such an approach, like that of anthropology or cultural studies in general, can never be divorced from the implicit socio-political assumptions that affect the humanities and social sciences as a whole, it seems better equipped to illuminate the complex spectrum of human behaviour than do those critiques which focus on ethical, political or gender issues and conduct their analysis within these relatively restricted perspectives. Like the affirmed body, the contested body is only part of the ambivalent image which the examined body presents for our inspection and analysis.

11.22 An inoffensive and even vulnerable neoteny, affirming a less dominant or threatening image of male heterosexuality.

12.1 **CHAPTER 12** THE BODY IN CONTEXT
Whether or not we are consciously aware of its cultural antecedents, we cannot read
the developed body without at least an implicit reference to them.

12

THE BODY IN CONTEXT

THE BODY'S LEGACY

Disrobed for our approving inspection in advertising images, stripped for military or pugilistic combat on cinema or TV screens, flaunted in strip-shows, paraded in bodybuilding contests and muscle magazines, provocatively bared in erotic centrefolds, the male body today has acquired a public exposure without parallel in our history. Subjected both to the analytical eye of the camera and to the fantasising gaze of the spectator, it has been acclaimed, condemned and minutely deconstructed by social theorists, academic critics, commentators and feature writers alike. Yet for all this, the developed body remains a curiously elusive construct of the Western imagination —present, as we have seen, since ancient times and never entirely eclipsed, yet emerging at particular historical moments as if to encapsulate and define an aspiration, often dimly perceived, towards something beyond itself. To explore some of the stages in this evolution and to analyse the codes of presentation that make the developed body readable in contemporary society has been the aim of the preceding chapters.

Having marked out the salient features of this bodily landscape, it is time to take stock of our surroundings and ask what kind of overview is possible. Is there a single unifying theme, or set of themes, which will allow us to set the developed body in an overall context and illuminate its metaphorical power to captivate the Western expressive consciousness? To this question we can now turn our attention.

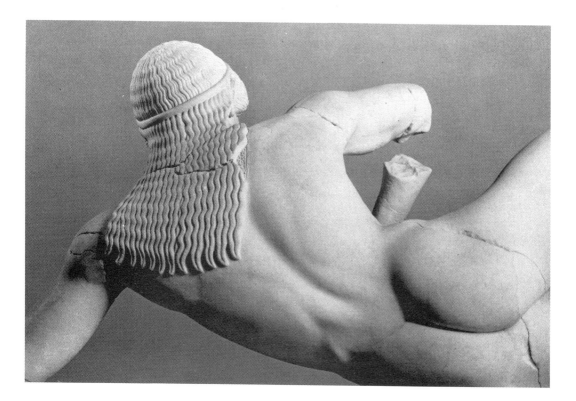

My overriding purpose in this study has been to account for the contemporary cult of the muscular body by reference to its cultural antecedents, and in so doing to seek to explain why it is that its symbolic significance in modern Western societies has not been paralleled in other social systems. To search for the deeper historical causes of those movements in Western society that have added to, or modified, our consciousness of the developed body is outside the scope of the present work: I have attempted merely to single out these shifts in perspective, whatever their causes, noting how each has built upon those that preceded it so as to endow our contemporary view of the body with a 'cultural baggage' of visual interpretation and social expression which (however unconsciously) conditions our understanding.

From this historical overview, it emerges that there have been three periods in particular (apart from our own) in which an important shift has taken place in our Western consciousness of the expressive power of the developed body. These are: the age of Greek Classicism and Hellenism; the age of the Italian Renaissance and its artistic successors; and the period in which high art began to give way to modern popular culture towards the end of the nineteenth century and beginning of the twentieth. In each of these periods, a particular conjunction of historical events and advances in cultural inventiveness or artistic creativity acted as the catalyst for a fresh and largely original mode of understanding of the human, and particularly the male, body as a symbolic vehicle.

In the Greek civilisation of the fifth century B.C., the appreciation and enjoyment of male physical beauty was emancipated for a time from the overlay of sexual reticence or taboo which has generally been applied by earlier and later societies anxious to preserve their social and sexual cohesion and to discourage the open display of homosexual attraction. Decisively, this development took place at precisely that period of relative social stability when the artistic, literary and philosophical endeavour of Greek society reached their apogee, becoming the basis on which much of the European cultural tradition would later be founded. If the Western world was the inheritor of artistic and philosophical forms first developed in classical Greece, it thereby became the heir to a cultural order in which (unlike most other philosophico-religious systems of the ancient world) the physical body mattered *in its own right*. The body's inherent status, as an emblem and incorporation of divine beauty, strength and harmony, was one of the chief legacies which Greece was to bequeath to the cultures which underwent its influence.

Despite the early impact of some Greek thought-forms (and even artistic conventions), the dominant ascetic-monastic tradition within Christianity managed to suppress the Greek view of the body until the time of the Renaissance, when once again an unusual conjunction of events occurred. At a time when humanist scholars were avidly re-reading, interpreting and incorporating classical Greek thought, there took place the re-discovery of a long-lost corpus of ancient sculpture which was to

12.2 Classical Greece bequeathed to Western Europe a tradition in which the body mattered in its own right, as an emblem and incorporation of divine beauty, strength and harmony. (Left: *Dying Warrior*, Temple of Athena Aphaea, Aegina, *c.* 500-480 B.C.)

359

provide inspiration for a new generation of artistic geniuses. By means of the concept of analogy, it was believed possible to reconcile both pagan and Christian conceptions of the body, so that an essentially Greek artistic treatment might be applied to Biblical themes. The breadth of Christian understanding of the body — particularly the notion of future resurrection — permitted such an extraordinary combination, quite alien to the medieval mind. In so doing, it enabled the Christian West to enunciate a visual language of physical perfection which is without parallel in any cultural system since antiquity.

Scientific, medical and technological advances in the post-Renaissance West confirmed and strengthened the understanding of the body as an object capable of improvement by scientific (or, in some cases, pseudo-scientific) regimens. From the time of the Industrial Revolution onwards, a new interest in physical exercise (required by a more urbanised society) went hand in hand with a belief in secular perfectibilism including the improvement of health and even the improvement of human breeding.

The body, in this process, became more and more an object of attention in its own right, the more so as religious influence waned and interest passed from the inner life (and mortification of the flesh) to notions of material progress and modern achievement. Photography opened up the 'real' body to public scrutiny as never before, and its inheritance of the Greek artistic canon soon turned it to the reproduction of images of physical beauty. At the same time, new 'sciences' of physical development were democratising the well-formed body and turning it into an attainable commodity.

By the end of the nineteenth century, the developed body had taken on such interest and attained such immediacy that the display of actual bodies, notable for their physical 'perfection', became an unprecedented form of public spectacle. A third unusual conjunction now took place. The death of representational high art meant the end of the heroic representation of the body, which now passed from the world of art into the 'real' world of actual display and of attainment through exercise. At the same time, while serious art became more and more limited to restricted coteries capable of appreciating cubism, abstractionism and expressionism, the popular media of visual representation underwent a remarkable development by way of the cinema and the adventure comic. Here, the heroic figure re-emerged in the form of fictitious characters, often of great strength and prowess. Illustrators trained in the art academies endowed these figures with the traditional muscularity of the inherited Greek anatomical canon, whilst their on-screen personifications were increasingly drawn from those who had devoted themselves to the pursuit of muscular development. As film and television increasingly conditioned the popular image of

12.3 The Renaissance managed to accommodate the classical Greek bodily canon within a Christian world-view, just as successive ages would adapt it to suit their growing scientific interest in the body's potential. (Left: Michelangelo's Adam, Vatican, Sistine Chapel, 1511.)

the normative male physique, so advertising and mass-circulation magazines were to appropriate the developed body for their own commercial ends, transforming it into a commodity precisely geared to the aspirations of Western consumerist societies.

Of the three ages that I have singled out as occupying a crucial place in the evolution of our modern consciousness of the developed body, the second and third each built upon and further elaborated the visual language and acquired meanings invented or refined by the age or ages preceding it, so that our contemporary reading of the muscular tradition in male iconography is inescapably conditioned by the sum of what has gone before. It is not necessarily the case that we consciously understand the developed body of today in terms of its avatars or its incarnations in high art or even early photography —any more than, in using the English language, we are conscious of the successive ages of folk-wandering, foreign influence and normative literary usage which have given it its characteristic modern form. Yet all of these things are there, embedded in our written and spoken linguistic codes just as our cultural antecedents lie hidden within the visual language by which we mediate external reality and its implicit meanings.

12.4 By the end of the
nineteenth century,
largely under the
influence of
photography,
representation of the
developed body had
moved from the world of
high art to that of live
display: its domain
would increasingly be
that of popular media.
(Left: Eugen Sandow.)

It has not escaped our attention, in analysing the portrayal of the male body in the three periods mentioned, that a curiosity as to the expressive capacity of the muscular physique has been accompanied by the unusually high social visibility of male homosexuality. Whether in fifth-century Athens, Renaissance Italy or *fin de siècle* Europe, the issue of homosexuality can hardly be avoided, the more so as many of those who devoted their artistic skill to the depiction of the muscular male body were (or are thought to have been) homosexually inclined. This observation, however, is both obvious and — as an explanation — over-simple. The appeal of the great exemplars of visible muscularity, whether in high art or even in photography and popular media such as the movie or the comic-book, has never been exclusively to a homosexual audience, and the very existence of the muscular male ideal as a well-nigh universal token of visual currency in Western society could never have been founded upon the predilections of a small sexual minority.

Without denying the inclinations of a number of the most creative artists, sculptors and photographers who have contributed to the visual language of the developed body, we must look to a less facile explanation if we are to understand the circumstances which led to the significant advances in representation referred to above. Each of these three ages, in fact, was a period of radical re-evaluation of man's place within the total scheme of things — whether the universe itself or the more limited confines of the social order. It is no accident that the age of the classical Greek representations was also that of the great Greek philosophers, and that their common theme was the exploration of human autonomy and the classification of human experience (including desire) according to canons of perfection which made sense in human terms. Or that the sculptors of the Renaissance were the contemporaries (and often the friends) of the humanist philosophers, attempting a new synthesis of ancient wisdom and Christian revelation in which man could be both 'the measure of all things' and at the same time a reflection or type of a more perfect reality lying beyond the visible world. Nor is it completely fortuitous that the age of the impetus towards physical development and the display of the living body, free of metaphysical or spiritual adumbrations yet striving towards a more perfect form of *human* being, should also have been the age of Nietzsche and Darwin. In every case, the representation of the developed body has been related to, even inextricably bound up with, the issue of human perfection, of what it means to be perfectly human — an issue with which each age has had to grapple in a radically new way according to its changing view of ultimate reality.

12.5 The notion of bodily
perfectibility is
essentially a Western
preoccupation –
Western in its
concentration on
outward visibility, on
physical striving and
action.

For all its metamorphoses, however, this search for human perfection has remained an essentially *Western* preoccupation. Western, that is, in its concentration on external activity, on outward visibility, on physical striving and action. To return to Gilbert Andrieu's evocative image, it has remained in one form or another a working-out of the myth of Hercules rather than that of Narcissus, a quest for salvation — or at least (in modern times) for the attainment of identity and significance, for the denial of human meaninglessness — through individual achievement rather than through the exploration of inner consciousness or its attunement to the undifferentiated absolute. Only in societies which understand the individual self, and its metaphor the body, as somehow transcending their temporary localisation does the pervasive Western belief in physical perfection make sense. That certain configurations of naked flesh in particular should come to be singled out as objects of contemplation in their own right, eliciting either admiration or desire (or both), reflects a view of reality in which the body is more than just a haphazard and transitory assemblage and becomes the symbolic embodiment of an aspiration towards a reality and a meaning which lie beyond itself.

Although earlier chapters have called attention to the less commendable social ends to which the pursuit of physical development has lent itself, the overall aim of my historical account has been investigative rather than polemical. I have been concerned primarily to register these negative aspects as part of the total spectrum of attitudes and applications to which the cult of the perfectible body may give rise. It is equally relevant, however, to point out that such aberrations must be placed alongside the capacity of the developed body to evoke a sense of inventive and productive fascination. For generations of artists, it acted as an imaginative symbol of self-transcendence, of the capacity of the physical body to operate as a metaphor or representation of a reality lying beyond and above itself. Even in contemporary Western culture where less exalted aims and meanings attach to the human condition, it can still function symbolically as the diversionary exercise of one form of human potential. Like the cultivation of a fine singing voice or advanced mathematical ability, the optimisation of human physical endowment can be a source of potent curiosity and even wonderment, a celebration of the suggestive capacity of that mutable frame of flesh in which our inner being is mysteriously embodied.

THE BODY TODAY

Like the human body in general, the developed body has historically functioned as a symbol, a metaphor of what we ourselves are or seek to be. To aim at physical perfection, or even at the less ambitious goal of bodily improvement, both implies a view of human nature itself as perfectible and points to the constitutive role of the body in that imaginative construct. Our physical being does not exist independently of the self, but is its exteriorisation, the embodied being that we present to the world outside ourselves for its inspection and judgment. The particular meanings we attribute to the body, as we seek to understand its language, are the meanings we read into the persona lying underneath. Though no more than an external surface, it is nonetheless the most immediate instrument of our transaction with the world and the most readily apprehended sign of our individual identity. Its depiction in art is founded on the premise that the body's very configuration — its structure, proportion, attitude and gestures — can express more than mere physical presence and can render legible a world of latent meanings. If the heroic Greek statues embody and define an intelligible view of man, so too (at a less exalted and more immediate level) do the advertising images, film heroes, strippers and pin-ups of contemporary male iconography.

What, then, are we to say of the developed body in Western society today? Do the closing years of the twentieth century mark a fourth decisive period in its representation, building on the earlier three but exhibiting its own distinctive characteristics? The hypothesis is certainly tempting, though like any attempt to explicate one's own age or to account for it by a general theory it must inevitably lack that clarifying perspective and sense of proportion which only the hindsight afforded by a certain removal in time can bring. If it is indeed the case that we are living in such a fourth age, it follows from our earlier analysis that the portrayal of the body will tend to incorporate contemporary values, aspirations and anxieties, a number of which have been discussed in the preceding chapters in so far as they have conditioned the mode of presentation of the body.

12.6 The body is our most immediate means of transaction with the world: though no more than an external surface, it is not semantically neutral but rich in possibilities of imaginative interpretation.

By way of summary, the closing years of the millennium are marked by a deep uncertainty as to ultimate human meanings and transcendent values. While traditional organised religion flounders and a minority take refuge in populist fundamentalism or faddish 'new Age' mysticism, most retain a vague and ill-defined belief in overriding purpose which (except at times of personal calamity) interferes minimally with practical hedonism and a morality based on self-interest. 'Lifestyles' have, in urbanised Western societies, largely taken the place of life-meanings. The rise of television has further accentuated the Western 'post-modernist' preoccupation with the visual surface of things (including the human body), as the growth of technology and increasingly sedentary lifestyles have both reduced the need for physical effort and, paradoxically, increased the popular vogue of physical exercise. Images of success in a competitive society are associated with youth, vitality and fitness; along with the fear of ageing, these factors have led to a remarkable burgeoning in the 'fitness industry' which — like almost every other aspect of contemporary Western society — seeks validation by reference to the visual outcome it produces. The male icons of this culture tend to be characterised by an advanced (if not extreme) degree of muscularity.

The uncertainties of the age are reflected in the paradoxical and often conflicting messages our society sends to itself: these condition the uncertain and ambiguous status we attribute to the body as values shift and ultimate meanings are individually, rather than collectively, defined. Examples of the self-contradiction inherent in contemporary Western society, and its reference to commonly-held views of the body, are to be found in a wide variety of fields. In a troubled and self-analytical society, the post-modernist concern with surface, spectacle and the images of things takes precedence over things themselves, and 'bodyism' has emerged as a particular form of narcissism or preoccupation with the self and especially with the external, visible self. In an age when holistic medicine, encounter groups and ecological awareness stress the interconnectedness of the natural world, obsessive behaviour and the use of drugs arising from an ethos of possessive individualism nonetheless treat the body as an object to be controlled by the ego as if it were a machine rather than a part of the self. At a time of widespread disillusionment with the culture of mass technology, the possibility of the 'improvement' of the body by instrumental techniques renders it subject to the dictates of fashion, popular images and exploitative commercialism so that the body itself becomes a mere commodity, an object of mass consumerism. At the close of the twentieth century, when the fear of sexually-transmitted diseases and the devastation wrought by the AIDS virus have rendered sexual relationships at best problematic and at worst dangerous, there is (perhaps for this very reason) an unprecedented fascination with thinking, talking and writing about sex — as well as a remarkable efflorescence of visual images of eroticism. As the range of politically acceptable sexual behaviour has narrowed, so the scope afforded by the visual media to openly sexual voyeurism has widened: never before in our social history have we been presented with such all-pervading public representations of the naked or near-naked body as an object of erotic desire.

In no sphere, however, are the uncertainties and contradictions of modern society more clearly evident than in that which affects male and female gender-roles. The entry of women into hitherto exclusively male domains, and a new assertiveness in the demand for sexual equality, have often left men defensive or unsure as to what are appropriate or acceptable expressions of masculinity. While some men have willingly embraced the new male sensitivity, others have sought solace in 'male bonding' or have adopted a more reactionary stance by way of the macho quasi-militarism to which Stallone's Rambo-figure has lent his name (and his physique). The identification of masculine physical traits, especially muscular development, with a tendency towards domination — at the personal, group or national level — has tended to turn the cult of the perfectible body into a species of physical elitism which is socially dismissive and may become socially repressive. The public visibility of homosexuality, since the first Kinsey Report drew attention to its social incidence, has led to the sense of liberation and acceptance exemplified by the 'gay pride' movement and the introduction of gay studies into some campus curricula, notwithstanding the darker fears and suspicions associated with the AIDS epidemic and the 'outing' campaigns directed at a number of public figures. The well-documented homosexual interest in the cultivation of the male body has affected the popular portrayal of well-built males as desirable sex objects and has provided sexually emancipated women with a frankly erotic pictorial language previously restricted to the portrayal of women, while the recent recognition of gays as consumers has broadened the language of implicit sexual appeal woven into commercial images.

At the close of the twentieth century, the developed male body has become the subject of an unprecedented volume of discussion and analysis which reflects the heightened visibility it has assumed over the past twenty-five years or so. As one element (perhaps the crucial element) of the contemporary deconstruction of masculinity, the male body itself is seen at its most symbolically identifiable when characterised by such visual images of hyper-masculinity as mesomorphy and developed muscularity. The question of male identity, in its various guises including its visual symbolism, is increasingly seen as an open rather than (as for earlier generations) a closed issue, its prospective new status emerging only from tentative reconstruction following a relentless process of deconstruction. In this process, various perspectives have been brought to bear upon the semiotics of masculinity, whether in terms of social patriarchy or of sexual dominance; of these none has had more significant (and perhaps more lasting) public currency than the male-female dialectic. Two of the most articulate opponents of male-dominated society, Naomi Wolf and Susan Faludi, have both predicted that the objectified male body will remain a leading motif of social discussion throughout the 1990s.[1]

12.7 The emblematic significance of the male body has become a central issue in contemporary Western societies, embodying many of the uncertainties and contradictions of the late 20th century.

12.8 Hotly contested and still unresolved issues of sexual politics have called into question the traditional Western descriptors of masculine identity and left the way open for a more caring and sensitive image of masculinity.

As 'men's studies' courses spring up in the trendier universities and sociologists debate the issue of whether traditionally male characteristics (strength, aggression, violence) are inherent biological traits or culturally conditioned behaviour patterns, a new dichotomy has arisen between those mainly middle-class males who seek to adapt their consciousness to the new sexual politics and those, usually lower down the social scale, whose reaction is to meet the vexed question of male identity with an exaggerated machismo which seeks to re-establish traditional sexual roles. For the latter group, the gym culture and the movie cult of kick-boxers and Terminators provide a last bastion against a confused world of disappearing sexual stereotypes.

It may well be that the feminist struggle to overcome stereotypical images and open up to women a range of options as to the roles they may wish to play, free of the male-imposed constraints of traditional socio-sexual expectation, is yet to find its masculine counterpart. Conditioned still by the need to define themselves and establish their identity by reference to the 'masculine' criteria of outward performance, social success and approved image rather than by a heightened level of access to their own deeper affections and hidden emotions, many men remain insecure and uncertain as to what they are actually entitled to feel — indeed, as to what contemporary women expect of them, or find acceptable as expressions of masculinity. As more women have entered the workforce and gained economic independence, they have also become sexually more assertive, demanding greater sensitivity in their partner, the right to say no to sex or to walk out on a relationship. The traditional descriptors of male role-play, whether social or sexual, no longer seem to be defined as sharply as for earlier generations, or to be appropriate in an age of anxious transition to an as yet untested sexual equilibrium. On the one hand, as we have seen, men may seek to magnify those gender-markers still available to them, by a pursuit of the mesomorphic image of super-masculinity; on the other, they may seek to reject or at least attenuate the phallic dominance-imagery of the male body by a reversion to the visual language of youth or adolescence in which male-female distinctions are minimised. At either of these extremes, or hovering uncertainly between them, the desirable self-images held up to men by popular media and the culture at large rely as heavily as ever before on the power of the visible body to define and express an inner identity and aspiration.

There are signs, however, that feminism itself is undergoing a radical re-appraisal in the wake of the social upheaval which has affected men's, as well as women's, self-understanding over the last decade.[2] For some intellectually serious contemporary feminists, authors such as Susan Faludi and Marilyn French represent not so much the cutting edge of feminist thought as the last hurrah of the reactive and simplistic feminism of the 1970s and 80s, which split the world neatly into male and female sexuality. Sexual identity is increasingly seen as more variable, uncertain and elusive than classical feminism had admitted, especially in an age when the Janus Report on Sexual Behavior has drawn attention to the protean varieties of

12.9 The muscular mesomorph may continue to occupy one end of the imaginative spectrum of masculinity, but his privileged symbolic position may disappear as physical perfectibility loses its former overtones of higher purpose.

sexual activity in which 'middle Americans' actually engage. The expression of sexuality tends more and more to be understood as a continuous spectrum rather than a battle-ground between two sides, two genders or two discrete sexual orientations. A number of feminist authors, while stopping short of the radicalism of a Camille Paglia or a Katie Roiphe, have sought to modify or qualify their earlier positions: Naomi Wolf's *Fire With Fire*[3], amongst other recent works, has pointed to the counterproductive nature of some Second-Wave feminism (including the 'women as victims' mentality). Even within the homosexual movement, there has been a reaction against the categorising approach of the 70s and 80s, in which 'gay identity' was proclaimed as the sole means of defining and expressing one's true nature as a gay or lesbian person: the newer movement, sometimes under the banner of 'queer theory', recognises that the line between straight and gay is less rigidly drawn than had been earlier proposed, and affirms both the diversity within gay communities and between lesbians and gay men. An increasing number of 'new wave' lesbian nightclubs now cater for an erotic display of the female body which traditional feminism would have denounced as sexist and exploitative. Within the homosexual community, as within the Women's Movement, there is an emerging sense that the political battles of earlier decades — however necessary they may have been at the time in the face of discrimination and overt oppression — are no longer relevant, and that a new understanding and recognition of the varieties of sexual identity and expression has significantly altered the face of sexual politics.

How far this contemporary shift in attitude will affect the visual images by which we filter and mediate our social environment remains to be seen. The muscular mesomorph may continue to represent one end of the spectrum of a masculinity which is as much a symbolic construct of the imagination as a biological reality; but he may well cease to occupy the privileged position assigned to him by the Western visual tradition. Melody Davis may perhaps be correct in finding the handicapped black nudes of George Dureau[4] a more authentic representation of contemporary masculinity than the perfectly-formed, idealised physiques of Robert Mapplethorpe. Unlike the centuries of widespread religious faith, when the developed body could symbolically point to a transcendent reality, our own age has retained the paradigmatic language of physical perfectibility but without any intimation of higher reference. The developed body may today symbolise power and dominance, sexual attractiveness, hedonistic self-absorption or even enviable status as a consumer commodity, but the deeper emotions of wonderment, awe and reverence are more likely to be excited by contemporary advances in astronomy or quantum physics than by contemplation of the emblematic power of the human body. Whether twenty-first-century Western man will seek, or wish, to re-define himself in terms appropriate to his society by recourse to the inner self rather than to outward symbolism — to follow the way of Narcissus rather than that of Hercules — it is impossible to predict. The 2500-year-old tradition of the ideal representation of 'Western man' has perhaps reached its most critical phase.

N O T E S

INTRODUCTION

1. See Michel Henry, *Philosophy and Phenomenology of the Body* (transl. Gerard Etzkorn), The Hague: Martinus Nijhoff, 1975, pp.2-8.

2. See Leonard Barkan, *Nature's Work of Art: The Human Body as Image of the World*, New Haven and London: Yale University Press, 1975, p.2.

3. John Passmore, *The Perfectibility of Man*, London: Duckworth, 1970.

4. Passmore, *op. cit.*, pp.12-27. Cf. Martin Foss, *The Idea of Perfection in the Western World*, Lincoln: University of Nebraska Press, 1946, p.10.

5. See, e.g. Jonathan Benthall and Ted Polhemus [eds], *The Body as a Medium of Expression*, Allen Lane/Dutton: New York, 1975; Ted Polhemus [ed.], *Social Aspects of the Human Body*, Harmondsworth: Penguin, 1978; Mary Douglas, *Natural Symbols: Explorations in Cosmology*, Harmondsworth: Penguin, 1973; Erving Goffman, *The Presentation of Self in Everyday Life*, Harmondsworth: Penguin, 1971; Bryan S. Turner, *The Body and Society: Explorations in Social Theory*, Oxford: Basil Blackwell, 1984; Peter Brown, *The Body and Society: Men, Women and Sexual Renunciation in Early Christianity*, New York: Columbia University Press, 1988; Thomas Laqueur, *Making Sex: Body and Gender from the Greeks to Freud*, Cambridge, Mass./London: Harvard University Press, 1990.

6. See R.D. Guthrie, *Body Hot Spots: The Anatomy of Human Social Organs and Behavior*, New York: Van Nostran Reinhold, 1976, p.vii.

7. Marcel Mauss, 'The Techniques of the Body', *Economy and Society*, 2, I (Feb. 1973), pp.70-88.

8. Kenneth Clark, *The Nude: A Study of Ideal Art*, Harmondsworth: Pelican, 1960, p.10.

CHAPTER 1 - THE EMERGING BODY

1. Clark, *op. cit.*, p.3.

2. *Ibid.*, p.22.

3. *Ibid.*, pp.13-33, *passim*.

4. See George M.A. Hanfmann, *Classical Sculpture*, London: Michael Joseph, 1967, p.19.

5. Oswyn Murray, 'Life and Society in Classical Greece', in John Boardman, Jasper Griffin and Oswyn Murray [eds], *The Oxford History of the Classical World*, Oxford: OUP, 1986, p.226.

6. See Robert Parker, 'Greek Religion', in Boardman *et al.*, *op. cit.*, p.256.

7. G. Andrieu, 'La Respiration reflet de nos aspirations', in Gilbert Andrieu [ed.], *Sports, Arts et Religions* (Proceedings of International Congress, Larnaca, Cyprus, 11-18 December 1988), Paris, Université de Paris X Nanterre, 1989, pp.20-33.

8. *Art cit.*, pp.23-24 [my translation].

9.   See Jean Boisselier *et al., The Image of the Buddha*, Paris: UNESCO/London: Serindia Publications, 1978, p.71-72, p.314.

10. See Kenneth K.S. Ch'en, *The Chinese Transformation of Buddhism*, Princeton, NJ: Princeton University Press, 1973, p.8. For an alternative interpretation based on the harmony of two triangles, see Helmut Uhlig, *Das Bild des Buddha*, Berlin: Safari Verlag, 1979, p.12.

11. Clark, *op. cit.*, p.239; cf. John Griffiths Pedley, *Greek Art and Archaeology*, London: Cassell, 1993, pp.338-340.

12. See Edward Lucie-Smith, *Eroticism in Western Art*, New York: Praeger, 1972, *passim.*

13. See E. Norman Gardiner, *Athletics of the Ancient World*, Oxford: Clarendon Press, 1965, pp.54, 56-57.

14. John Boardman, 'Greek Art and Architecture', in Boardman *et al., op. cit.*, p.276.

15. See Gardiner, *op. cit.*, p.61.

16. See Nicholas Bornoff, *Pink Samurai: The Pursuit and Politics of Sex in Japan*, London: Grafton Books, 1991, p.426.

17. See Murray, *op. cit.*, p.225.

18. Michel Foucault, *The Uses of Pleasure (The History of Sexuality*, Vol. 2, transl. Robert Hurley), New York: Pantheon Books, 1985, p.187.

19. Thomas Laqueur, *Making Sex: Body and Gender from the Greeks to Freud*, Cambridge, Mass./London: Harvard University Press, 1990, p.52.

20. See Richard Davenport-Hines, *Sex, Death and Punishment: Attitudes to Sex and Sexuality in Britain since the Renaissance*, London: Collins, 1990, p.78.

21. Hanfmann, *op. cit.*, p.30.

22. K.J. Dover, *Greek Homosexuality*, London: Duckworth, 1978, p.70.

23. *Ibid.*, p.125.

24. See *Ibid.*, p.130.

25. See Hanfmann, *op. cit.*, pp.202-205.

26. John Webb, 'Reading Bodies', in *XY: Men, Sex, Politics*, Summer 1991/92, p.15.

27. Dover, *op. cit.*, pp.134-135.

28. Rosalind Miles, *The Rites of Man: Love, Sex and Death in the Making of the Male*, London: Grafton Books, 1991, p.146.

29. See Michael Gill, *Image of the Body: Aspects of the Nude*, New York: Doubleday, 1989, p.127.

30. See Gardiner, *op. cit.*, p.49.

31. See Hanfmann, *op. cit.*, pp.35-38.

32. R.J.A. Wilson, 'Roman Art and Architecture', in Boardman *et al., op. cit.*, p.796.

33. *Ibid.*, p.336; cf. Clark, *op. cit.*, p.35.

CHAPTER 2 - THE BODY RE-BORN

1. Joseph Campbell, *Myths to Live By*, London: Souvenir Press, 1992 (1st ed. 1972), pp.69-70.

2. See Sydney Cave, *The Christian Estimate of Man*, London: Duckworth, 1957, p.36.

3. See Foss, *op. cit.*, pp.28-29.

4. See Cave, *op. cit.*, pp.74-78.

5. Peter Brown, *The Body and Society: Men, Women and Sexual Renunciation in Early Christianity*, New York: Columbia University Press, 1988, p.168; cf. *ibid.*, pp.130-132.

6. See Passmore, *op. cit.*, p.83.

7. See Henry, *op. cit.*, pp.208-209.

8. John Romer, *Testament: The Bible and History*, London: Michael O'Mara, 1988, p.231.

9. See Hanfmann, *op. cit.*, p.42.

10. See Marcel Simon, *La Civilisation de l'antiquité et le christianisme*, Paris: Arthaud, 1972, pp.370-371.

11. See Turner, *op. cit.*, p.36.

12. See Hanfmann, *op. cit.*, p.343.

13. See Barkan, *op. cit.*, pp.50-51.

14. See Clark, *op. cit.*, p.9.

15. See *ibid.*, p.230.

16. See Foss, *op. cit.*, p.76.

17. Gill, *op. cit.*, p.189.

18. See P.P. Bober and R.O. Rubinstein, *Renaissance Artists and Antique Sculpture*, London: Harvey Miller Publishers, 1986.

19. Clark, *op. cit.*, pp.48-50.

20. Margaret Walters, *The Nude Male: A New Perspective*, New York/London: Paddington Press, 1978, pp.116-117.

21. See Edward Lucie-Smith, *The Body: Images of the Nude*, London: Thames & Hudson, 1982, p.13.

22. Frederick Hartt, *David by the Hand of Michelangelo: The Original Model Discovered*, New York: Abbeville Press, 1987, p.94; cf. Ruth Westheimer, *The Art of Arousal*, New York: Abbeville Press, 1993, p.22.

23. Webb, *loc. cit.*

24. Gill, *op. cit.*, p.191; cf. *ibid.*, p.215.

25. Francis Haskell and Nicholas Perry, *Taste and the Antique: The Lure of Classical Sculpture 1500-1900*, New Haven/London: Yale University Press, 1981, pp.6-15, *passim*.

26. See Edward Lucie-Smith, in Stephen Boyd [ed.], *Life Class: The Academic Male Nude 1820-1920*, London: GMP Publishers, 1989, Introduction, p.8.

27. Gill, *op. cit.*, p.262.

28. See Haskell and Perry, *op. cit.*, pp.100-102.

29. Passmore, *op. cit.*, p.260.

30. Quoted by Graham Ovenden and Peter Mendes, *Victorian Erotic Photography*, New York: St Martin's Press/ London: Academy Editions, 1973, p.7.

31. See W.A. Hale, *The World of Rodin 1840-1917*, Nederland, Time-Life Library of Art, 1969, pp.51, 79; *Rodin Sculptures* (introd. Sommerville Story), London: Phaidon, 1970, pp.115-116.

32. See Peter Cannon-Brookes, *Emile-Antoine Bourdelle: An Illustrated Commentary*, 1984, pp.63-64, cf. Marina Lambraki-Plaka, *Bourdelle et la Grèce*, Athens: Akademia Athenon, 1985, pp.64-69.

33. Sir Leigh Ashton, 'Sculpture', in Alan Pryce-Jones [ed.], *The New Outline of Modern Knowledge*, London: Gollancz, 1956, p.303.

CHAPTER 3 - THE VISIBLE BODY

1. See Susan Sontag, *Photography*, Harmondsworth: Penguin, 1979, p.28.

2. See Aaron Scharf, *Art and Photography*, London: Allen Lane/The Penguin Press, 1968, p.90.

3. See Stephen Kern, *Anatomy and Destiny: A Cultural History of the Human Body*, Indianapolis/New York: Bobbs-Merrill, 1975, p.31.

4. See Clark, *op. cit.*, p.4.

5. See Sontag, *op. cit.*, p.134; William H. Gerdts, *The Great American Nude*, Phaidon, 1974, pp.118-124; cf. Naomi Rosenblum, *A World History of Photography*, New York: Abbeville Press, 1989, p.220.

6. See Lucie-Smith, *The Body*, p.26; Peter Weiermair, *The Hidden Image: Photographs of the Male Nude in the Nineteenth and Twentieth Centuries* (transl. Claus Nielander), Cambridge, Mass./London: The MIT Press, 1988, p.14.

7. See Robert Hughes, *The Shock of the New: Art and the Century of Change*, London: British Broadcasting Corporation, 1980, pp.44, 52.

8. See Kern, *op. cit.*, p.25.

9. See Weiermair, *op. cit.*, pp.13-14; cf. Robert Sobieszek, 'Addressing the Erotic: Reflections on the Nude Photograph', in Constance Sullivan [ed.], *Nude: Photographs 1850-1980*, New York: Harper & Row, 1980, p.172.

10. See Walters, *op. cit.*, pp.288-289.

11. Weiermair, *op. cit.*, pp.15-17; Emmanuel Cooper, *Fully Exposed: The Male Nude in Photography*, London: Unwin Hyman, 1990, Ch. 8 (pp.149-163).

12. See Weiermair, *op. cit.*, p.17.

13. See Allen Ellenzweig, *The Homoerotic Photograph*, New York: Columbia University Press, 1992, p.104.

14. See Cooper, *op. cit.*, Ch. 9 (pp.165-182).

15. See Horst Ueberhorst, *Friedrich Ludwig Jahn 1778-1978*, Bonn/Bad Godesberg: Inter Nationes, 1978, p.103.

16. *Ibid.*, p.93.

17. Quoted by David Chapman, 'Making Muscles', *Muscle & Fitness*, July 1988, pp.137-138.

18. *Loc. cit.*

19. For information concerning Sandow's life, see David Chapman, 'Sandow: Portrait of a Strongman', *Muscle & Fitness*, June 1986, pp.209 *ff*.; Bill Dobbins, *Encyclopedia of Modern Bodybuilding*, London: Pelham Books, 1985, pp.30-31.

20. Cf. Passmore, *op. cit.*, p.314.

21. See Ben Maddow, 'Nude in a Social Landscape', in Constance Sullivan [ed.], *op. cit.*, p.185; cf. Timothy Foote, *The World of Bruegel c.1525-1569*, Nederland, Time-Life Library of Art, 1968, p.60.

22. On the nudist movement, see Vern L. Bullough and Bonnie Bullough, *Sin, Sickness and Society: A History of Sexual Attitudes*, New York: Garland, 1977, Chapter 11 'Nudism and Clothing', pp.177-196, *passim*. See also Cooper, *op. cit.*, Ch. 4, 'Nakedness in Nature' (pp.73-89).

23. See Magnus Clarke, *Nudism in Australia: A First Study*, Victoria: Deakin University Press, 1982, p.229 *ff*.

24. See Cooper, *op. cit.*, p.76 *ff*.

25. See Jack D. Douglas and Paul K. Rasmussen, with Carol Ann Flanagan, *The Nude Beach*, Beverly Hills: Sage (Sociological Observations: 1), 1977, p.225.

26. *Ibid.*, pp.225-226.

27. Stephen Bayley, *Taste: The Secret Meaning of Things*, London: Faber & Faber, 1991, p.148.

28. Maddow, *op. cit.*, p.184.

29. See Clarke, *op. cit.*, p.259.

CHAPTER 4 - THE BODY BUILT

1. See David Chapman, 'Sandow: Portrait of a Strongman', *Muscle & Fitness*, June 1986, pp.209 *ff*.

2. Harry Paschall, 'The Little Giant', in *Strength and Health*, Jan 1956, pp.16 *ff*.; Earle Liederman, 'The Muscle Peddling Era', *Muscular Development*, March 1967, p.23 *ff*.

3. David Chapman, 'Albert Treloar', *Ironman*, Feb 1990, p.90.

4. David Chapman, 'Sieymund Klein', *Ironman*, July 1990, p.90.

5. See David Chapman, *Adonis: The Male Physique Pin-Up 1870-1940*, London: GMP Publishers, 1989, Introduction pp.7-9.

6. David Chapman, 'Posing for Glory: Pioneers of Physique Photography', *Muscle & Fitness*, March 1988, pp.122 *ff*.

7. David Chapman, 'Tony Sansone', *Ironman*, Aug 1991, p.74.

8. David Chapman, *Adonis*, p.9.

9. Weiermair, *op. cit.*, p.19.

10. See Dobbins, *op. cit.*, pp.39-40.

11. See George Butler, *Arnold Schwarzenegger: A Portrait*, New York: Simon and Schuster, 1990, pp.50, 52.

12. Quoted in Charles Gaines, *Pumping Iron: The Art and Sport of Bodybuilding*, London: Sphere Books, 1977, p.48.

13. Statistics quoted by Ben Weider, President, IFBB, in *Bodypower* (UK), Vol. 11, No. 1 (Jan. 1992), pp.50-51.

CHAPTER 5 - THE POPULAR BODY

1. See George Perry and Alan Aldridge [eds], *The Penguin Book of Comics*, Harmondsworth: Penguin, 1967, pp.128-129.

2. See *ibid.*, p.156.

3. Phillip Adams, 'Revenge of the Comix', *The Australian*, 10-11 Oct. 1992.

4. See James R. Parrish *et al.* [eds], *The Great Movie Series*, South Brunswick/New York: A.S. Barnes, 1971, pp.304-306. See also David Zinman, *Saturday Afternoon at the Bijou*, [New Jersey]: Castle Books, 1973, pp.19-41.

5. Michael Malone, *Heroes of Eros: Male Sexuality in the Movies*, New York: Dutton, 1975, p.83.

6. David Chapman, 'Maciste (Bartolomeo Pagano)', *Ironman*, Feb 1991, p.66; Robin Cross, *The Big Book of B Movies, or How Low Was My Budget*, London: Frederick Muller (Charles Heritage Books), 1981, p.165;; Derek Elley, *The Epic Film: Myth and History*, London: Routledge & Kegan Paul, 1984, pp.81-84.

7. Cross, *op. cit.*, p.165.

8. Adam Bowen, 'Groaning Sambals', *Sydney Morning Herald*, 14 Jan 1991.

9. James Harding, *The Rocky Horror Show Book*, London: Sidgwick & Jackson, 1987, p.20.

10. See Arnold Schwarzenegger with Douglas Kent Hall, *Arnold: The Education of a Bodybuilder*, New York: Pocket Books, 1977, pp.17-20.

CHAPTER 6 - THE SOCIAL BODY

1. Ernest Becker, *The Birth and Death of Meaning: An Interdisciplinary Perspective on the Problem of Man*, Harmondsworth: Penguin, 2nd ed. 1972, p.88.

2. See *ibid.*, p.162.

3. Kern, *op. cit.*, p.x.

4. Polhemus, *Social Aspects of the Human Body*, p.176.

5. Clark, *op. cit.*, p.9.

6. Bernard Rudofsky, *The Unfashionable Human Body*, New York: Doubleday, 1971, p.74.

7. See Robert Brain, *The Decorated Body*, London: Hutchinson, 1979, p.64.

8. See Bornoff, *op. cit.*, p.75, 300 *ff.*, 401.

9. See Gardiner, *op. cit.*, p.59.

10. See Fenja Gunn, *The Artificial Face: A History of Cosmetics*, Newton Abbot: David and Charles, 1973, p.151, pp.161 *ff.*

11. See J. Maisonneuve, 'Le corps et le corporéisme aujourd'hui' ('The Body and Bodyism Today'), *Revue française de sociologie*, 17, 4 (Oct-Dec 1976), pp.551-571.

12. See Daniel J. Boorstin, *The Image*, Harmondsworth: Penguin, 1963, pp.208 *ff.*

13. See Brain, *op. cit.*, pp.84 *ff.*, p.103.

14. *Ibid.*, pp.97-99.

15. Naomi Wolf, *The Beauty Myth*, London: Chatto & Windus, 1990, *passim.*

16. See Turner, *op. cit.*, pp.182-197.

17. See Rudofsky, *op. cit.*, p.111; Paschall, *op. cit.*, p.55.

18. See Kern, *op. cit.*, pp.16-17, p.200.

19. Reported in *Sydney Morning Herald*, 20 March 1992.

20. American statistics reported in *Sydney Morning Herald*, 20 March 1992. For European figures, see interview with Dr Jean-Claude Dardour, cosmetic surgeon, in *Le Nouvel Observateur* (Paris), 19-25 Dec 1991, p.11.

21. Australian research reported in *Sun-Herald*, Sydney ('Muscle Mania: Boys with a Weight on their Shoulders'), 26 July 1992; US research quoted by Miles, *op. cit.*, p.111.

22. Reuter news report, reprinted in *Newcastle Herald* (Australia), 14 April 1993.

23. See Arline and John Liggett, *The Tyranny of Beauty*, London: Victor Gollancz, 1989, pp.11-12.

24. Pascal Bruckner, 'Les hommes aussi', in *Le Nouvel Observateur* (Paris), 19-25 Dec 1991, pp.10-11.

25. Turner, *op. cit.*, see esp. pp.110-112; cf. Polhemus, *Social Aspects of the Human Body*, pp.21-23.

26. Desmond Morris, *The Human Zoo*, London: Transworld (Corgi Books), 1971, pp.175-176.

27. Roland Barthes, 'Le monde où l'on catche', in *Mythologies*, Paris: Editions du seuil, 1957.

28. Roland Barthes, *Système de la mode*, Paris: Editions du seuil, 1967.

CHAPTER 7 - THE BODY POLITIC

1. See Johann Winckelmann, *On the Imitation of the Painting and Sculpture of the Greeks [1755]*, in *Winckelmann: Writings on Art* (selected and edited by David Irwin), London: Phaidon, 1972, p.61.

2. See Ueberhorst, *op. cit.*, *passim.*

3. See Siegmund Klein, 'Friedrich Ludwig Jahn, Founder of the Turnvereins', *Strength and Health*, Nov 1958, p.54.

4. See Siegmund Klein, 'Louis Hart', *Strength and Health*, Dec 1958, p.54.

5. See Harold Aspiz, *Walt Whitman and the Body Beautiful*, Chicago: University of Illinois Press, 1980, pp.3-4; Kern, *op. cit.*, pp.80 ff.

6. See Sontag, *op. cit.*, p.29.

7. See Aspiz, *op. cit.*, p.194.

8. *Ibid.*, p.192.

9. See Kern, *op. cit.*, pp.62-63; Passmore, *op. cit.*, p.248.

10. See Ueberhorst, *op. cit.*, pp.72-74.

11. See David Chapman, 'Siegmund Breitbart', *Ironman*, Oct 1990, p.82.

12. See Ueberhorst, *op. cit.*, pp.77-79.

13. See Igor Golomstock, *Totalitarian Art*, London: Collins Harwill, 1990, pp.220-224.

14. See Cooper, *op. cit.*, pp.73-74.

15. Richard D. Mandell, *The Nazi Olympics*, New York: Souvenir Press, 1971, pp.56-57.

16. See Malone, *op. cit.*, pp.98-100.

17. See Perry and Aldridge, *op. cit.*, pp.98-99, 140-141.

18. Malone, *op. cit.*, pp.101-102.

19. See Graham McCann, *Rebel Males: Clift, Brando and Dean*, London: Hamish Hamilton, 1991, p.186.

20. Quoted by Chris Watson, *Newcastle Herald* (Aust.), 5 Sept 1991, p.3.

21. Yukio Mishima, (Introduction to) *Young Samurai: Bodybuilders of Japan* (transl. M. Wetherby and Paul T. Konya), New York: Grove Press, 1967, p.vii.

22. See Peter Wilson, 'The Mishima Madness', *The Australian*, 24-25 Nov 1990, p.23.

23. Butler, *op. cit.*, pp.21-22, 25.

24. Quoted by Butler, *ibid.*, p.34.

25. See Wendy Leigh, *Arnold: An Unauthorized Biography*, London: Pelham Books, 1990, p.6, pp.238-239.

26. See Alan M. Klein, 'Fear and Loathing in Southern California: Narcissism and Fascism in Bodybuilding Subculture', *Journal of Psychoanalytic Anthropology*, 10, 2 (Spring 1987), pp.117-137; cf. Alan M. Klein, 'Pumping Irony: Crisis and Contradiction in Bodybuilding', *Sociology of Sport Journal*, 3, 2 (June 1986), pp.112-133.

27. Sam Fussell, *Muscle: Confessions of an Unlikely Bodybuilder*, London: Sphere Books (Cardinal), 1991, p.95.

CHAPTER 8 - THE SEXUAL BODY

1. Kern, *op. cit.*, p.103.

2. Chris Sare, 'Exercise Makes You Sexy', *Muscle & Fitness*, Jan 1990, pp.83, 84.

3. Morris, *op. cit.*, p.42.

4. *Ibid.*, p.53.

5. See Jared Diamond, *The Rise and Fall of the Third Chimpanzee*, London: Radius, 1991.

6. See Gregory Rochlin, *The Masculine Dilemma: A Psychology of Masculinity*, Boston: Little, Brown & Co., 1980, pp.84-85.

7. Jonathan Dollimore, *Sexual Dissidence: Augustine to Wilde, Freud to Foucault*, Oxford: Clarendon Press, 1991, p.267.

8. Webb, *art. cit.*, p.15.

9. Diamond, *op. cit.*, p.64

10. Miles, *op. cit.*, p.111.

11. Research first reported in *Village Voice* (New York), 1972, and published in *Sunday Times Magazine*, 26 Feb. 1973, pp.36-37.

12. See Jan Govan, 'Women Working on their Bodies', *Momentum*, Dept of Anthropology and Sociology, Monash University, 1991, p.7; Robert W. Duff, 'Self-Images of Women Bodybuilders', *Sociology of Sport Journal*, 1, 4 (Dec 1984), pp.374-80.

13. Lucie-Smith, *The Body*, p.30.

14. See Kern, *op. cit.*, pp.209 *ff.*, 214 *ff.*

15. See, e.g., *Torso* (Variety Communications, Inc., N.Y.), *Male Pictorial* (Liberation Publications, Inc., N.Y.).

16. Reprinted in *Cleo* (Australia), September 1992, p.75; cf. Leigh, *op. cit.*, p.134.

17. See Walters, *op. cit.*, p.289.

18. See David Chapman, 'Posing for Glory: Pioneers of Physique Photography', *Muscle & Fitness*, March 1988, p.123.

19. Walters, *op. cit.*, pp.293 *ff.*

20. *Ibid.*, p.295.

21. See A.K. Hussain, 'Evaluators' Physique and Self-evaluation as Moderating Variables in Opposite-sex Physique Attraction', *Perspectives in Psychological Researches*, 5, 1 (April 1982), pp.31-36.

22. Quoted in Leigh, *op. cit.*, pp.60-61.

23. See Clark, *op. cit.*, p.6

24. Mark Gabor, *The Pin-Up: A Modest History*, London: Pan Books, 1972, p.205.

25. *Ibid.*, pp.203-205.

26. See Teagan, 'Musclephobia: The Cause, the Cure', *Ironman*, July 1990, pp.62 *ff.*

27. Toby Miller, 'Sport, Media and Masculinity', in David Rowe and Geoff Lawrence [eds], *Sport and Leisure: Trends in Australian Popular Culture*, Sydney: Harcourt Brace Jovanovich, 1990, p.78.

28. See Frank Jakeman, *Being Frank*, London: Guild Publishing, 1987, p.129.

29. Cooper, *op. cit.*, p.125.

30. John Leland, Maggie Malone, Marc Peyser and Pat Wingert, 'The Selling of Sex', *Newsweek/The Bulletin* (Australia), 3 Nov. 1992, pp.68-69.

31. Webb, *art. cit.*, p.15.

32. IFBB, *Guide Book for Judges, Competitors and Organizers*, pp.4-5.

33. IFBB, *Rules for Professional Bodybuilders and Contest Organizers*, p.37.

34. See, e.g., the 'human form' photography in the magazine *Exercise for Men Only* (Chelo Publishing, Inc., N.Y.); cf. [Kal Yee], *Perfect Form: Photography by Kal* [from *Men's Fitness* magazine], Beverly Hills, CA: Second Glance, Inc., 1991.

35. Walters, *op. cit.*, p.295.

36. Anne Honer, 'Beschreibung einer Lebenswelt: zur Empirie des Bodybuilding' ('Description of a Life-World: Bodybuilding'), *Zeitschrift für Soziologie*, 14, 2 (April 1985), pp.131-139.

37. See W.E. Thompson and J.H. Bair, 'A Sociological Analysis of Pumping Iron', *Free Inquiry in Creative Sociology*, 10, 2 (Nov 1982), pp.192-196.

38. See, e.g., the examples quoted in Teagan, *art. cit.*, Butler, *op. cit.*, pp.50-53; cf. review of Fussell, *op. cit.*, *The Australian*, 28 Sept 91.

39. Johan Huizinga, *Homo Ludens: A Study of the Play Element in Culture*, London: Granada Publishing (Paladin), 1970, pp.19-29, *passim.*; cf. Dennis Brailsford, *Sport and Society: Elizabeth to Anne*, London: Routledge & Kegan Paul, 1969, pp.260-261.

40. Christopher Lasch, *The Culture of Narcissism: American Life in an Age of Diminishing Expectations*, New York: Norton, 1978, pp. 104-105.

41. See Guthrie, *op. cit.*, p.101.

42. See Bayley, *op. cit.*, p.145.

43. Greg Callaghan, 'Dropping their Daks', in *Australian Women's Forum*, Vol. I, No. 7 (June 1992), p.51.

44. Zak Jane Keir, 'Girls on Top — The Dreamboys Exposed', in *For Women* (UK), Spring 1992, p.23.

CHAPTER 9 - THE SELF-ABSORBED BODY

1.   See Sontag, *op. cit.*, pp.153 *ff.*

2.   Lasch, *op. cit.*, pp. 91-92.

3.   Diana, Princess of Wales; news report, ABC TV (Australia), 28 April 1993.

4.   Quoted in Butler, *op. cit.*, p.124.

5.   Quoted in Gaines, *op. cit.*, p.48.

6.   Clive James, *Fame in the 20th Century*, London: BBC Books, 1993, p.149.

7.   Ronald Conway, *The Rage for Utopia*, Sydney: Allen & Unwin, 1992, p.188.

8.   See *ibid.*, p.240.

9.   See R.S. Laura and K.R. Dutton, *The Matrix Principle*, Sydney: Allen & Unwin, 1991, pp.78-82.

10. See, e.g., John Bubb, 'Steroids: One Man's Story', *Muscle Mag International*, May/June 1990, pp.17 *ff.*

11. Fussell, *op. cit.*, p.140.

12. *Ibid.*, p.51.

13. *Ibid.*, p.38.

CHAPTER 10 - THE SELF-CONTAINED BODY

1.   See, e.g., Lucie-Smith, *Eroticism in Western Art*, p.50.

2.   Rudofsky, *op. cit.*, p.52.

3.   See references in Chapter 13.

4.   Alan Hollinghurst, 'Robert Mapplethorpe' in *Robert Mapplethorpe 1970-1983*, London: Institute of Contemporary Arts, 1983, p.8 *ff.*

5.   See Passmore, *op. cit.*, pp.313-314; cf. Walters, *op. cit.*, p.15; Morris, *op. cit.*, p.188.

6.   Clark, *op. cit.*, p.25.

7.   Butler, *op. cit.*, p.13.

8.   In *Lady: Lisa Lyon*, London: Blond & Briggs, 1983, p.12.

9.   Walters, *op. cit.*, p.295.

10. Clark, *op. cit.*, p.199.

11. Robert Kennedy, *Reps!*, New York, Sterling Books, 1985, pp. 98-99.

12. See Rudofsky, *op. cit.*, p.212.

13. See Gunn, *op. cit.*, p.31.

14. See Rudofsky, *op. cit.*, p.94.

15. See Polhemus [ed.], *Social Aspects of the Human Body*, p.141.

16. Brain, *op. cit.*, pp.146-147.

17. Guthrie, *op. cit.*, p.67 (cf. *ibid.*, p.69).

18. *Loc. cit.*

19. *Ibid.*, p.159.

20. Malone, *op. cit.*, pp.73-75.

21. *Ibid.*, pp.75-77.

22. See Tony Crawley, *Screen Dreams: The Hollywood Pin-Up* (Photographs from the Korbal Collection), London: Sidgwick & Jackson, 1982, pp.62, 77.

23. Suzanne Mostyn, 'In Trim for the Hair-free Alternative', *Sydney Morning Herald*, 10 Oct 1991.

24. See, e.g., Guthrie, *op. cit.*, p.84.

25. E.W. Delph, *The Silent Community: Public Homosexual Encounters*, Beverly Hills, Calif.: Sage (Sociological Observations, 8), 1978, p.71.

26. See Guthrie, *op. cit.*, p.176; Gunn, *op. cit.*, pp.164-165; Bayley, *op. cit.*, pp.151-153.

27. Jennifer Montagu, *Bronzes*, London: Weidenfeld & Nicholson, 1963, pp.9, 16.

CHAPTER 11 — THE BODY OBSERVED

1. On the American congressional debates concerning Mapplethorpe, see Allen Ellenweig, *The Homoerotic Photograph*, New York: Columbia University Press, 1992, p.205 ff.; Robert Hughes, *Culture of Complaint*, New York: New York Public Library/Oxford University Press, 1993, pp.158-161.

2. See *Robert Mapplethorpe Black Book*, New York: St Martin's Press, 1986. Cf. the note on Tom ('Joe') Simmons in John Patrick [ed.], *The Best of the Superstars 1993*, Sarasota, FL: STARbooks Press, 1993, p.242.

3. See Richard Marshall, 'Mapplethorpe's Vision', in Marshall [ed.], *Robert Mapplethorpe*, London: Secker and Warburg, 1988, p.14; cf. Germano Celant, 'Eine Welt in zwei Welten', in *Robert Mapplethorpe: Photographien 1984-1986*, München: Schirmer/Mosel, 1987, pp.[1-2].

4. Melody Davis, *The Male Nude in Contemporary Photography*, Philadelphia: Temple University Press, 1991, p.23.

5. Ellenzweig, *op. cit.*, p.138.

6. See *Bruce Weber* [ed. John Cheim], München-Paris: Schirmer/Mosel, 1989; *An Exhibition by Bruce Weber at Fahey/Klein Gallery ...*, [Tokyo]: Treville, 1991.

7. Quoted by Ellenzweig, *op. cit.*, p.167.

8. See *Duo: Herb Ritts Photographs Bob Paris and Rod Jackson*, Twin Palms Publishers, 1991.

9. See Jim French, *Opus Deorum*, Calif.: State of Man Publishing, 1992, p.[7]; cf. [Victor Skrebneski], *Skrebneski: Black, White & Color*, Boston: Little, Brown & Company, 1989.

10. See Tom Bianchi, *Out of the Studio*, New York: St Martin's Press, 1991; *Extraordinary Friends*, New York: St Martin's Press, 1993.

11. See Edward Lucie-Smith, in Boyd [ed.], *op. cit.*, p.10.

12. Quoted by Kate Halfpenny, 'Men as Sex Objects', *Newcastle Herald* (Australia), 19 Sept. 1992.

13. Deirdre Macken, 'Selling by Male', *Sydney Morning Herald* magazine, 24 April 1993, pp.8-11.

14. Beatrice Faust, 'Art v. Pornography: The Thin Blue Line', *Sydney Morning Herald*, 28 Sept. 1991.

15. Andrew Wernick, 'From Voyeur to Narcissist: Imaging Men in Contemporary Advertising', in Michael Kaufman [ed.], *Beyond Patriarchy: Essays by Men on Pleasure, Power and Change*, Toronto: OUP, 1987, p.278.

16. Davis, *op. cit.*, p.158.

17. 'Introducing Grace Lau', *Ludus* (Essex, UK), Vol. 1, Issue 1, 1992, p.42.

18. Hiromi Nakamura, *The Male Nude: Visions of 60 Sensual Photographs*, Tokyo: Treville, 1991.

19. Richard Dyer, 'Don't Look Now', in Angela McRobbie [ed.], *Zoot Suits and Second-Hand Dresses: An Anthology of Fashion and Music*, London: Macmillan, 1988, pp.199-200.

20. *Ibid.*, p.202.

21. *Ibid.*, pp.205-6, *passim*.

22. Quoted in *Sydney Morning Herald* magazine, 24 April 1993, p.12.

23. Webb, *art. cit.*, p.16.

24. Greg Callaghan, 'In Search of the Body Beautiful', *Campaign* (Australia), June 1992, p.40.

25. Marc E. Mishkind, Judith Rodin, Lisa R. Silberstein and Ruth H. Striegel-Moore, 'The Embodiment of Masculinity: Cultural, Psychological and Behavioral Dimensions', in Michael S. Kimmel [ed.], *Changing Men: New Directions in Research on Men and Masculinity*, Newbury Park: Sage, 1987, p.46.

26. *Ibid.*, p.47.

27. Wernick, *art. cit.*, p.293.

28. *Ibid.*, p.294.

29. Mick Carter, 'The Look of Love', *Australian Journal of Cultural Studies*, Vol. III, No. 1, 1985, p.108.

30. *Ibid.*, p.118.

31. Colin McDowell, *Dressed to Kill: Sex, Power and Clothes*, London: Hutchinson, 1992, pp.16-17.

32. *Ibid.*, p.17.

33. *Loc. cit.*

34. *Loc. cit.*

35. *Ibid.*, pp.102-103.

36. *Ibid.*, p.105.

37. *Ibid.*, p.17.

38. Quoted in *Sydney Morning Herald* magazine, 24 April 1993, p.11.

CHAPTER 12 – THE BODY IN CONTEXT

1. Quoted in *The Australian*, 27-28 June 1992; *Sydney Morning Herald.*, 20 June 1992.

2. See, e.g., Julia Neuberger, *Whatever's Happening to Women? Promises, Practices and Pay Offs*, London: Kyle Cathie, 1991, p.205.

3. Naomi Wolf, *Fire With Fire: The New Female Power and How It Will Change the 21st Century*, New York: Chatto & Windus, 1993.

4. See Davis, *op. cit.*, pp.88-107; cf. *George Dureau: New Orleans*, London: GMP Publishers Ltd, 1985.

ACKNOWLEDGEMENTS

Thanks are due to the following: Anne Lang and Eileen O'Donohue for their assistance, advice and unfailing encouragement; Marj Kibby, Ron Laura and Imre Salusinszky, who kindly read through early drafts and offered valuable comments; Pam Delbridge, Frank Morgan, Geoffrey Samuel and John Shea, who provided helpful information; Robin Bates, Michael Birchill, Max Bristow and Allan Richards for photographic documentation; Laurel Graham for word-processing; and Daniel Dacey for computer graphics.

I am most grateful to those who acted as models for the photographs specially taken for this book: Mose Alatise, Robert Allum, Cardigan Connor, Peter Fitzgerald, Clayton Fitts, Hayden Francis, Peter Grant, Paul Haslam, Charles Haywood, Robert Jovanovski, Jeremy Kang, Jason Low, Michael Lynch, Richard Marshall, Steven Meakes, Yves Moanda, Samuel New, Lee Priest, Dennyse Seow, Lauro Sottovia, Paul Stolk, John Sullivan, John Terilli, Paul Wright and Simon Zablotsky.

My special thanks go to Liane Audrins and Toni Shuker for their photographic collaboration, their patience and support. Photos 0.1, 5.1, 6.1, 6.4, 6.7, 6.8, 8.1, 8.8, 8.17, 8.18, 8.24, 9.1, 11.1, 11.7, 11.8, 11.9, 11.10, 11.11, 11.12, 11.13, 11.14, 11.16, 11.18, 11.19, 11.20, 12.1, 12.2b, 12.7, 12.8 and 12.9 by Lianne Audrens and Toni Shuker. Photos 4.2, 6.11, 6.12, 6.13, 7.1, 8.6, 8.9, 8.14, 8.16, 8.19, 8.20, 8.23, 10.1, 10.5, 10.7, 10.9, 10.13, 10.20, 10.21, 11.15, 11.17, 12.3b, 12.5 and 12.6 by Carl Hensel. Photos 3.6, 6.6, 10.3, 11.6, and 12.4b by John Freund. Photos 8.4, 8.21, 10.10 and 10.16 by Kim Emsermann. Photos 10.11 and 11.22 by David Adermann. Photo 10.19 by Graham Hynds. Photos 3.15, 5.9, 6.9, 7.10, 7.11, 7.12a and b, 7.13, 7.14, 7.17, 8.15, 8.22, 9.2, 9.7, 9.9, 10.14, 10.17 and 11.21 courtesy Newcastle Herald (Australia). Photos 0.2 - 0.6 and 3.1 courtesy Lauro Sottovia. Photos 6.10, 6.14 and 8.25 courtesy John Terilli. I am very much indebted to Tom Bianchi for permission to reproduce photos 11.2 - 11.5.

Every effort has been made to obtain copyright permission where required, but it has not always been possible to trace copyright holders. Any omission brought to our attention will naturally be rectified in future editions.

Finally, my particular gratitude to Rhys Palmer for design and layout, and for his valuable suggestions.

SELECTED BIBLIOGRAPHY

This bibliography lists books and significant journal articles only. Magazine and newspaper articles are not included.

ANDRIEU, G., 'La respiration reflet de nos aspirations', in ANDRIEU, Gilbert [ed.] *Sports, Arts et Religions* (Proceedings of International Congress, Larnaca, Cyprus, 11-18 December 1988), Paris, Université de Paris X Nanterre, 1989, pp.20-33.

ASHTON, [Sir] Leigh, 'Sculpture', in Alan Pryce-Jones [ed.], *The New Outline of Modern Knowledge*, London: Gollancz, 1956, pp.299-320.

ASPIZ, Harold, *Walt Whitman and the Body Beautiful*, Chicago: University of Illinois Press, 1980.

BARBOUR, Alan G., *Days of Thrills and Adventure*, London: Collier-Macmillan Limited (Collier Books), 1970.

BARKAN, Leonard, *Nature's Work of Art: The Human Body as Image of the World*, New Haven/London, Yale University Press, 1975.

BARTHES, Roland, 'Le Monde où l'on catche', in *Mythologies*, Paris: Editions du seuil, 1957.

BARTHES, Roland, *Système de la Mode*, Paris: Editions du seuil, 1967.

BARTHES, Roland, [Introduction to] *Taormina: Wilhelm von Gloeden*, Altadena, Calif.: Twelvetrees Press, 2nd ed. 1990.

BAYLEY, Stephen, *Taste: The Secret Meaning of Things*, London: Faber & Faber, 1991.

BECKER, Ernest, *The Birth and Death of Meaning: An Interdisciplinary Perspective on the Problem of Man*, Harmondsworth: Penguin Books, 2nd edition 1971.

BENTHALL, Jonathan and POLHEMUS, Ted, *The Body as a Medium of Expression*, New York: Allen Lane/Dutton, 1975.

BIANCHI, Tom, *Out of the Studio* (Foreword by Paul Monette), New York: St Martin's Press, 1991.

BOARDMAN, John, 'Greek Art and Architecture', in Boardman *et al.*, *The Oxford History of the Classical World*, q.v., pp.275-310.

BOARDMAN, John, GRIFFIN, Jasper and MURRAY, Oswyn [eds], *The Oxford History of the Classical World*, Oxford: OUP, 1986.

BOBER, P.P. and RUBINSTEIN, R., *Renaissance Artists and Antique Sculpture*, London: Harvey Miller Publishers, 1986.

BOISSELIER, Jean, *et al.*, *The Image of the Buddha*, Paris: UNESCO/London: Serindia Publications, 1978.

BOORSTIN, Daniel J., *The Image*, Harmondsworth: Pelican Books, 1963.

BORNOFF, Nicholas, *Pink Samurai: The Pursuit and Politics of Sex in Japan*, London: Grafton Books, 1991.

BRAILSFORD, Dennis, *Sport and Society: Elizabeth to Anne*, London: Routledge & Kegan Paul, 1969.

BRAIN, Robert, *The Decorated Body*, London: Hutchinson & Co., 1979.

BROWN, Peter, *The Body and Society: Men, Women and Sexual Renunciation in Early Christianity*, New York: Columbia University Press, 1988.

BULLOUGH, Vern and BULLOUGH, Bonnie, *Sin, Sickness, & Sanity: A History of Sexual Attitudes*, New York: Garland Publishing, Inc., 1977.

BUTLER, George, *Arnold Schwarzenegger: A Portrait*, New York: Simon & Schuster, 1990.

BUTLER, Ruth, *Western Sculpture: Definitions of Man*, Boston: Little, Brown and Company (New York Graphic Society), 1975.

CAMPBELL, Joseph, *Myths to Live By*, London: Souvenir Press, 1992 (1st ed. 1972).

CANNON-BROOKES, Peter, *Emile-Antoine Bourdelle: An Illustrated Commentary*, London: Trefoil Books, 1984.

CAVE, Sydney, *The Christian Estimate of Man*, London: Duckworth, 1957.

CELANT, Germano, 'The Buried Body' (translated by John Mitchell), in *The Power of Theatrical Madness: Jan Fabre*, photographs by Robert Mapplethorpe, London: Institute of Contemporary Arts, 1986.

CELANT, Germano, *Robert Mapplethorpe Photographien 1984-1986*, Munich: Schirmer/Mosel, 1986.

CHAPMAN, David, *Adonis: The Male Physique Pin-Up 1870-1940*, London: GMP Publishers, 1989.

CH'EN, Kenneth K.S., *The Chinese Transformation of Buddhism*, Princeton, NJ: Princeton University Press, 1973.

CLARK, Kenneth, *The Nude: A Study of Ideal Art*, Harmondsworth: Pelican Books, 1960.

CLARKE, Magnus, *Nudism in Australia: A First Study*, Victoria: Deakin University Press, 1982.

CONWAY, Ronald, *The Rage for Utopia*, Sydney: Allen & Unwin, 1992.

COOPER, Emmanuel, *Fully Exposed: The Male Nude in Photography*, London: Unwin Hyman, 1990.

CRAWLEY, Tony, *Screen Dreams: The Hollywood Pinup* (Photographs from the Kobal Collection), London: Sidgwick & Jackson, 1982.

CROSS, Robin, *The Big Book of B Movies, or How Low Was My Budget*, London: Frederick Muller Limited (a Charles Herridge Book), 1981.

DAVENPORT-HINES, Richard, *Sex, Death and Punishment: Attitudes to Sex and Sexuality in Britain Since the Renaissance*, London: Collins, 1990.

DAVIS, Melody, *The Male Nude in Contemporary Photography*, Philadelphia: Temple University Press, 1991.

DELPH, Edward William, *The Silent Community: Public Homosexual Encounters*, Beverly Hills, Calif.: Sage Publications (Sociological Observations, No. 3), 1978.

DIAMOND, Jared, *The Rise and Fall of the Third Chimpanzee*, London: Radius, 1991.

DOLLIMORE, Jonathon, *Sexual Dissidence: Augustine to Wilde, Freud to Foucault*, Oxford: Clarendon Press, 1991.

DOUGLAS, Jack D., and RASMUSSEN, Paul K., with Carol Ann FLANAGAN, *The Nude Beach*, Beverly Hills: Sage (Sociological Observations: 1), 1977.

DOUGLAS, Mary, *Natural Symbols: Explorations in Cosmology*, Harmondsworth: Penguin, 1973.

DOVER, K.J., *Greek Homosexuality*, London: Duckworth, 1978.

DUFF, Robert W., 'Self-Images of Women Bodybuilders', in *Sociology of Sport Journal*, I, 4 (Dec. 1984), pp.374-80.

ELLENZWEIG, Allen, *The Homoerotic Photograph*, New York: Columbia University Press, 1992.

ELLEY, Derek, *The Epic Film: Myth and History*, London: Routledge & Kegan Paul, 1984.

EMRICH, Bill, *Photographs of Men*, Berlin: Volker Janssen, 1992.

FOOTE, Timothy, *The World of Bruegel c.1525-1569*, Nederland: Time-Life Library of Art, 1968.

FOSS, Martin, *The Idea of Perfection in the Western World*, Lincoln: University of Nebraska Press, 1946.

FOUCAULT, Michel, *The Use of Pleasure* (Volume 2 of *The History of Sexuality*), translated from the French by Robert Hurley, New York: Pantheon Books, 1985.

FRENCH, Jim, *Opus Deorum*, Calif.: State of Man Publishing, 1992.

FUSSELL, Sam, *Muscle: Confessions of an Unlikely Bodybuilder*, London: Sphere Books (Cardinal), 1991.

GABOR, Mark, *The Pin-Up: A Modest History*, London: Pan Books, Ltd, 1972.

GAINES, Charles, *Pumping Iron: The Art and Sport of Bodybuilding*, London: Sphere Books, 1977.

GERDTS, William H., *The Great American Nude*, London: Phaidon, 1974.

GILL, Michael, *Image of the Body: Aspects of the Nude*, New York: Doubleday, 1989, p.127.

GOFFMAN, Erving, *The Presentation of Self in Everyday Life*, Harmondsworth: Penguin, 1971.

GOLOMSTOCK, Igor, *Totalitarian Art in the Soviet Union, the Third Reich, Fascist Italy and the People's Republic of China*, London: Collins Harwill, 1990.

GOVAN, Jan, 'Women Working on their Bodies', in *Momentum*, Dept. of Anthropology and Sociology, Monash University, 1991, pp.1-10.

GUNN, Fenja, *The Artificial Face: A History of Cosmetics*, Newton Abbot: David & Charles, 1973.

GUTHRIE, R. Dale, *Body Hot Spots: The Anatomy of Human Social Organs and Behavior*, New York: Van Nostrand Reinhold, 1976.

HALE, W.A., *The World of Rodin 1840-1917*, Nederland: Time-Life History of Art, 1969.

HANFMANN, George M.A., *Classical Sculpture*, London: Michael Joseph, 1967.

HARDING, James, *The Rocky Horror Show Book*, London: Sidgwick & Jackson, 1987.

HARTT, Frederick, *David by the Hand of Michelangelo: The Original Model Discovered*, New York: Abbeville Press, 1987.

HASKELL, Francis and PENNY, Nicholas, *Taste and the Antique: The Lure of Classical Sculpture 1500-1900*, New Haven/London: Yale University Press, 1981.

HENRY, Michel, *Philosophy and Phenomenology of the Body* (translated by Gerard Etzkorn), The Hague: Martinus Nijhoff, 1975.

HOLLINGHURST, Alan, 'Robert Mapplethorpe', in *Robert Mapplethorpe 1970-1983*, London: Institute of Contemporary Arts, 1983, pp.8-17.

HONER, Anne, 'Description of a Life-World: Bodybuilding' (Beschreibung einer Lebenswelt: Zur Empirie des Bodybuilding), in *Zeitschrift für Soziologie* (1985) 14, 2, pp.131-139.

HUGHES, Robert, *The Shock of the New: Art and the Century of Change*, London: British Broadcasting Corporation, 1980.

HUGHES, Robert, *Culture of Complaint: The Fraying of America*, New York: New York Public Library/Oxford University Press, 1993.

HUIZINGA, Johan, *Homo Ludens: A Study of the Play Element in Culture*, Boston: Beacon Press, 1944.

HUSSAIN, A.K. 'Evaluators' Physique and Self-evaluation as Moderating Variables in Opposite-sex Physique Attraction', in *Perspectives in Psychological Researches*, 5, 1 (April 1982), pp.31-36.

JAKEMAN, Frank, *Being Frank*, London: Guild Publishing, 1987.

JAMES, Clive, *Fame in the 20th Century*, London: BBC Books, 1993.

KENNEDY, Robert, *Reps*, New York: Sterling, 1985.

KERN, Stephen, *Anatomy and Destiny: A Cultural History of the Human Body*, Indianapolis/New York: The Bobbs-Merrill Company, Inc., 1975.

KLEIN, Alan M., 'Fear and Self-loathing in Southern California: Narcissism and Fascism in Bodybuilding Subculture', in *Journal of Psychoanalytic Anthropology*, (1987) 10, 2, pp.117-137.

LAMBRAKI-PLAKA, Marina, *Bourdelle et la Grèce*, Athens: Akademia Athenon, 1985.

LAQUEUR, Thomas, *Making Sex: Body and Gender from the Greeks to Freud*, Cambridge, Mass./London: Harvard University Press, 1990.

LASCH, Christopher, *The Culture of Narcissism: American Life in an Age of Diminishing Expectations*, New York: W.W. Norton, 1978.

LAURA, R.S. and DUTTON, K.R., *The Matrix Principle*, Sydney: Allen & Unwin, 1991.

LEIGH, Wendy, *Arnold: An Unauthorized Biography*, London: Pelham Books, 1990.

LIGGETT, Arline and John, *The Tyranny of Beauty*, London: Victor Gollancz, 1989.

LUCIE-SMITH, Edward, *Eroticism in Western Art*, New York: Praeger, 1972.

LUCIE-SMITH, Edward, *The Body: Images of the Nude*, London: Thames & Hudson, 1982.

LUCIE-SMITH, Edward, 'Life Class', Introduction to Stephen Boyd [ed.], *Life Class: The Academic Male Nude 1820-1920*, q.v., pp.5-13.

LULLIES, Reinhard [ed.], *Greek Sculpture*, London: Thames und Hudson, 1957.

[LYNES, George Platt], *George Platt Lynes* (ed. Peter Weiermair), Berlin: Bruno Gmünder Verlag, 1989.

McCANN, Graham, *Rebel Males: Clift, Brando and Dean*, London: Hamish Hamilton, 1991.

MADDOW, Ben, 'Nude in a Social Landscape', in Sullivan, *Nude*, q.v., pp.183-196.

MAISONNEUVE, Jean, 'The Body and "Bodyism" Today' (Le Corps et le corporéisme aujourd'hui), in *Revue française de sociologie* (1976), 17, 4, pp.553-571.

MALONE, Michael, *Heroes of Eros: Male Sexuality in the Movies*, New York: E.P. Dutton (Dutton Paperbacks), 1979.

MANDELL, Richard D., *The Nazi Olympics*, New York: Souvenir Press, 1971.

MAPPLETHORPE, Robert, *Lady: Lisa Lyon* (text by Bruce Chatwin), London: Blond & Briggs Ltd., 1983.

MAPPLETHORPE, Robert, *Certain People — A Book of Portraits*, Pasadena, Calif.: Twelvetrees Press, 1985.

[MAPPLETHORPE, Robert], *Robert Mapplethorpe Black Book* (Foreword by Ntozake Shange), New York: St Martin's Press, 1986.

MARSHALL, Richard, *Robert Mapplethorpe*, London: Secker & Warburg, 1988.

MASCALL, E.L., *Existence and Analogy*, London: Longmans, Green & Co., 1949.

MAUSS, Marcel, 'The Techniques of the Body', in *Economy and Society*, 2, I (Feb. 1973), pp.70-88.

MILES, Rosalind, *The Rites of Man: Love, Sex and Death in the Making of the Male*, London: Grafton Books, 1991.

MILLER, Jonathon, *The Body in Question*, New York: Random House, 1978.

MILLER, Toby, 'Sport, Media and Masculinity', in David Rowe and Geoff Lawrence [eds], *Sport and Leisure: Trends in Australian Popular Culture*, q.v., pp.74-95.

MISHIMA, Yukio, (Introduction to) *Young Samurai: Bodybuilders of Japan* (Photographs by Tamotsu Yato), translated into English by M. Weatherby and Paul T. Konya, New York: Grove Press, 1967.

MISHKIND, Marc E., RODIN, Judith, SILBERSTEIN, Lisa R., and STRIEGEL-MOORE, Ruth H., 'The Embodiment of Masculinity: Cultural, Psychological and Behavioral Dimensions', in Michael S. Kimmel [ed.], *Changing Men: New Directions in Research on Men and Masculinity*, Newbury Park: Sage, 1987, pp.37-52.

MONTAGU, Jennifer, *Bronzes*, London: Weidenfeld & Nicholson, 1963.

MORRIS, Desmond, *The Human Zoo*, London: Corgi Books, 1971.

MURRAY, Oswyn, 'Life and Society in Classical Greece', in Boardman *et al.*, *The Oxford History of the Classical World*, q.v.., pp.204-233.

MUYBRIDGE, Edweard, *The Human Figure in Motion* (Introd. by Robert Taft), New York: Dover Publications, Inc., 1955.

NAKAMURA, Hiromi, *The Male Nude: Visions of 60 Sensual Photographs*, Tokyo: Treville, 1991.

NEUBERGER, Julia, *Whatever's Happening to Women? Promises, Practices and Pay Offs*, London: Kyle Cathie, 1991.

OVENDEN, Graham, and MENDES, Peter, *Victorian Erotic Photography*, New York: St. Martin's Press/London: Academy Editions, 1973.

PARKER, Robert, 'Greek Religion', in Boardman *et al.*, *The Oxford History of the Classical World*, q.v., pp.254-274.

PARRISH, James Robert *et al.* (eds.) *The Great Movie Series*, South Brunswick & New York: A.S. Barnes & Co./London: Thomas Yoseloff Ltd., 1971.

PASSMORE, John, *The Perfectibility of Man*, London: Duckworth, 1970.

PATRICK, John [ed.], *The Best of the Superstars 1993: The Year in Sex*, Sarasota, FL: STARbooks Press, 1993.

PEDLEY, John Griffiths, *Greek Art and Archaelogy*, London: Cassell, 1993.

PERRY, George, and ALDRIDGE, Alan, *The Penguin Book of Comics*, Harmondsworth: Penguin Books, 1967.

POLHEMUS, Ted [ed.], *Social Aspects of the Human Body*, Harmondsworth: Penguin, 1978.

RITTS, Herb, *Herb Ritts Photographs Bob Paris & Rod Jackson*, [USA]: Twin Palms Publishers, 1991.

ROCHLIN, Gregory, *The Masculine Dilemma: A Psychology of Masculinity*, Boston: Little, Brown & Co., 1980.

[RODIN], *Rodin Sculptures* (introd. Sommerville Story), London: Phaidon, 1970.

ROMER, John, *Testament: The Bible and History*, London: Michael O'Mara, 1988.

ROSENBLUM, Naomi, *A World History of Photography*, New York: Abbeville Press, 1989.

ROWE, David and LAWRENCE, Geoff (eds.), *Sport and Leisure: Trends in Australian Popular Culture*, Sydney: Harcourt Brace Jovanovich, 1990.

RUDOFSKY, Bernard, *The Unfashionable Human Body*, New York.

SCHARF, Aaron, *Art and Photography*, London: Allen Lane/The Penguin Press, 1968.

SCHWARZENEGGER, Arnold, with Douglas Kent Hall, *Arnold: The Education of a Bodybuilder*, New York: Pocket Books, 1977.

SCHWARZENEGGER, Arnold, *Encyclopedia of Modern Bodybuilding* (with Bill Dobbins), London: Pelham Books, 1985.

SIMON, Marcel, *La Civilisation de l'antiquité et le christianisme*, Paris: Arthaud, 1972.

[SKREBNESKI, Victor], *Skrebneski: Black, White & Color*, Boston: Little, Brown & Company, 1989.

SOBIESZEK, Robert, 'Addressing the Erotic: Reflections on the Nude Photograph' in Sullivan, Constance, *Nude, q.v.*, pp.169-179.

SONTAG, Susan, *Photography*, Harmondsworth: Penguin Books, 1979.

SULLIVAN, Constance (ed.), *Nude: Photographs 1850-1980*, New York: Harper & Row, 1980.

THOMPSON, W.E., and BAIR, J.H., 'A Sociological Analysis of Pumping Iron', in *Free Inquiry in Creative Sociology*, 10, 2 (Nov. 1982), pp.192-196.

TURNER, Bryan S., *The Body and Society: Explorations in Social Theory*, Oxford: Basil Blackwell, 1984.

UEBERHORST, Horst, *Friedrich Ludwig Jahn 1778-1978*, Bonn/Bad Godesberg: Inter Nationes, 1978.

UHLIG, Helmut, *Das Bild des Buddha*, Berlin: Safari Verlag, 1979.

von der FUHR, Rein, 'Robert Mapplethorpe', in *Robert Mapplethorpe, fotografie*, a cura di Germano Celant, Idea Books Edizione [n.d.]

WALTERS, Margaret, *The Nude Male: A New Perspective*, New York/London: Paddington Press Ltd., 1978.

WEBB, John, 'Reading Bodies', in *XY: Men, Sex, Politics*, Summer 1991/92, pp.14-18.

[WEBER, Bruce], *Bruce Weber* (ed. John Cheim), Munich & Paris: Schirmer/Mosel, 1989.

[WEBER, Bruce], *An Exhibition by Bruce Weber at Fahey/Klein Gallery ...*, [Tokyo]: Treville, 1991.

WEIERMAIR, Peter, *The Hidden Image: Photographs of the Male Nude in the Nineteenth and Twentieth Centuries*, translated by Claus Nielander, Cambridge, Mass.: the MIT Press, 1988.

WERNICK, Andrew, 'From Voyeur to Narcissist: Imaging Men in Contemporary Advertising', in Michael Kaufman [ed.], *Beyond Patriarchy: Essays by Men on Pleasure, Power and Change*, Toronto: OUP, 1987, pp.277-297.

WESTHEIMER, Ruth, *The Art of Arousal*, New York: Abbeville Press, 1993.

WILSON, R.J.A., 'Roman Art and Architecture', in Boardman *et al.*, *The Oxford History of the Classical World, q.v.*, pp.771-806.

[WINCKELMANN, Johann], *Winckelmann: Writings on Art* (selected and edited by David Irwin), London: Phaidon, 1972.

WOLF, Naomi, *The Beauty Myth*, London: Chatto & Windus, 1990.

WOOD, Susan, *Roman Portrait Sculpture 217-260 A.D.*, Leiden: E.J. Brill, 1986.

[YEE, Kal], *Perfect Form: Photography by Kal*, Beverly Hills, CA: Second Glance, Inc., 1991.

ZINMAN, David, *Saturday Afternoon at the Bijou*, [New Jersey]: Castle Books, 1973.

INDEX

Figures in italics refer to illustrations